"Harvey and Rathbone have written a gem of a book! *Dialectical Behavior Therapy* is a must-read for all practitioners who treat this population, regardless of thei tion. DBT practitioners will find much in this book to deepen and enhance the with other orientations will find ideas, skills and techniques to add to their c … The authors are clearly dedicated to providing the most effective treatment possible for adolescents and their families. Through this book, they generously share their knowledge with the rest of us. This book represents a major contribution to DBT and all therapy that involves working with adolescents."

—**Judi Sprei, PhD**, psychologist and contributor at www.dbtpsychologist.com, Bethesda, MD

"I highly recommend *Dialectical Behavior Therapy for At-Risk Adolescents* to practitioners. Harvey and Rathbone skillfully review DBT and articulate sound reasoning for its use with at-risk adolescents. The reader will find detailed tools and interventions targeting challenging adolescent emotions and behaviors. The sample dialogues, practice assignments, and handouts designed specifically for work with adolescents also provide the reader with concrete tools that can be easily incorporated into practice. Harvey and Rathbone have crafted a clear rationale and comprehensive guide for clinicians seeking practical and straightforward interventions for using dialectical behavior therapy with adolescents."

—**Christy Matta, MA**, author of *The Stress Response*

"This book provides a sympathetic view of the adolescent in crisis and has smart, accessible ideas for therapists and parents."

—**Anne Kendall, PhD**, DBT psychologist at The Wake Kendall Group, Washington, DC

"*Dialectical Behavior Therapy for At-Risk Adolescents* is a welcome addition to the scant resources available for using DBT with this population—the very population that so desperately needs DBT. The text is immediately accessible and doesn't rely on jargon, making it the ideal introduction for those who would like to begin to use this powerful technology but may have been intimidated by other sources. For those who have more experience with DBT for adults, it provides key concepts and modifications to help extend their practice to adolescents. Additionally, the authors' use of charts, summarizing bullet points, concise language, case examples, and exercise suggestions provide experienced practitioners with an effective refresher and quick reference that supports their continued growth and commitment as a DBT provider."

—**Abby Sarrett-Cooper, MA, LPC**, licensed professional counselor in private practice in New Jersey

"Full of practical examples and concrete tools, this book provides invaluable strategies for working with the toughest adolescents. Regardless of your DBT background, this book will prove useful to any professional seeking to help young people whose intense emotional reactions get in the way of building the lives they want. Harvey and Rathbone draw on their years of clinical experience to lay out an evidence-based treatment that is compassionate to youth and parents alike."

—Simona Dumitrescu Murnick, MD, child and adolescent psychiatrist

"Harvey and Rathbone have created a clear, comprehensive, and accessible guide for clinicians who use DBT with adolescents and their families. … This book is filled with practical how-to steps, including case examples and worksheets that practitioners can turn to again and again. It could be invaluable for any therapist who wants to use DBT with adolescents and their families."

—Brian Corrado, PsyD, psychologist in Bethesda, MD

"This book offers readers an understanding of at-risk behavior that conveys respect and compassion for adolescents and their caregivers. The collaborative treatment strategies highlighted throughout the text provide hope that change and relief are possible for families that have struggled with the endless challenges that accompany behaviors such as self-injury, substance abuse, and aggression."

—Elizabeth Fessenden, MA, LMHC, assistant director of dialectical behavior therapy services at The Bridge of Central Massachusetts, Inc.

"Reading this book by Pat Harvey and Britt H. Rathbone felt to me like having incredibly warm, expert DBT colleagues sitting with me while I was treating a challenging, even frightening, kid and family. They are sophisticated and practical when providing tips and examples of how to talk with teens and parents; how to introduce DBT, mindfulness, dialectics, behavioral chain analysis, diary cards (wisely renamed daily logs); and a multitude of other typical and difficult tasks. They give a wonderful guide to the five modules of DBT, along with examples, handouts, and worksheets for how to teach them. Their section on how to apply DBT for coaching parents is a real advancement to this evolving treatment. Having read their book, I know I will be a more balanced, skilled, and validating DBT therapist with teens and families."

—Charles Swenson, MD, associate clinical professor of psychiatry for University of Massachusetts Medical School

"DBT has moved beyond diagnostic groups and specific target symptoms. By making DBT skills more broadly accessible, the authors provide powerful tools to at-risk adolescents and their parents. The skill sets in this book target the prevention of emerging psychiatric problems, and will endure as essential guidelines for effective living beyond crises. This book is a wonderful, alternative—and yet essential—guide to raising teens who are both at risk and not at risk!"

—Blaise Aguirre, MD, staff psychiatrist at Harvard's McLean Hospital

Dialectical Behavior Therapy *for* At-Risk Adolescents

A Practitioner's Guide to Treating
Challenging Behavior Problems

PAT HARVEY, ACSW, LCSW-C
BRITT H. RATHBONE, ACSW, LCSW-C

New Harbinger Publications, Inc.

Publisher's Note

Distributed in Canada by Raincoast Books

Copyright © 2013 by Pat Harvey and Britt H. Rathbone
          New Harbinger Publications, Inc.
          5674 Shattuck Avenue
          Oakland, CA 94609
          www.newharbinger.com

Cover design by Amy Shoup
Acquired by Tesilya Hanauer
Edited by Jean Blomquist

Library of Congress Cataloging-in-Publication Data

Harvey, Pat.
  Dialectical behavior therapy for at-risk adolescents : a practitioner's guide to treating challenging behavior problems / Pat Harvey, ACSW, LCSW-C, and Britt H. Rathbone, ACSW, LCSW-C.
    pages cm
  Summary: "At-risk adolescents may exhibit signs of moodiness, aggression, and even self-injury, and these behaviors often cause parents, teachers, and clinicians to become extremely frustrated. Adolescents themselves may even believe that change is impossible. Drawing on proven-effective dialectical behavior therapy (DBT), Dialectical Behavior Therapy for At-Risk Adolescents is the first reader-friendly and easily accessible DBT book specifically targeted to mental health professionals treating adolescents who may be dangerous to themselves or others"-- Provided by publisher.
  Includes bibliographical references and index.
  ISBN 978-1-60882-798-5 (pbk.) -- ISBN 978-1-60882-799-2 (pdf e-book) -- ISBN 978-1-60882-800-5 (epub) 1. Dialectical behavior therapy. 2. Behavior disorders in adolescence--Treatment. 3. Problem children--Behavior modification. I. Rathbone, Britt H. II. Title.
  RC489.B4H378 2014
  616.89'142--dc23
                   2013039165

Printed in the United States of America

15   14   13

10   9   8   7   6   5   4   3   2   1

First printing

To the parents of past, present, and future adolescents who have allowed me to witness their courage and strength in living lives filled with frustrations, challenges, willingness, acceptance, and hope.

—PH

To my family, especially Susan and Huntly, and all the adolescents whose strength and growth continue to inspire me.

—BHR

Contents

Acknowledgments

I am grateful to the administration of the Bridge of Central Massachusetts. Their dedication to implementing DBT in residential programs meant that I had the opportunity to receive excellent training in DBT and to implement DBT in a residential program for transition-age adults while developing an adolescent program that fully incorporated DBT. In those programs, I began to develop and implement skills groups for the parents of the residents. I want to thank Steve Murphy, my supervisor and the DBT skills group facilitator, who coined the term "The Story of Emotion." I am especially grateful to Christy Clark Matta, the DBT project director, for teaching me the concepts, philosophy, and skills of DBT, for showing me what it meant to be part of a consultation team, for sharing with me the information she received from Alec Miller about the middle path, and for instilling in me my love of DBT.

I am grateful to Jeanine Penzo, my friend and coauthor of my first book, for sharing what it means to parent a "child" with emotion dysregulation. Her thoughtful insights, her willingness to share, and the strength and courage she shows in living her life and appreciating every possible moment prompted and continues to inspire my ongoing work with parents.

I have been lucky along the way to attend trainings by Marsha Linehan and the late Cindy Sanderson, as well as Charlie Swenson and Alec Miller, all superb teachers. I am grateful to Charlie for his continued teaching; for sharing his sensitivity, caring, and mindfulness in action; and for demonstrating how to implement DBT in a holistic and personal way.

I am grateful to the Tuesday morning consultation team—Jean Lauderback, Wyneshia Hicks, Mark Becker, Betty Bae, and Sara Rothhelder—who have given me the opportunity to train seasoned and new clinicians in the DBT framework and to learn along the way. Witnessing their journeys toward incorporating DBT into their personal and professional lives has been rewarding in many ways. I thank this consultation team for helping me to further understand how to use DBT with adolescents and for making every Tuesday morning a wonderful and fulfilling experience.

I also am very appreciative of my colleagues (and friends) at the Metro DBT Consortium—Brian Corrado, Judi Sprei, and my coauthor, Britt Rathbone—who have been my invaluable supporters and teachers for the past two years. I have come to count on your help in finding the middle path and learning to be more accepting, and you remind me to always think dialectically. I value our time together, and it has helped me to become a much more effective DBT practitioner. And, Britt, your patience and collaboration in writing this book and in teaching me so much about DBT and adolescents is much appreciated. I am continually impressed by your ongoing devotion to providing the most effective treatment to adolescents, and I am so pleased that I have been able to come along with you as we have learned together.

I am grateful, as always, to my family of friends, whose support is always appreciated. They have witnessed my personal and professional changes (and, amazingly, how I brought mindfulness into my life), and they have willingly spent long hours listening to me extol the virtues of DBT.

I am grateful for my growing family, for Jenn and Neil and Sarah and Brady, for the joy you bring me as well as for providing opportunities for me to practice these skills. And I am most appreciative of Josh and Molly, my two grandchildren, whose arrival into my life has provided me with the greatest pleasure and the most incredibly wonderful distractions that I have ever experienced. And I can never adequately express my appreciation to my husband, Brad, whose ongoing support of my efforts and whose belief, confidence, and pride in me has provided me with the strength to take risks and continue to grow. My family has enabled me to create balance in my life and to be more aware of its beauty and wonder.

—Pat Harvey

This book would not be possible without the support and guidance from my teachers and colleagues over the years. I am especially grateful to Susan Loughman for teaching me the role of biology and its interaction with the environment in mental health; and to my fellow DBT consultation team members—John Dunn, Phyllis Pomerantz, JoJo Gaul, Anu Lukk, Betty Bae, Ben Pleasure, and Pat Harvey—who all have made sacrifices to learn, implement, and improve their delivery of DBT; and to my colleagues on the Metro DBT Consortium—Pat Harvey, Brian Corrado, and Judi Sprei—who have helped me grow personally and supported the development of high-quality DBT services for adolescents by being collaborative and encouraging. And I would never have had the time to do this were it not for Kathy Myers helping with practice-related administrative tasks.

I am very appreciative that Pat Harvey relocated to the Washington, DC, area and took the lead in pulling providers together who share an interest in DBT, and for guiding me through the process of writing this book.

My family has been especially understanding and supportive as this book came together. I so appreciate their understanding of my passion for my work and allowing me the time to pursue it.

My love for DBT would probably never have developed were it not for the inspiration and information I received by attending trainings years ago with Marsha Linehan, Alec Miller, and Sherri Manning, as well as the continued development of DBT knowledge and skill through advanced training with Charlie Swenson and consultation with Ed Shearin. The distinctive personalities of each of these individuals has helped me see that DBT does not rely solely on the personality of the therapist, and that therapists who want to help adolescents can learn the skills to do so.

My greatest gratitude is to every one of the adolescents with whom I have worked over the years. Each has taught me something. They all have given back to me, through their hard work and growth, ongoing optimism, and respect for each person's individual struggles and how these struggles lead to incredible growth.

—Britt Rathbone

We would like to thank our colleagues who helped us become more effective in our work with adolescents. We want to thank Judi Sprei and Brian Corrado for helping us develop our practice with adolescents and parents, and for supporting our efforts toward increasing effectiveness in all that we do. We would like to thank Judi Sprei, JoJo Gaul, Donna Firer, Wyneshia Hicks, Mark Becker, Jean Lauderback, Anu Lukk, and Abby Sarrett-Cooper for taking the time to read parts of this manuscript and for providing us with much appreciated feedback and support. Thank you for helping us write a clearer and more understandable book. And we would like to thank our consultant, Ed Shearin, for teaching us how to use DBT in more flexible ways while also holding us to a high level of fidelity to the model as it was developed. And our great appreciation goes to him for reading the entire manuscript, sharing with us his vast knowledge, and providing invaluable feedback.

The folks at New Harbinger have been so helpful from the very beginning as we pulled this book together. We would like to thank Tesilya Hanauer for helping us develop the ideas for this book and then giving us the opportunity to write it. We would also like to thank Jess Beebe and the rest of the developmental editors for their always-positive feedback and for helping us write in a clear, concise, and understandable way. We wrote with ever-present mindfulness of your invaluable advice. Finally, we want to extend our appreciation to our copy editor, Jean M. Blomquist, for her insights, patience, and commitment to helping us create a coherent, organized, and well-written book.

—PH and BHR

Introduction

It's not easy being an adolescent. The world becomes more complex and the adolescent brain develops at its own pace, often glaringly a step behind the demands placed on it for judgment, emotional maturity, and achievement. We know kids suffer. Britt sees it in his office every day, and Pat hears the painful stories that parents tell about their adolescent children. One estimate finds that "approximately one in every four to five youth in the US meets criteria for a mental disorder with severe impairment across their lifetime" (Merikangas et al., 2010, p. 980). Many receive ineffective treatments, and many of them do not receive treatment at all. The need for effective treatment has never been more pronounced.

In the twenty-five years that Britt has spent working exclusively with adolescents and Pat has spent working with adolescents in residential care and in families, it has become very clear that several factors contribute to effective treatment:

- conveying respect for the adolescent in a nonjudgmental manner

- avoiding power struggles when possible

- maintaining a transparent style

- taking the role of a detective with the adolescent, and making no assumptions

- offering structure within the treatment

- teaching the skills needed to live a satisfying and healthy life

When Britt sought the most effective way to provide services to adolescents, he was excited when he discovered these same elements present in dialectical behavior therapy (DBT). His initial DBT training led to the ability to develop and facilitate skills training groups. The idea of teaching skills that are essential for mental health and not systematically taught elsewhere immediately appealed to Britt. Initially, he started a skills group as an adjunct to treatment as usual. Teaching the skills meant that he really had to know them, and he found that knowing the skills improved his work with all adolescents. Seeing teenagers who have significant difficulties improve, some dramatically, reinforced the commitment to DBT and led to developing a DBT treatment and consultation team within his practice.

The demand for DBT consistently outstrips capacity, which has led to an increase in the number of therapists and number of skills groups within the practice. Training therapists, learning skills, and orienting adolescents to a new form of treatment have all presented challenges that we continue to address. The learning curve continually challenges us all. However, we have also found that learning DBT both stimulates us and encourages our creativity.

Why take on a treatment that is labor intensive, includes so many modalities, and brings the riskiest and most difficult clients? Because it works. It enables you to provide state-of-the-art treatment to your adolescent clients, allows you to literally save lives, and enables you to witness the ultimate transformation of anger, pain, and suffering into competency, satisfaction, and success. The elegance of DBT is that it takes tried and true psychological skills and packages them in a format that allows adolescents to learn them, apply them, and integrate them into their lives in a structured and organized way.

DBT is a treatment that has been proven effective with suicidal and self-harming adolescents and has been adapted for use with at-risk adolescents. Adolescents have the reputation for being notoriously challenging for practitioners, given their tendency to blatantly question authority and be actively unengaged in therapy. Some practitioners avoid working with adolescents altogether as a result. DBT structures the treatment in such a way that you develop confidence and effectiveness with this challenging population. DBT engages adolescents, gives them crucial skills they are not taught elsewhere, and helps them change their behaviors. In short, DBT changes lives. It offers a clear, concrete treatment that guides you while it also helps the adolescent; it allows you to use the therapeutic relationship in the service of change. This treatment will help you be a more effective therapist, be more effective in your own life, and become increasingly rejuvenated by the change in your clients.

Providing DBT is professionally rewarding. It instills hope in adolescents, parents, and practitioners. One DBT graduate asked his school if he could teach the DBT skills to his special education program. Another wrote to us from college to say she felt significantly more prepared to manage the difficulties life brought her, and another wrote the following letter to future DBT participants when she graduated from skills group:

> At first I didn't think I needed to attend….[N]ow I think everyone, even the happiest person in the world, should join a DBT group. I learned so many skills, and I have found one or two that really help pull me out of the depression I feel sometimes. Even if you only like one skill, I urge to you to use it as often as possible. I have even taught my friends skills…and those friends, who have never cut or tried to hurt themselves, use those skills as often as I do. DBT saved my life. I no longer feel the need to cut when I'm upset or bored, and I can communicate with people so much easier, which makes me feel less alone. I am so glad to have taken part.

These types of unsolicited reactions from adolescents who have participated in DBT are not unusual. They are the bonus for solid and effective treatment.

This book is about treating adolescents who have emotional intensity, engage in high-risk and, at times, life-threatening behaviors, and have not responded to other therapies. In it, we provide guidance to practitioners who search for ways to use DBT in their practices, want to develop a DBT practice for adolescents, or seek to become more effective in DBT practices that are already underway. We provide answers to the questions we had as we began to integrate DBT into our therapeutic practice and looked for material to help us know where and how to start. The process of DBT implementation is ongoing and ever changing; we continue to evaluate our practice and to learn new ways to become more effective. Our hope is that this book helps you start the process of DBT implementation or helps enhance the work you are already doing. We also hope it encourages the continued questioning and learning that is a hallmark of DBT.

About This Book

This book is the result of the collaboration within two separate consultation teams, that unique entity that so enhances the effectiveness of DBT. One consultation team—started by Pat—consisted of clinicians who were new to DBT and were learning how to implement skills groups and then how to provide individual therapy with adolescents. Together the members of the team worked on understanding each skill and how it would be useful to adolescents, developing new materials that were relevant to adolescents, and practicing DBT skills in their own lives. Some of the worksheets in this book are the result of the work of that team. That team continues to meet and question and learn as we implement DBT in our practices and in our lives, and Pat serves as facilitator and mentor.

At the same time, we (Britt and Pat) joined two other experienced practitioners who had already implemented DBT into their therapeutic work; we came together to form a consultation team to enhance our clinical work. Just as we did when we began, our consultation team continues to discuss how to provide the most comprehensive and effective DBT treatment to the adolescents and their families with whom we work. We are passionate about the needs of adolescents—and their parents, whose needs can sometimes be overlooked in other treatment approaches. This dual passion continues to fuel our ongoing discussions. Many of the ideas in the following pages resulted from these consultation team discussions.

We chose to write this book for "practitioners," regardless of discipline or the setting in which you work, because we know that DBT is used by many professionals in many settings, a development we hope will continue over time. If you are a professional who works with youth and tries to engage adolescents in the work of change, this book is for you.

How to Use This Book

We designed this book to help you in your clinical work by focusing on the behavioral symptoms that are caused by emotion dysregulation. This is consistent with the cognitive behavioral approach that underlies dialectical behavior therapy. Directly targeting behaviors causes a reduction in those that interfere with the quality of life and an increase in healthier behaviors. This book helps you respond effectively to behavioral syndromes, not to specific diagnoses.

We have divided this book into four parts. Part one provides an overview of adolescence and why DBT helps the practitioner who works with challenging and high-risk adolescents. This section also provides an overview of DBT treatment. It enables you to think about how to implement DBT and how much DBT to implement. We suggest you read part one first, especially if you are new to DBT or beginning to implement it with adolescents for the first time.

Part two provides a summary of the various modalities of DBT treatment—individual therapy (including coaching between sessions), skills training, work with families, and consultation teams. In order to provide comprehensive DBT, you have to be familiar with these modalities, and find a way to provide them. Most of the specific lessons of DBT are contained in these chapters.

The third part provides ways that you can work with adolescents who have specific emotionally driven behaviors. It gives very specific guidance on interventions, and dialogues for use with adolescents with specific emotional and behavioral challenges—self-harming and suicidal behaviors, substance abuse, anxiety-driven behaviors, disordered eating, and disruptive behaviors. Find the chapter that relates to the specific problem behaviors you are experiencing with an adolescent.

The last part is a summary. It provides directions for beginning or continuing your DBT practice as well as resources and references.

Throughout the book, you will find new and unique worksheets and practice assignments designed for adolescents and their parents. These materials can be used directly with your clients. You will also find exercises that will enable you to understand DBT more personally and help you become a more effective therapist. Finally, you will find examples of adolescents—composite characters, male in some chapters and female in others—who experience a variety of behavioral symptoms of emotion dysregulation. Along with these, we offer dialogues and specific interventions that will help you engage difficult adolescents, and help them make a commitment to treatment and change their behaviors to develop the life they would like to have.

The skills, examples, interventions, and homework practices found within this book are based on the concepts and materials originally developed by Linehan (1993a, 1993b) and Miller, Rathus, & Linehan (2007), and are used by us, our colleagues, and those we train. They are tried and true and ready to go. Our goal is to provide you with the knowledge we have learned through our experiences. Dialectics teaches us that change is constant, so we are constantly learning and our skills are constantly evolving. We hope that this book will be the beginning, or continuation, of your own exploration of learning and the evolution of your professional skills.

PART 1

The Challenge of Adolescence and the Benefits of DBT

CHAPTER 1

Adolescents and DBT

An adolescent is brought to your office, clinic, program, or facility. She may be brought by her parents, referred by a family doctor or psychiatrist, or sent by a juvenile justice program, a residential program, or a hospital. The young person in your office may or may not want to be there, believe she has a problem, or be willing to talk or cooperate in the process. She may recognize that she is having difficulty in her life with her peers, family, or school, or she may believe that she is doing just fine. Even if the adolescent has recently tried to harm herself or run away, been in trouble with the law, or otherwise displayed high-risk behavior, she may now believe that her problems are all behind her. She may believe that it is her parents, other authority figures, or larger institutions that have the problem. Or she may feel so overwhelmed by her feelings that she thinks that nobody can understand or help her. Those who choose to work with adolescents who have high-risk and/or challenging behaviors know the difficulties in connecting, understanding the problem, and helping the adolescent commit to the therapeutic process.

The parents who bring in the adolescent may experience a variety of thoughts and feelings:

- blamed, judged, overwhelmed, disappointed, and frustrated

- anxious that their adolescent will continue to engage in dangerous behaviors and afraid of how dangerous these behaviors are

- scared that they do not know how to keep their child safe

- worried that if their son or daughter does something dangerous, it will be their fault

- despairing that their home is chaotic

- angry that they cannot talk to their son or daughter

- burned out from numerous ineffective prior treatments

- hopeless and helpless

While you may be the first practitioner the adolescent has seen, it is more likely that you are one in a long list of professionals from whom the parents have sought help. Previous practitioners might have felt overwhelmed by the adolescent, finding it difficult to engage someone who blames others for her problems. The level of risk, possibility of an unsatisfactory outcome (suicide, arrest, incarceration, worsening symptoms, refusal to participate in treatment), and pressure to "fix" the adolescent may at times have caused practitioners to refuse to treat the adolescent, to refer out, or to recommend a residential program or other higher level of care.

It is understandable that the family feels hopeless. It is up to you, the present practitioner, to communicate that change is possible and that the family can be helped. The first and most important step you will take, as in most treatment frameworks, will be to establish a relationship with the adolescent. While DBT is a cognitive-behavioral approach to treatment (with a focus on behavioral change), it is also very much focused on the nature and importance of the relationship between the practitioner and the client. It is through the therapeutic relationship that learning, and change, can occur.

The Paradox

The behaviors that are viewed as problematic for the adults in the adolescent's life paradoxically are actually quite effective and helpful for the adolescent, as they help her feel better immediately. Thus, the adolescent sees little reason to change these behaviors. The adolescent is not "resistant to change" or "unmotivated"; the behaviors actually help her feel better in the moment. She may be reluctant to talk about the behaviors (or even think about them) after they have occurred because of feelings of shame and guilt. As a result, she has very little opportunity to learn from experience. The practitioner who understands how effective these behaviors are for the adolescent is better able to engage the adolescent in the difficult work of replacing dangerous behaviors with healthier, more adaptive behaviors.

The Challenges of Normative Adolescence

Adolescence, even for those who do not have emotional problems or difficulties, is a time of great emotional, physical, and neurological change. For many adolescents, identity and sense of self are developed by experimenting with friendships, activities, belief systems, and sexual encounters—and by challenging parents who they think hold them back. Adolescents develop the ability to think abstractly, which both allows and causes them to question long-held understandings. All of a sudden adolescents can see alternatives to their parents' choices and decisions. They need to separate from their parents in order to develop their own identity, and this separation is sometimes filled with anger and anxiety. While their adolescents work on separating, so, too, do the parents struggle to provide guidance and structure while also letting go. Friction and tension between adolescents and parents is a developmental norm.

Despite the fact that adolescents can now begin to think in an abstract way, their brain development is not complete. They often do not see the long-term consequences of their choices and decisions. Adolescents tend to take risks because they do not see the danger inherent in their decisions and they have a neurological predisposition to seeking out stimulating experiences. They often react emotionally and impulsively and see themselves as invincible.

The moods of adolescents can be labile and erratic. They are sometimes sullen, sometimes happy and joyful, sometimes depressed, sometimes almost manic in their exuberance. They are easily reactive to situations in which they feel challenged, threatened, or unsure. The same adolescent who rebels against conformity may desperately need to "fit in" with her peer group and will demand similar clothes, freedoms, and privileges. Feeling "different" is very uncomfortable. Adolescents may easily get angry, especially within the family when disappointed or unable to have desired privileges. Parents and teachers may become confused because the behaviors and moods of the adolescent can be so variable. The standout student may be a quiet and depressed son or daughter. The loyal friend who is always there for her friends may be unwilling to do chores or help out at home. The caring and sensitive preadolescent may become a demanding, angry, and self-absorbed teenager. The confusion felt by the adolescent is mirrored in the parents and family.

Complicating the emotional unpredictability of adolescents is the impact of the peer group, which directly and indirectly influences adolescent behavior. Teens begin to rely more on friends for emotional support, and parents may feel disconnected, "out of touch," or even rejected. Teens with behavior problems or mental health issues often seek out peers with similar issues, and practitioners are well aware of the contagion effect of substance abuse, self-harm, risk taking, and suicidal behaviors.

When parents bring an adolescent to a practitioner, they are often looking for guidance in understanding whether their adolescent's behaviors are developmentally "normal," or reflect a deeper problem. To answer this question, the practitioner will look at the behaviors, the level of risk, how long the behaviors have been occurring, and how much they impact the life of the adolescent. The practitioner will establish the function of the behaviors in question: Are they indicative of an adolescent who is experimenting with her identity? Are the behaviors being used to modulate and regulate emotions that feel intense, very reactive, and "out of control"? The answers to these questions will help the practitioner decide what, if any, kind of help the adolescent might need. We can look at these questions in light of Maria's situation:

Seventeen-year-old Maria's parents are concerned. Three months ago, they stumbled upon sexually explicit text messages on her phone, and when they investigated further, they found sexually suggestive photographs that she had sent to boys. They called the practitioner for an evaluation after they noticed scars on her thighs when they were vacationing. Maria admitted to them that she has been cutting herself, and while she claims that the text messages and photographs are not an ongoing issue, her parents are suspicious and don't want to take any chances. Up until this year, they had not been too worried about her. She has always earned excellent grades in school, and teachers have nothing but praise for her. Home life is another story. Maria has been

*challenging—at times breaking rules, becoming angry and yelling at her parents, refusing to coop-
erate with chores and expectations, and spending a lot of time alone in her room. Her parents
have wondered whether they do enough to help her with her temper and moodiness. They have
always thought that if she's doing well at school, then she must be okay overall.*

*In the first meeting with Maria, the practitioner discovers that she first cut herself in seventh
grade after a friend confided in her that she had been cutting her arms for several months; and
she started cutting more regularly at the end of eighth grade when she was having problems
getting along with her friends.*

*Maria is proud of her good grades and her athleticism. She has been on the track and basket-
ball teams this year and runs year round. Her doctor has expressed concern about the amount of
exercise she does. Maria says the exercise makes her feel so much better, and she will not follow
the doctor's guidelines.*

The Treatment Challenges and Practitioner's Responses

Adolescents face particular difficulties that present special challenges for mental health professionals. We can look at these difficulties, see how they are manifested in Maria's life, and explore the
challenges they pose to practitioners and the ways in which practitioners can respond.

**There is often a discrepancy between what the adolescent thinks is a problem and what the
parents are concerned about.** In the example above, Maria's parents are concerned about potentially dangerous behaviors (cutting, exercising too much, sending sexually explicit material) that
might lead to health issues or injury, while Maria minimizes the potential danger and believes that
she is fine. The adolescent looks for the practitioner to take sides and often expects the practitioner
to take the side of the parents.

- **Practitioner's response:** To validate the grain of truth (Burns, 1999) in both the adolescent's and the parents' perspectives by acknowledging the concerns and feelings of both.
  The practitioner works on engaging the adolescent in the process of change, despite her
  belief that her parents are overreacting and there really isn't any problem or danger in her
  behavior.

**Often, adolescents do not choose to go to a practitioner; instead, they have been "mandated" to
do so by parents, courts, or other authority figures.** The practitioner, by extension, becomes one
more adult who wants to change the adolescent and wants her to be different than she is. The
natural guardedness and lack of trust that adolescents feel with adults is transferred to the

practitioner, compromising the adolescent's willingness to participate. Some adolescents may have previously experienced treatment that has been ineffective or judgmental, increasing their hesitancy. And even the most willing adolescents may feel apprehensive sharing their private experiences with someone they have just met.

- **Practitioner's response:** To immediately prioritize the development of a collaborative and trusting working relationship with the adolescent so that she comes, over time, to accept that the practitioner wants to help her make chances that are meaningful for her and that help her meet her own goals.

Adolescents who are brought to a practitioner may be embarrassed or ashamed. It can be difficult for adolescents to ask for or use the help of adults. Stigma plays a role in keeping adolescents from accepting help; they are worried and anxious about how they will be perceived by others, and they fear that they will be seen as different and "abnormal." Maria, a good student and athlete, is probably held in high regard by her peers. She may not know how to explain that she is seeing a practitioner—and her parents may have similar feelings. They may feel that seeking out mental health treatment is a sign of failure on their part, and they may feel (unjustified) shame and guilt about their parenting.

- **Practitioner's response:** To provide a comforting, welcoming environment (providing snacks, drinks, age-appropriate magazines, comfortable furniture, and so on) and to "normalize" the process as much as possible. The practitioner can list well-known individuals who have accessed therapy, such as musicians, artists, and sports figures. Comparing therapy to other medical treatments for chronic or acute problems is also useful, and an accurate orientation to treatment is critical.

Ongoing and incomplete brain development makes it difficult for adolescents to see the long-term impacts of their behaviors. It is therefore difficult to engage them in the process of therapy or convince them of the need to change dangerous behaviors. Because they often do not believe that the risks they take can result in negative consequences, injury, or death, they do not see the necessity of avoiding those risks. Maria does not accept that her excessive exercise may be harmful and does not acknowledge that cutting can cause physical harm.

- **Practitioner's response:** To help the adolescent understand the links among triggers, behavior, and consequences, and to learn how to problem solve and choose safer ways to manage her feelings. The practitioner accomplishes this by remaining concrete and direct and by providing clear feedback.

The chart below summarizes the ways in which adolescents, in general, may challenge practitioners and some of the ways that DBT practitioners respond to those challenges.

Challenge	DBT-Influenced Responses by the Practitioner
Adolescent does not believe there is a problem.	Help the adolescent to examine and assess positive and negative impact of behaviors, and to evaluate the long-term consequences
Adolescent is forced to participate in treatment.	Acknowledge that treatment is being required by others and offer some choice about which therapy to engage in Provide a validating and nonjudgmental therapeutic environment
Adolescent has had unsatisfactory experiences in previous treatments.	Take responsibility for treatment effectiveness, communicate this to client, and do not blame the client if treatment is ineffective
Adolescent or family experiences treatment as shaming.	Validate feelings Expose the adolescent to feelings of shame Normalize the process
Adolescent has executive functioning impairment.	Structure treatment and explain it in ways that are understandable to the adolescent
Adolescent has neurological predisposition to taking risks.	Provide skills training Help the adolescent evaluate the impact of behavioral choices

The Philosophy and Structure of DBT

DBT provides a welcome guide through the jungle of working with adolescents and their families, especially when high-risk and challenging behaviors are present. DBT philosophy and skills help lessen the practitioner's anxiety and enable the practitioner to target symptomatic behaviors in a strategic and logical manner.

The Philosophy of DBT

The DBT philosophy that emotion dysregulation is the underlying issue that leads to behavior dysregulation helps the practitioner to remain nonjudgmental and accepting. DBT philosophy that encourages validation and transparency enables the practitioner to engage the adolescent in what will be the hard work of change.

Behaviors Manage Emotional Pain

The behaviors that are so dangerous and problematic in the adolescent's life are seen as ways that the adolescent has learned to manage emotional pain (Linehan, 1993a). These behaviors are not "attention seeking" or "manipulative." The adolescent is not "lazy," "disobedient," or "oppositional." Neither the adolescent nor the parent is at fault, and nobody is blamed.

The practitioner who uses a DBT framework recognizes and acknowledges the pain, as well as the intense emotions that lead to dangerous behaviors and that bring the client and her family to treatment. Parents and the adolescent understand very quickly that if these behaviors have been learned, then new behaviors can be learned to take their place and DBT will provide specific ways for life to improve. Relief is evident; hope becomes possible. In a validating and accepting environment in which the adolescent does not feel "bad" or blamed, the adolescent is better able to accept the feedback she is given and look less defensively at her own behaviors.

Treatment Is Transparent and Collaborative

The practitioner takes great pains to explain the process, theory, and structure of the treatment to the adolescent and her family so that it is transparent, and to engage them in a collaborative process. The adolescent learns from the DBT practitioner that the work they will do together will help her to meet her own goals for life; the process of developing goals engenders trust, as does the practitioner's ongoing explanation of how each skill (explained in more detail in chapter 4) will be helpful to her. The practitioner may even self-disclose her own use of skills. Explanations about the reasons for using skills occur continuously. This approach increases the adolescent's willingness to be involved in the process of change.

The Structure of DBT Treatment

DBT demands that practitioners teach new skills and behaviors in an organized, structured way that moves adolescents and families from feeling miserable to developing the life they want (Linehan, 1993a). DBT guides the practitioner to target symptomatic behaviors in a strategic and logical manner. Throughout the following chapters, we will discuss these important components of DBT:

- commitment strategies

- validation strategies

- priority targets

- dialectical approaches and strategies

- behavioral analysis

- change strategies

You will learn practical ways to incorporate these components into your practice that will enable you to treat adolescents more effectively. To do this, however, you must first be able to identify which adolescents will benefit from DBT.

Is DBT Recommended for This Adolescent?

DBT will be most effective with adolescents whose behavioral problems are the result of emotion dysregulation—that is, the adolescent's behavioral difficulties are the result of her attempts to regulate painful and intense emotions. Because of DBT's strong focus on gaining commitment to treatment, it is often the most effective treatment for adolescents who have either dropped out of other treatments or been "fired" by other treatment providers.

When to Use DBT: Adolescents and Emotional Dysregulation

You may see adolescents in your practice who will exhibit an ongoing pattern of one or more of the following behaviors:

- angry outbursts

- rages

- threatening behaviors, especially in response to disappointment

- abusiveness to other family members

- intensity in relationships

- decision making that is driven by how someone *feels* about them

These behaviors may be indicative of emotion dysregulation (Miller, Rathus, & Linehan, 2007) if they are being used to manage painful and overwhelming emotions, and indicate that DBT may be an effective treatment choice.

Commitment to Treatment

To be accepted into DBT, a client must be willing to make a commitment to staying alive and to reducing self-harming behaviors. Some adolescents may not be ready to commit to changing unsafe behaviors, or may not be willing initially to be involved in comprehensive treatment. Some adolescents may have to work with their practitioner in an early stage of treatment to make these commitments. Commitment strategies will be discussed further in chapter 3.

Limits to Effectiveness

DBT may not be the most effective treatment for certain adolescents:

- those who have severe psychotic symptoms that may interfere with integrating the cognitive aspects of DBT

- those who have severe cognitive impairment or severe receptive or expressive language problems (Miller, Rathus, & Linehan, 2007)

- those who have eating disorders or substance-use disorders, unless other evidence-based treatments have been found ineffective (Koerner, Dimeff, & Swenson, 2007)

- those who have obsessive-compulsive disorder or other anxiety disorders, unless the evidence-based treatment for these disorders has been proven ineffective

In addition, see the decision tree (below) that we developed to assess whether a particular adolescent is a candidate for DBT:

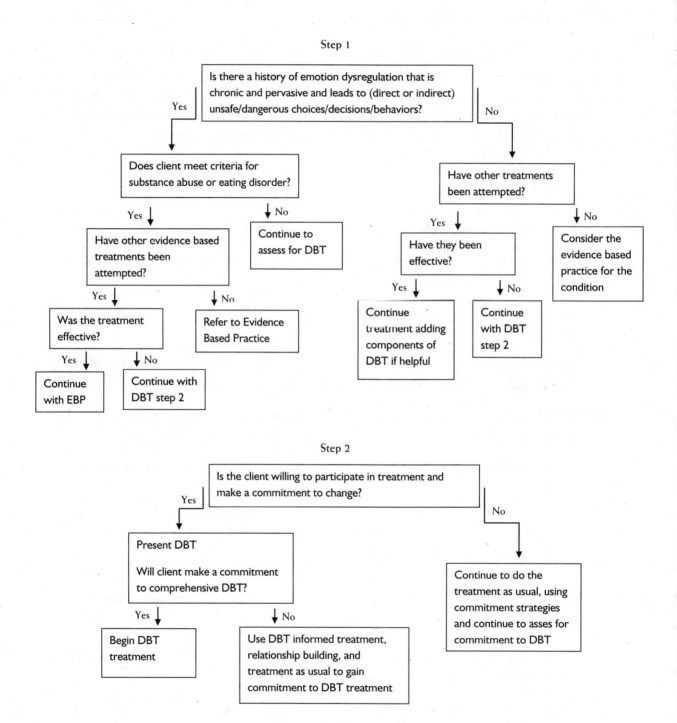

Summary

In this chapter, we discussed the special circumstances and challenges involved in treating adolescents and the ways in which DBT philosophy, structure, and tools can help practitioners provide more effective treatment to this population. These concepts will be revisited throughout the book as we address how to apply DBT treatment to specific behavioral problems. The next chapters will provide more specific details about the structure and tools of DBT and how they are applied to individual therapy, skills training groups, and family work.

CHAPTER 2

DBT Orientation

The first contact with the practitioner is usually a parent or caregiver, who may be aware of the effectiveness of DBT or who may simply be looking for a way to help end the misery and the high-risk or challenging behaviors of an adolescent child. The practitioner's first task is to orient the adolescent and parents or caregivers to DBT, regardless of their prior knowledge about DBT.

Explaining DBT

The transparent and collaborative nature of DBT begins during the intake and assessment process when DBT is explained fully and completely to any client for whom DBT is being considered:

- DBT was developed by Marsha Linehan, who, adapted a *cognitive behavioral approach* (one that focuses on changing thoughts, feelings, and behaviors) by adding *acceptance* (behaviors that communicate empathy and acceptance of the way things are in this moment) to make it more effective in helping individuals lessen their self-harming and suicidal behavior (Linehan, 1993a).

- DBT is an *evidence-based therapy*, its effectiveness proven by research, which has been adapted for individuals with a variety of emotional difficulties.

- DBT is a structured treatment that includes structured individual therapy (focused on goals and "target behaviors") and skills training groups (that include five modules of skills, adapted for adolescents).

- Out-of-session coaching is available by phone or text to help clients when they are in crisis.

- DBT is hard work and will require the adolescent's willingness to make a commitment to life, which includes eliminating self-harming behaviors.

The practitioner begins to develop a dialectical stance (one that accepts contradictions) to treatment by acknowledging that drug use, self-harm, aggressive behaviors, eating disorders, and/ or other high-risk behaviors can serve to regulate emotions *and* that the adolescent will have to replace these behaviors with safer behaviors if he is to develop the life he wants.

Adolescents, Families, and the Biosocial Theory

The *biosocial theory* (Linehan, 1993a) is a nonjudgmental and nonblaming explanation of the complex transaction between a child's biology (hard-wired vulnerability to emotional intensity that a child is born with or develops early in life) and the environment (those individuals who respond to the experiences of the young child) that leads to *emotional dysregulation* as the child develops—that is, emotional responses that overwhelm the individual and lead to behavioral dyscontrol. Adolescents and their parents are introduced to this theory during the initial phases of treatment.

Emotion Dysregulation/Intensity of Emotion

The theoretical underpinning of DBT is that the pain and emotional intensity that the adolescent experiences physiologically, emotionally, and behaviorally is caused by a biologically based vulnerability to emotion dysregulation (Linehan, 1993a); the adolescent has an emotional system that reacts more immediately and more intensely to emotional stimuli than would individuals who do not have this vulnerability. This physiological system causes emotions, when triggered, to remain intense longer and to take longer to return to the baseline mood. The adolescent's temperament and vulnerability may be impacted by an early childhood experience or a traumatic event that exacerbates an already sensitive emotion regulation system, or it may be a reflection of the child's biological temperament. Parents often report that their adolescent has "always" been highly reactive to emotional situations, and has "always" been challenging to them.

Individuals with this particular biological vulnerability are more likely to exhibit behaviors such as deliberate self-harm, delinquent behavior, substance abuse, conduct disorder, impulsivity, and other behavior problems (Crowell et al., 2011). An adolescent with emotion dysregulation uses his behaviors, even those that are dangerous, to try to regulate his emotions, not to be "manipulative," "scary," or disruptive to those around him.

This explanation resonates with adolescents who have not been able to understand why they feel the way they do or why they react to situations differently than others. These adolescents have often been told that these strong emotions are somehow their fault and are unacceptable, that they can feel better if they try harder, or that they should "just get over it." These comments add to their sense of confusion, guilt, and shame. Having an explanation for why they might feel the way they do begins to bring them some relief.

The practitioner points out that intense emotions are not always a problem and are certainly not the fault of the adolescent. The practitioner explains that sometimes these emotions (and passions) can be extremely pleasurable and highly effective in getting the adolescent what he wants, may lead to creative work, and are probably reinforced by others. Intense emotions can lead to productive behaviors *and* harmful behaviors. The practitioner helps the adolescent see both the effectiveness and the negative consequences of his behaviors, all within the context of helping to normalize and accept the reality of his life situation.

Another way of looking at the concept of emotion dysregulation that adolescents find very helpful can be seen in the diagram below:

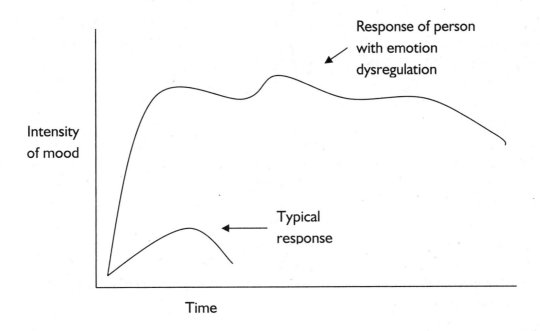

The adolescent with emotional intensity is in a state of emotional arousal more often and at higher levels. Therefore, subsequent events "bounce" the adolescent's distress up again before his mood has had a chance to settle from an initial event. (The drawing is exaggerated for effect.)

The Impact of the Environment

The biosocial theory further explains that the biological vulnerability to emotion dysregulation that the child is born with is met with responses from people in the young child's environment who do not understand what, to them, appear to be unreasonable emotional and behavioral responses to situations. The parent or caregiver may, in an attempt to help the child feel better, encourage the child "not to worry" or to "get over it," or may try to fix the situation without understanding its emotional components. These responses may directly or indirectly dismiss, minimize, or trivialize the reaction of the child, thereby invalidating him and causing pervasive emotion dysregulation as he grows into adolescence and adulthood. Often parents, teachers, relatives, or other child-care providers do not recognize the invalidating nature of what they say. This explanation does not blame the environment; instead, it recognizes the desire of the individuals in the environment to lessen the discomfort of the child they care about.

The Transaction of Emotion Dysregulation and the Invalidating Environment

The biosocial theory is a *transactional formulation*: the adolescent interacts with people who may invalidate what he experiences, and the adolescent may also behave in ways that cause the people around him, who might otherwise be supportive, to become dismissive, frustrated, and angry. We often explain to parents that just as their young child's behaviors as they develop into adolescence might be partly a response to how they parented, so too can parents' behaviors be a response to their child and their child's temperament.

Without the understanding that their child is, in fact, feeling emotions more intensely, parents may demand that their child get over whatever bothers him without realizing that he is physiologically incapable of doing so or does not have the skills to do so. The parent may see the adolescent as willful or oppositional. They do not realize that telling a child not to feel something is the same as asking a person with a migraine not to be sensitive to light and not to feel nauseated. It is impossible not to feel what someone feels. Suggesting that one should not feel their feelings directs more attention to the emotion, and increases the frustration and shame one feels for not being able to do what others appear to do so easily. The biosocial theory teaches parents to validate the pain that is present despite the fact that they cannot see it.

Biosocial Theory and Its Impact

The transaction of emotional vulnerability and an inadvertently invalidating environment can produce an adolescent or young adult who does not trust his own internal experiences. He will look to others to tell him how he is supposed to feel, and he feels bad about what he does feel. An invalidating environment also contributes to adolescents not learning how to manage difficult feelings; they are told they should just get over them without being taught or shown *how* to manage them. As a result, the adolescent learns that difficult and painful feelings can and should be avoided.

Adolescent Responses to Invalidation

Adolescents tend to respond to invalidation in one of two ways: by escalating their behaviors to let others know that they really do feel awful and need to be taken seriously, or by avoiding their own feelings, forcing them inward, and developing other ways to give them expression.

Either way, these adolescents may become unsafe (by behaving in ways that may cause harm, injury, or even death), dangerous, and aggressive, or they may exhibit other unhealthy ways to manage their emotions. Family members may find themselves responding to escalated behaviors in attempting to keep the adolescent safe. An unfortunate dynamic develops in which the adolescent is reinforced with attention (or by getting demands met) for unsafe and dangerous behaviors.

The Biosocial Theory in DBT Treatment

When the biosocial theory is explained to parents and adolescents who feel that nothing will ever change because there is something "wrong" with the adolescent, the relief they feel is palpable. The biosocial theory and the understanding that the behaviors of the adolescent are ways in which he has *learned* to manage his emotion dysregulation give hope to parents and adolescents that change is possible and that more effective behaviors can be learned. The biosocial theory provides practitioners with a starting point for understanding the adolescent and enables the development of an accepting, and therefore more effective, therapeutic environment, one in which the adolescent is taken seriously, listened to, and understood.

An Accepting Cognitive Behavioral Approach to Change

Dialectical behavior therapy is, at its core, a treatment framework that focuses on acceptance and change. The guiding principle of DBT is that change, the goal of any and all therapeutic practices, will not occur without acceptance. Practitioners who wish to use DBT in their work learn to accept and integrate this core dialectic: their clients are doing the best they can in this moment, based on the history and context of their lives, *and* that they have to make changes to their behaviors so that they can live the lives they want (Linehan, 1993a).

Mindfulness

A core component of DBT is acceptance, and a path to acceptance is *mindfulness*, the practice of being aware of the present moment (Linehan, 1993b). Many terms are used to describe mindfulness: paying attention to the present moment, noticing what is going on, or "present-focused, nonjudgmental awareness" (Barlow, Farchione, Fairholme, Todd, Ellard, & Ehrenreich-May, 2010, p. 91). One of the mindfulness skills in DBT is noticing and being aware, which encourages someone to slow down, pay attention, and experience the situation in the moment, thus enabling one to gain perspective, see things more clearly, and develop new understanding. Thus, mindful awareness enables change. For the adolescent who is impulsive and whose "out of control" behaviors are often the result of emotion dysregulation, mindfulness is a powerful tool for regulating emotions and choosing less impulsive behaviors.

Mindfulness skills, when used by practitioners allow them to accurately observe the adolescent and, thus, validate more effectively. Practitioners who maintain mindful awareness will be able to respond in ways that are more genuine and more genuinely accepting, which is more engaging to a guarded adolescent.

Mindfulness teaches doing what is effective and most helpful rather than what might feel "fair" or "right" (Linehan, 1993a). Many adolescents have been taught (directly or indirectly) to avoid unpleasant or distressing emotions, and, as a result, they have not learned the skills others have learned for managing their feelings. As adolescents fall further behind their peers in the ability to manage challenging emotions, behavioral "escapes" become more and more necessary, and when these escapes work (by helping the adolescent feel better), they are reinforced. Mindfulness skills enable exposure to painful emotions, allowing the adolescent to experience his emotions without escape or avoidance, allowing him to learn and ultimately use the skills taught throughout the treatment. (For more on skills, see chapter 4.)

A Mindfulness Practice for Practitioners

In order to understand how mindfulness practice can slow someone down and lead to new awareness, try the following exercise:

Take several minutes to write your name *very slowly*. *Notice* all aspects of the writing process:

- how you pick up the pen and get it into position in your hand

- which muscles you use

- whether you move your fingers or your wrist

- how hard you write on the paper

- how you position the paper

- what sensations you feel in your hand

Is your handwriting different? What was the experience like?

Now that you have practiced this exercise and experienced it for yourself, try it with an adolescent and/or his parents.

When the exercise is over, review with the client what he noticed, what new awareness he has, and whether or not he recognizes any difference in his handwriting or the experience of writing when he slows down. Adolescents (and parents) learn the importance of slowing down in order to change patterns and behaviors.

Acceptance

Many adolescents are brought into treatment by parents who want them to change. What the adolescent wants is someone to "get it," to understand how he feels. DBT practitioners understand the conflict and pain that the adolescent feels, and they accept and acknowledge that his behaviors are responses to that internal pain. As in the vignette below, when the adolescent feels heard and understood, he is then able to hear what the practitioner is saying, and together they are able to collaborate and work on change.

Scott is a fifteen-year-old high school freshman. He misses school often and spends many days in his room, in his bed under the covers, ignoring his friends and not communicating with his parents. His parents found drug paraphernalia in the bathroom and confronted Scott about this. He admitted that he has been smoking pot and drinking for the past year. This has led his parents to monitor his activities more closely.

In the initial session with his parents, Scott sits quietly in his chair, with his face hidden by the hood of his sweatshirt. His parents talk about how "disrespectful" Scott is to them, that he explodes in a rage when they do not allow him to do what he wants to do, and that he is not doing any work in school. His parents fear that he will not be able to get into a good college. Eventually, they admit that they also fear Scott will hurt himself seriously.

When the practitioner sees Scott alone, he remains quiet. As the practitioner begins to talk about DBT, about the pain that he must be feeling inside, Scott begins to talk. He says that nobody understands him. The practitioner listens intently to Scott, making eye contact whenever possible.

In the very first session, the practitioner makes it clear that he can understand why Scott might find drugs helpful and that he wants to help Scott figure out what he wants to change to make his life better. The practitioner explains to Scott that he will be taught new skills so that he can manage his emotions safely and that they will, together, decide on what target behaviors and goals they will work on. Even though Scott is not sure of his goals or what he wants to work on, he begins to understand that this treatment will help him change his behaviors, something he thinks he might be willing and able to do. He already likes the positive and validating attention he feels from the practitioner.

As can be seen from this vignette, in order to help adolescents change, the practitioner acknowledges that the behaviors of the adolescent have actually been effective in helping him regulate his emotions. When Scott smokes pot or drinks, he feels better. However, these behaviors also have had some negative consequences, which is why Scott's parents brought him to treatment. Generally, adolescents will not make changes that are imposed on them by others; treatment with adolescents necessitates that the adolescent "buy in" to the work and to the goals, which he must have a role in developing. The DBT therapeutic collaboration assures the adolescent that the changes he works on will be meaningful and helpful for him. Practitioner-client agreement on goals for treatment correlates with effectiveness of therapy, and DBT is no exception to this rule.

In the above scenario, Scott may not want to give up smoking pot and drinking. Scott likes the fact that the practitioner does not make him feel ashamed of his behaviors and understands that smoking and drinking help him "get some relief," something other adults have not understood. Scott begins to acknowledge that his smoking and drinking have some negative impact on his life (such as declining grades, less freedom, and more monitoring) that he is not happy about. Scott and the practitioner discuss what changes Scott might have to make in order for him to have the freedoms that he used to have. In this way, the practitioner's acceptance of Scott and his needs enables them to address behavioral change.

This discussion about change could not have happened had the practitioner not first acknowledged the function of the behavior that brings Scott to treatment. This type of honest and forthright interaction is particularly useful with adolescents. The atmosphere of respect is an important and essential aspect of this treatment.

Validation and Acceptance

Validation is a way of saying "I get it" to the adolescent, of letting the adolescent know that you understand what he feels in the context of his life, even if you don't agree with it or like it. Validation is the tool that is used to express acceptance. Conveying acceptance is necessary for change to occur. The various validation strategies that are outlined in DBT (Linehan, 1993a) help practitioners genuinely acknowledge and understand the feelings of the adolescent and help engage guarded adolescents in treatment. A practitioner's active awareness of the need to be validating ensures that the treatment setting does not become another invalidating environment. This enables the work of change.

Many practitioners equate validation and *empathy*, communicating to someone else that you understand what he is going through. In fact, validation includes empathy and also a willingness on the part of the practitioner to search for what is valid in what the person is saying. It is also not one-size-fits all; validation is considered "validating" only if the person hearing it feels as if he has been understood; each practitioner has to individualize validation to each adolescent client. Validation usually leads to more disclosure (Fruzetti, 2005). If the client is not communicating, you may want to reassess whether or not your client feels understood by you.

If a client says, "You suck," what is valid about the statement? The truth may be that the adolescent is not feeling heard and is probably angry. The practitioner, using mindful awareness, can acknowledge the client's disappointment and anger and the practitioner's own shortcomings in that moment, without becoming defensive. He can acknowledge his *lack* of effectiveness. The practitioner can then search for ways, together with the adolescent, to be more validating and more effective. This removes the practitioner from the power struggle with the adolescent and allows the relationship to move forward.

A practitioner who becomes dysregulated or emotional in a session cannot be as effective in validating clients. The practitioner may need to step back, gain perspective, seek the validity in the statement, recognize that the client is "doing the best he can" in this situation, and seek a way to communicate acceptance to the client. It is in these moments when mindfulness—just observing the situation without judgment—may be most helpful to the practitioner. Steps for validating a client (Linehan, 1993a; Miller, Rathus & Linehan, 2007) are described in the chart below.

HOW TO VALIDATE ADOLESCENT CLIENTS EFFECTIVELY

Step 1. Listen. Be interested.

Step 2. Get perspective. Stop, step back, observe, and think.

- Take a moment before responding—slow down your response time.
- Let go of problem solving; focus on the affect in the moment.
- Step back and observe your client without judgment.
- Remain nonjudgmental.
- Do not assume what you cannot observe.
- Do not confuse the intention of a behavior with its consequences.

Step 3. Search for what is valid to the adolescent. Remember, the client is doing the best the client can do under the circumstances. What affect is your client feeling? If you don't know, ask. How would other people feel in similar circumstances? What is going on for this adolescent? Is something in the environment triggering old memories? Old feelings?

Step 4. Genuinely acknowledge what is valid, what makes sense in what the client says. Find a way to show your client you take him seriously. Be aware of what you say both verbally and nonverbally. Be careful not to validate what is actually invalid (behaviors that are not useful in changing target behaviors, such as punching a teacher).

Step 5. If you have trouble validating or find yourself in a power struggle with your client, ask yourself these questions:

- What vulnerabilities do I bring to this situation?
- What is this situation triggering for me?
- Am I personalizing what is going on or what is being said?
- Am I being judgmental?
- Am I moving too fast to fix the problem or the situation? Is the power struggle a signal that even though I am trying to be validating, the client does not feel validated?

Step 6. Check out whether or not your understanding of your client is accurate. Ask whether your client is feeling understood and accepted.

Understanding Validation

Validation is a very complex strategy that requires ongoing training and practice. It is important to receive feedback from clients to ensure that practitioner behaviors are not inadvertently invalidating. It helps to know what, according to Koerner (2012) and Manning (2011), validation does *not* mean:

- agreeing with everything the client says or does

- doing whatever the client asks you to do (which actually can disempower and invalidate a client)

- telling the client that you understand when you don't

- supporting the client's unsafe behaviors, not acknowledging an unsafe behavior, or supporting invalid statements or behaviors

- saying something contrary to what the client says to help him feel "better" (for example, telling a client he is smart when he thinks he is not)

- defending yourself against what a client says about you

- telling the client he is "right"

- telling the client how to do something better in the future

- insisting you know why the client does what he does despite his protests to the contrary

- telling the client how he "should" feel or behave

- being insincere or untruthful

- being unrealistic about the client's capabilities and expressing unrealistic confidence

Just as it is important to know what validation does not mean, it is also important to know what validation, again according to Koerner (2012) and Manning (2011), *does* mean:

- listening intently without judgment

- focusing all your attention in the moment on your client

- listening actively or reflectively by repeating what your client says (for example, "By that, you mean _____")

- asking your client if you are reflecting accurately (for example, "Did I get that right?")

- active listening by listening for the underlying emotion (for example, "Others in this situation might feel _____ . Is that how you feel?")

- acknowledging in a nonblaming way why your client might be behaving this way given his history (for example, "It is understandable that you do _____ , given your history.")

- encouraging your client by letting him know you believe in his capabilities

- meaning what you say—being genuine and reflecting your true reaction to your client (for example, "It breaks my heart to hear that.")

- believing in your client

We think it is important to genuinely understand DBT concepts on a personal level so that you can teach them instinctively to your clients. In order to understand how it feels to be validated (or invalidated), try the exercise below:

Understanding the Value of Validation in Your Own Life Experience

Think about attending a meeting in which you want to discuss a problem you have with a client. Imagine the others at the meeting telling you how you can work with the client more effectively. Think of all the advice that you might receive. Think about how you feel about this advice, the way it is being given, and your own abilities. Do you feel resentful that everyone has a better idea? Do you feel incompetent? Do you feel heard? Do you feel like others are not understanding what you really need?

Now imagine that others at the meeting validate you. They tell you that they recognize the difficulties you are having, which are understandable given the complexities of the situation you describe. Imagine they tell you that they understand and would feel the same way given a similar situation. How do you feel now? Is it easier for you to take the advice and guidance given to you after the validation? Do you leave the meeting feeling better about yourself and better about the direction you will take with your client?

Below we have filled in a Validation Practice Worksheet for a practitioner meeting with Scott from the vignette.

EXAMPLE: VALIDATION PRACTICE WORKSHEET

Your emotions make validating harder: remember to slow down your response and gain perspective.

What do I want to validate? (Look at nonverbal and verbal behaviors that indicate emotions.)

The thoughts or feelings that lead to Scott sitting quietly with his hood covering his face.

I am aware of the following judgments and assumptions that make it harder to validate the other person:

"He doesn't want to cooperate or engage in treatment." "I wish he were more motivated to participate in treatment." "This is frustrating for me."

(Remember to separate the words from the feelings and concentrate on the feelings.)

What is valid for the client?

What I think the other person is feeling or experiencing:

Scott is in pain and may distrust adults because of past experiences.

After listening intently and without judgment,

I can let the other person know that I hear, understand, and accept him or her by making the following validating statement:

"You seem uncomfortable. It seems like you don't want to be here."

You can practice effectively validating your client by filling out the following worksheet. As with all skills, you can also use this worksheet to teach your clients how to validate others.

VALIDATION PRACTICE WORKSHEET

Your emotions make validating harder: remember to slow down your response and gain perspective.

What do I want to validate? (Look at nonverbal and verbal behaviors that indicate emotions.)

I am aware of the following judgments and assumptions that make it harder to validate the other person:

(Remember to separate the words from the feelings and concentrate on the feelings.)

What is valid for the client?

What I think the other person is feeling or experiencing:

After listening intently and without judgment, I can let the other person know that I hear, understand, and accept him or her by making the following validating statement:

Change Strategies in DBT

DBT practitioners need to continually balance validation and acceptance with change and problem solving. A focus solely on either acceptance or change will be ineffective. DBT provides a number of change strategies (see chart below). In order to maintain the transparent and collaborative nature of DBT, clients are given explanations about why a particular change strategy is being utilized at a certain time.

Change Strategies in DBT

Change Procedure	Behaviors to Increase	Behaviors to Decrease
Skills Training	• mindful awareness • emotion modulation • use of safer behaviors with fewer long-term negative consequences • dialectical thinking, accepting alternative perspectives • effectiveness in social situations	• avoidance of uncomfortable emotional experiences • labile affect/emotional outbursts • impulsivity/aggression/self-harm • rigid, all-or-nothing thinking • interpersonal problems/fears of abandonment
Cognitive Restructuring	• ability to accept alternative possibilities • reasonable and wise thinking	• negative belief systems and interpretations of events
Exposure	• ability to experience and/or tolerate painful emotions	• classically conditioned response to emotion • escape and avoidance of emotions
Contingency Management	• use and generalization of skillful behaviors • adaptive behaviors	• unsafe behaviors • aggressive behaviors

Applying Change Strategies

In the vignette above, Scott and his individual practitioner will target behaviors for change that help him meet his goals. To do this, they will implement the four DBT change strategies (Linehan, 1993a):

- *skills training* that teaches him to manage emotions, behaviors, and life situations more skillfully

- *cognitive restructuring* to shape more effective ways of thinking, which leads to different emotional experiences and, ultimately, more effective behavior

- *exposure* to the cues that trigger painful emotions while reducing escape or avoidant behaviors, enabling Scott to experience emotions and practice the skills he is learning for managing those emotions in a safe and healthy manner

- *contingency management*, which is the strategic use of reinforcers to increase effective behaviors, with Scott's practitioner reinforcing him for effective behaviors in the session and for making a commitment to treatment (This includes working with his parents to teach them to be more validating of Scott's concerns, more reinforcing of adaptive behaviors, and more mindful of not inadvertently reinforcing behaviors they want to eliminate.)

We will discuss each of these change strategies further in the following chapters. First, however, we want to discuss the synthesis of validation strategies and change strategies, which is the dialectical approach that informs DBT.

A Dialectical Approach: Acceptance *and* Change

The dialectical approach within DBT, which is one of its unique aspects, encourages DBT practitioners to accept contradictions and conflicting points of view and to recognize that there can be validity in opposing viewpoints (Linehan, 1993a). The ability to move between points of view, to accept alternative perspectives, and to change course when necessary is incredibly helpful and necessary when working with adolescents, who are always changing and often prone to engage in power struggles. As the practitioner seeks a synthesis between opposing ideas, the client learns to do the same. The adolescent will learn that he can be very angry with his parents and really love them at the same time (and the parents will learn the same). He can learn that the practitioner will observe limits and still be flexible in adapting to some of his needs.

This dialectical approach guides the practitioner's interventions and is also a core treatment concept. For example, the practitioner will accept that the adolescent sees no point in changing, and at the same time acknowledge the need for change in order for the adolescent's mood and functioning to improve. The practitioner will artfully and strategically stay out of a power struggle with the adolescent while at the same time encouraging the adolescent to make changes. This will be described in more detail in future chapters. The concept of dialectics also directly addresses the black-and-white/either-or thinking so prevalent in depressed and angry teens. We look for ways to accept both perspectives—black *and* white (not gray)—and to teach the adolescent to think more flexibly and realistically.

Finding a resolution to problems that balances different points of view, needs, expectations, limits, and hopes within a family is often a goal of DBT work with adolescents and their families. This dialectical approach enables the practitioner to accept and validate each member of the family and minimizes the desire of the practitioner to seek "the truth" and to take sides or think about who is "right" and who is "wrong." Instead, the practitioner seeks, and helps the family to seek, a middle ground (Miller, Rathus, & Linehan, 2007). In a dialectical framework, truth is not absolute; it evolves and changes over time, much as adolescents continually evolve and change.

DBT Goals and Modalities

Comprehensive DBT involves five modalities of treatment that address the five goals of DBT (Linehan, 1993a). The goals, or functions, of DBT are explained to adolescents and their families during the intake process:

- help motivate the client to make a commitment to change

- teach the client to become more capable of taking care of himself by learning new skills

- ensure that the skills learned generalize to the natural environment and beyond the treatment setting

- structure the environment to ensure that adaptive behaviors are reinforced, unsafe behaviors are not inadvertently reinforced, and practitioners can observe their own behavioral limits in their own practice settings

- help practitioners maintain competence and commitment to effective treatment

Each of these goals of DBT is addressed within the modalities of DBT. These five modalities will be discussed at length in part 2:

1. Individual therapy

2. Skills training group or a second individual session that is devoted to skills training

3. Out-of-session phone coaching and consultation in a crisis

4. Family therapy and other consultations to help others in the adolescent's environment encourage him to generalize the skills he learns through behavioral contingencies and validation at home and at school

5. DBT consultation team in which all DBT practitioners in a setting validate one another and discuss how to provide the most effective treatment

Comprehensive DBT vs. DBT-Informed Treatment

Comprehensive DBT includes all five modalities listed above. In contrast, DBT-informed treatment incorporates only some of these modalities into the treatment, and practitioners will determine what is most effective in their practice or for each individual adolescent client. Some practitioners have concerns about providing coaching outside of therapy sessions and may feel overwhelmed by the idea of being so available to such a high-risk population. Other practitioners may find that they do not have enough adolescent clients to fill a group or that it is hard to find other practitioners with whom to develop a consultation team. The research done on comprehensive DBT does not clearly indicate which of the modalities, if used independently, are effective.

Many practitioners and programs begin by offering a skills training group. As practitioners receive more training in DBT philosophy and skills, they may begin to provide individual therapy for those clients who are in skills training. Other practices may decide that any client who is at risk for suicidality or self-harm must be in both individual DBT and skills training.

If you implement DBT-informed treatment, it is important to monitor and evaluate your work and the modalities used for effectiveness. Make changes to the treatment as indicated.

The Pros and Cons of DBT

In DBT, the pros and cons skill (Linehan, 1993a) is taught to help clients make choices, and it, like all DBT skills, can be used by the practitioner as well. We have developed a worksheet for you to evaluate the positive and negative impact of the decision to use some or all of the DBT modalities in your practice. We have already listed some of the issues you will face as you think about using DBT in your practice. We encourage you to fill out the worksheet to help you establish whether you wish to provide comprehensive DBT treatment or to incorporate some of the philosophy and not all of the modalities into DBT-informed treatment. These are personal, professional, and business decisions, and they should not be taken lightly. As you fill in the last set of boxes, remember that you can start with DBT-informed treatment and grow your work into comprehensive DBT. Evaluating the positive and negative impact may not answer all of your questions; it will, however, help provide guidelines with which to make your choices and decisions. You can also fill in your own pros and cons on the lines provided.

The Pros and Cons of DBT

Incorporating DBT vs. Treatment as Usual

Positive impact of incorporating DBT	Negative impact of incorporating DBT
Structures treatment	*Paradigm shift—learning new and different approach*
Prioritizes teaching skills	*Overwhelming new materials and strategies*
Teaches accepting and nonjudgmental focus of treatment	
Positive impact of continuing your treatment as usual	**Negative impact of continuing treatment as usual**
Practitioner's comfort and familiarity	*Effectiveness may be limited*

Comprehensive DBT vs. Treatment as Usual

Positive impact of doing comprehensive DBT	Negative impact of doing comprehensive DBT
Proven effectiveness with high-risk and challenging clients	*Time commitment and disruptions to do telephone coaching in crisis*
Support to practitioners built into treatment	*Significant learning curve*
Increased referrals	*Labor intensive*
Positive impact of doing treatment as usual	**Negative impact of doing treatment as usual**
Decreased stress of learning new model and new strategies	*Do not grow or learn new skills*
Less accountability to consultation team	*May not be as effective with high-risk clients*
Comfort of doing what is familiar	

Comprehensive DBT vs. Informed Treatment

Positive impact of doing comprehensive DBT	Negative impact of doing comprehensive DBT
Positive impact of doing DBT-informed treatment	**Negative impact of doing DBT-informed treatment**

Whatever decision you make, you will find helpful DBT strategies and skills for working with specific categories of high-risk adolescents throughout the rest of this book.

Assumptions for Practitioners

DBT holds practitioners to a very high standard, expecting them to maintain an ongoing balance in treatment between acceptance and change and a nonjudgmental stance with multiproblem clients. This high expectation for both practitioner and adolescent bonds them in a treatment that can be difficult *and* incredibly rewarding for both.

The following assumptions, adapted from the work of DBT trainers (Linehan, 1993a; Miller, Rathus, & Linehan, 2007; Swenson, 2012), will provide guidance for your work:

DBT Assumptions for Practitioners

- There has to be acceptance in order for there to be change.

- Practitioners do not make assumptions about clients; they develop theories, ask questions, and are willing to change if their theories are inaccurate.

- Commitment to treatment is necessary for therapeutic work. Practitioners must continually gain commitment from adolescents to do the work.

- Taking a nonjudgmental and dialectical stance is essential to the work.

- Practitioners need to teach skills to adolescents who need to replace unhealthy behaviors with healthier behaviors.

- All work in DBT is transparent and collaborative.

- Practitioners will prioritize work in sessions to stay focused on the goals and will minimize responding to the "crisis of the moment" unless it is related to a treatment goal.

- Practitioners will develop an environment that reinforces adaptive behaviors and that attempts to extinguish unsafe and unhealthy behaviors.

- Practitioners will notice, acknowledge, and target unsafe behaviors.

- Practitioners need to be aware of their own limits, communicate them clearly, and respond in ways that consistently maintain them.

- Practitioners who work with adolescents who are "at risk" need the support, validation, and skill development that comes from participation in a consultation team.

- Practitioners will honestly examine their own work and maintain their competence and effectiveness.

- Practitioners will use DBT skills in their own lives.

- Practitioners who use or incorporate DBT in their work need to have integrated the concepts and skills so that they flow from the practitioner in a natural way.

Summary

In this chapter, we introduced you to the foundations of DBT treatment and to the theoretical dialectic of acceptance and change that will guide your work when you provide DBT treatment. We have provided several specific ways to practice both acceptance (validation) and change when you work with adolescents. Finally, we have presented assumptions that will guide your work as a DBT practitioner.

PART 2

DBT Treatment for Adolescents: An Overview of DBT Modalities

CHAPTER 3

Individual Therapy

Individual DBT therapy begins with the understanding that a practitioner can be most caring and effective by helping a client change in ways that bring her closer to her own goals for life. In therapy with adolescents, practitioners treat the adolescent, the family, and the transaction between the two, doing what is effective to help the adolescent behave in ways that make her life better (Sanderson, 2001). To be genuinely effective, DBT practitioners must be willing and able to maintain professional boundaries at the same time as they share relevant experiences about how DBT skills have been helpful in their own lives.

DBT treatment begins with the individual practitioner, who is responsible for orienting the adolescent to the process of treatment. This includes acknowledging the adolescent's hesitation and reluctance, validating her concerns, and beginning to explain the treatment framework and how it can help her. The individual practitioner enables the adolescent to see that she can achieve a life that fulfills her.

The Role of the Individual Practitioner

The first step in DBT is to develop a trusting, collaborative connection with the adolescent through which the practitioner will be able to work on the goals of treatment: "You are bringing the treatment into the relationship, not the other way around," as Swenson (2012) puts it. The DBT individual practitioner is the treatment coordinator and, as such, carries out these actions:

- assesses the client by getting a detailed history from the adolescent and her family

- orients the adolescent and her parents to the organization and philosophy of DBT

- develops treatment goals in collaboration with the adolescent and her family, emphasizing those goals that are most relevant to the adolescent

- prioritizes those goals that are life threatening, that interfere with treatment, and that interfere with the life that the adolescent wants to live

- gains commitment to treatment, monitors commitment to treatment, and returns to commitment strategies when the adolescent becomes less motivated to work in any modality of treatment

- introduces and orients the adolescent to the daily log (see "Daily Logs" on page 52)

- targets and completes a behavioral chain analysis (see "Chain Analysis" on page 60) on any target behavior or treatment-interfering behavior that occurs in any modality

- implements change strategies

- helps to structure the environment of the adolescent

- coaches the client to use skillful and safe behaviors during crises between sessions

- consults with the client about any difficulties she has with other members of the treatment team

We can see how practitioners meet these responsibilities when working with Rosa, whom we introduce in the vignette below. In this chapter, we will follow Rosa's experiences in individual therapy.

Rosa is eighteen years old. She was adopted from Russia in infancy and has lived with her adoptive parents ever since. Beginning in childhood and continuing through her adolescence, she has had a stormy relationship with her two adopted sisters and her parents. She is often left out of family activities as a result of her past behaviors, and she doesn't feel understood or accepted by anyone in the family. Rosa attended a therapeutic high school because her behavior was so disruptive in the classroom. She has destroyed property in the home when she has been upset, has had parties in the house in which valuables were stolen and/or damaged, has physically assaulted her parents and sisters, and has burned herself with cigarettes. She has seen a string of practitioners, none of whom she connected with or liked.

Rosa is referred for DBT after being arrested for DUI when she crashed her car into a tree, injuring herself and her passenger quite seriously. She faces incarceration for the offense, and her attorney recommended DBT with the hope that participating in DBT and maintaining safe behaviors will keep her out of jail. She is adamantly opposed to medication, is suspicious of the effectiveness of therapy, and says she only comes to the sessions because her attorney recommends it.

The First Phase of Treatment

The DBT practitioner spends as long as is necessary in the beginning phase of treatment, orienting the adolescent to DBT and gaining the adolescent's commitment to the work of the treatment.

This early phase of treatment may resemble "treatment as usual" in that the practitioner uses many interpersonal skills to develop trust and a working connection with the adolescent. In these early sessions, the practitioner focuses more on acceptance and validation than on change, although the practitioner will look for opportunities to introduce change strategies when they will be effective. The treatment cannot move too quickly into change protocols, or the adolescent may resist, and actually defend and strengthen the very behaviors that bring her to treatment. A practitioner who emphasizes change too early, without a commitment from the adolescent to the work and goals of treatment, will find that the work stalls because the adolescent is not contributing to the effort. It is thus very important to put the effort into gaining commitment early in the treatment, and to revisit this commitment whenever necessary.

By the time the practitioner and the adolescent are ready to shift from this early phase of treatment, the adolescent understands what is expected of her in DBT and has made a commitment to participate, to stay alive, and to work on reducing her target behaviors. At this point, the work of change can begin in earnest.

Consultation to the Client

One of the goals of DBT treatment is to help clients learn to manage real-life situations effectively, and practitioners need to be aware of teaching "life lessons." In this regard, the DBT practitioner acts as a "consultant" to the client, helping her to navigate her natural environment, guiding her in the process, and not advocating directly for her unless absolutely necessary (Linehan, 1993a).

Helping the Adolescent to Negotiate Her Environment and Self-Advocate

If an adolescent has problems at home, the DBT practitioner will help the adolescent learn and practice skills for talking to her parents and advocating on her own behalf. If the practitioner and the adolescent choose to have a family meeting so that the practitioner can coach and model the behaviors more directly with the parents present, the practitioner and the adolescent will practice skills and strategies prior to the session. The preparation for the meeting provides opportunities for the practitioner to directly model skills for the adolescent. The goal is to increase the adolescent's sense of mastery of her ability to handle situations that come up in her life.

The individual practitioner may also spend time helping an adolescent negotiate problems at school, intervening directly only when the adolescent does not yet have the skills to manage the situation or after she has run into barriers in the environment that impede effective resolutions to the problem.

If the adolescent articulates a problem with the skills trainer, medicating psychiatrist, other staff, or another member of the DBT team, the individual practitioner typically does not go to the other member of the team and express the concerns of the adolescent. Rather, the practitioner coaches the adolescent on discussing the situation directly with the other member of the team, goes over possible barriers and ways to manage those barriers, and encourages the adolescent's attempts at self-advocacy.

Practitioners recognize that adolescents feel better when they feel capable, and advocating for themselves is one of the ways they can experience their own strengths and abilities. However, there may be times when more direct intervention is necessary (with parents, schools, psychiatrists, and so on), because the adolescent does not always have the power to negotiate with other systems or because the practitioner must intervene to keep the adolescent safe (Miller, Rathus, & Linehan, 2007). This should be done in consultation with the adolescent as often as possible, and with attempts by the practitioner to model the skills that the client will need to use when advocating for herself.

Priority Targets

DBT treatment focuses on priority targets (Linehan, 1993a) and minimizes discussion of ongoing problems of the moment or whatever is bothering the client when she walks into the session (such as fights with parents or peer conflicts). Because clients with emotion dysregulation often face difficult situations and often are "in crisis" (both perceived and real), they understandably want each session to focus on what is bothering them at that moment. If the practitioner follows the client's agenda in this way, the client may feel better briefly; however, she will not have learned the skills necessary to avoid a similar situation and to manage the situation in a safer or more effective way in the future. The dilemma when working with high-risk adolescents is that if you become overly focused on the adolescent's immediate needs and the problem of the moment, you will not have the time or opportunity to teach the skills necessary for change.

DBT makes explicit what is usually implicit: a client has to be alive to participate in treatment, and she must be engaging in the treatment to use it effectively and make necessary changes. For this reason, DBT is structured around the following priority targets: behaviors that threaten the client's life, interfere with her participation in treatment, and keep her from having the quality of life she desires (Linehan, 1993a).

The chart below delineates, in the order in which they are prioritized and addressed, the target behaviors that the practitioner will focus on within the session (Linehan, 1993a):

Target Category	Specific Behaviors
Priority 1—life-threatening behaviors: any behavior that causes or could likely cause physical harm to the client	• attempts suicide • engages in suicide ideation/communication • carries out self-harm—with intent to cause bodily damage • uses substances that cause physical harm • engages in other behaviors with high risk for lethality or physical harm (such as physical fights with police, drunk driving, life-threatening disordered eating, and so on)
Priority 2a—client treatment-interfering behaviors: any behavior on the part of the client that interferes with treatment	Adolescent: • misses or cancels individual or group sessions for various reasons, including excessive hospitalization • arrives late to sessions • does not bring the daily log to sessions • does not bring homework to skills group • does not call the practitioner when in crisis • abuses phone coaching by calling at times and for reasons that are outside the client-practitioner agreement, or otherwise does not observe the practitioner's limits • does not respond in sessions • engages in destructive behavior in the office
Priority 2b—practitioner treatment-interfering behaviors: any behavior on the part of the practitioner that interferes with treatment	Practitioner: • arrives late • does not return phone calls • does not look at or integrate daily logs in treatment • does not complete chain analysis • is judgmental of the client • focuses exclusively on either change or acceptance • engages in power struggles with the client
Priority 3—quality of life–interfering behaviors: any behavior that gets in the way of the client's being able to have the life she wants	• uses and abuses substances • has eating disorders that are not life threatening • fights with parents or peers • does not attend school or work • withdraws from or avoids responsibilities and activities • has poor or minimal peer relationships • experiences financial, housing, or educational problems

Self-Harming Behaviors

There is some question about where to place self-harming behaviors in the context of priority targets. All behaviors that cause physical harm to an adolescent and all stated self-harm ideation, whether or not there is intent to die, are considered life-threatening behaviors and targeted as a priority. Self-harm and talk of self-harm is a predictor of suicide and may leave permanent scarring or result in accidental death, and must be seriously addressed. Additionally, practitioners need to acknowledge self-harm as a way to show deep concern and send the message that it is unacceptable behavior (Miller, Rathus, & Linehan, 2007).

Adolescent Treatment-Interfering Behaviors

DBT practitioners recognize the importance of the adolescent's participation and compliance within the treatment if change is to occur. DBT, uniquely and strategically, prioritizes behaviors that interfere with the treatment and guides practitioners in how to respond to those behaviors. Here is a description of these behaviors and the skills used by practitioners to respond to them:

Adolescent Treatment-Interfering Behavior	Impact of Treatment-Interfering Behavior	Practitioner Responses
Canceling, missing, or being late to sessions	Inconsistent attendance impedes progress and does not enable the maximum benefit of treatment.	• Some practitioners observe a limit that an adolescent who misses four sessions in a row is out of DBT and may return at a later time. (Other practitioners do not observe that limit so that an adolescent is given every opportunity to engage and participate in treatment.) • The behavior is prioritized and explored through chain analysis, and adolescents cannot discuss other issues until these behaviors are addressed. • The practitioner helps the adolescent resolve the barriers that come up in the chain.
Not bringing in or completing the daily log or homework	The practitioner does not know what has occurred during the week. The adolescent misses opportunities to observe and describe her own behaviors.	• Contingency management is used by having the adolescent complete the log in session prior to discussing other issues. • Chain analysis is conducted about the behavior so the adolescent and practitioner can work on identifying and resolving barriers.
Not using phone coaching	The adolescent is not able to get through difficult times using skillful behaviors.	• Chain analysis is conducted to highlight the choice made by the client to not contact the practitioner or the barriers to doing so. • Change strategies and contingency management encourage the adolescent to call the next time she is in crisis. • The practitioner desensitizes the adolescent to calling by scheduling a noncrisis call or text during the week.

Not observing practitioner limits	These behaviors burn out the practitioner, may cause less than effective treatment, or may cause the practitioner to not want to work with the client.	• The practitioner addresses each behavior that is not respectful of limits and may do a chain to understand the behavior further. • The practitioner assesses whether his or her own behaviors have allowed this behavior, and whether or not the limits have been clear and transparent. • The practitioner directly comments to the adolescent about the behaviors.
Lack of responsiveness in the session	This behavior is frustrating for the practitioner and does not allow the work to go forward.	• The practitioner uses an irreverent communication style to engage the adolescent. • The practitioner notes the possibility that there is inadequate validation or low commitment to treatment and, in response, supportively reviews and recommits to goals and focuses on validation. • The practitioner uses indirect communication (metaphors, fables, etc.) to bypass resistance and defensiveness.
Abusive behavior in the practitioner's office—damaging the office or being verbally abusive toward office staff, for example.	These behaviors may be some of the behaviors that brought the adolescent into treatment. They cannot be ignored or the adolescent will believe they are acceptable ways to behave. These behaviors also trigger feelings for the practitioner and may burn out the practitioner or otherwise cause less-than-effective practice.	• The practitioner comments on these behaviors and uses contingencies (such as removal of warmth) as a way to note that the behaviors are unacceptable. • The client can be asked to do a "repair" or otherwise "give back" for disrupting or hurting others, or for destroying property.

The practitioner targets treatment-interfering behaviors with the goal of minimizing them in the future. Each treatment-interfering behavior is addressed in treatment until it is no longer problematic (Linehan, 1993a). Practitioners will practice their own mindful awareness so that they can recognize behaviors that interfere with their ability to provide the most effective treatment for their clients (Swenson, 2012).

Practitioner Treatment-Interfering Behaviors

DBT also targets treatment-interfering behaviors on the part of the practitioner. If a practitioner is late to a session or does not return an e-mail or call, the practitioner may decide to do a repair or make an apology as a way to recognize that this behavior may have negatively impacted the treatment, and to model behavior for the adolescent. Repairs from the practitioner to the adolescent can be invaluable in developing trust and an effective working relationship. Practitioners cannot conduct effective DBT treatment without mindful awareness of themselves as practitioners, their limits, and the way in which they interact with clients. Practitioners who engage in power struggles with adolescents and get caught up in "opposing" their requests, demands, or expectations will find it helpful and effective (1) to be aware of dialectics, the fact that there is validity in the requests and concerns of the adolescent and the practitioner needs to search out this validity from the adolescent's point of view; and (2) to be self-aware and mindful throughout the session to avoid power struggles and to help the adolescent accept different points of view.

Observing and Maintaining Practitioner's Limits

Adolescents may behave in ways that even seasoned practitioners find offensive and that create emotions in the practitioner that make it difficult to work with the adolescent. Many clients come to us after having been "fired" by previous mental health professionals. DBT practitioners recognize that certain client behaviors may contribute to their own lack of desire to work with the client. To minimize the practitioner's possible frustration and burnout with high-risk clients, DBT encourages practitioners to recognize and observe their limits and to make those limits transparent and clear to the client by articulating the following expectations:

- what hours they will take phone calls from clients to coach them through a crisis

- what hours they will take phone calls for good news, for repairing the relationship, and for other issues

- what they are willing to discuss with clients between sessions

- behaviors that will be accepted or not accepted in the office

- the personal disclosure they are comfortable with

Practitioners use consistent contingency management to maintain limits when clients do not observe them. Many adolescents continue to ask for special consideration or they do not observe the limits of others—behaviors that frustrate and challenge the people around them—because they have been intermittently reinforced. These behaviors have the same impact on practitioners who do not observe their own limits. Practitioners must maintain their limits skillfully; it is critically important to preserve the positive relationship between the practitioner and the adolescent so that the treatment can continue. Let's return to Rosa, whom we met earlier, and see how her practitioner observes limits:

Rosa has been working with her DBT practitioner for several months when she has an increase in self-harming behavior. Her practitioner has told her that noncrisis calls can occur only between 8 a.m. and 10 p.m. One night, at midnight, Rosa calls the practitioner to discuss difficulties in her relationship with her boyfriend. The practitioner initially takes this call because of concerns about self-harm. When the practitioner recognizes it is not an emergency, he ends the call as gently as possible while telling Rosa that he can speak to her the next day during business hours. When Rosa calls later that week in the middle of the night, the practitioner, still concerned about self-harm, answers the call. As soon as he assesses that this is not an emergency, he, again, ends the call.

Since Rosa has been intermittently reinforced when the practitioner answers the calls, she continues to call even though the practitioner ends the call quickly. The practitioner continues to take these phone calls, make a quick assessment as to safety, and end the calls in a very business-like fashion. The practitioner chains this therapy-interfering behavior in the following session (see "Chain Analysis" below), helps Rosa to problem solve other ways to get her needs met, and uses feedback from his consultation team to develop an effective plan to address this behavior in sessions. When he does not receive any non-crisis after-hours phone calls the following week, the practitioner praises Rosa in the next session.

TREATMENT TOOLS AND STRATEGIES

DBT provides practitioners with a number of treatment tools, and strategies, for working with difficult adolescents and providing effective interventions. They include gaining commitment, daily logs, chain analysis, and coaching in the natural environment.

Gaining Commitment

Often, when a client initially meets the practitioner, she is in crisis and looking for immediate resolution to the problem. Practitioners feel pressure to help the client immediately and may move too quickly toward helping the client change behaviors. If the client has not committed herself to do the work of treatment, then little progress will be made. In DBT, practitioners will use commitment strategies to engage (initially) or reengage the client (if progress has slowed) in the work of behavioral change.

DBT practitioners ask for a commitment to life, safety, and behavioral change. If the client is not able to make these commitments initially, the practitioner will ask her to make this commitment until the next session. The practitioner asks for greater commitment while accepting the commitment the client is able to make, always balancing acceptance and change and the dialectic of promoting safety while providing outpatient treatment. For example, the practitioner asks for abstinence from self-harm while taking a nonjudgmental stance toward self-harm behaviors when they occur. Throughout treatment, the practitioner continues to request commitment to behavioral change while accepting that the client is doing the best she can. Practitioners reinforce and support increasing levels of commitment, and they encourage clients as the clients make greater commitments to change.

Commitment to Treatment Strategies

There are several strategies for gaining commitment to treatment (Linehan, 1993a):

- collaboratively establishing goals and looking for ways to link these goals to behavior changes (For example, Rosa wants to stay out of jail; in order to accomplish this, she commits to making a change.)

- going over the positive and negative impact of making changes, based on the concerns the client brings to treatment. (For example, in Rosa's case, the practitioner may say, "The positive impact is if you come to treatment and make changes, your parents may allow you to join family activities; you may stay out of jail. The negative impact is you will have to come to treatment and work hard; you will have to focus on your behaviors and their consequences.")

- asking for a greater commitment and then accepting a lesser commitment initially (For example, the practitioner may ask for the daily log to be filled out daily and then accept it initially being filled out several days of the week.)

- gaining commitment to an easier request first and then asking for more as the client becomes comfortable (For example, the practitioner may start with asking for only individual therapy and then ask the client to add skills group, or the practitioner may initially ask a client to delay a behavior rather than eliminate it.)

- suggesting to the client that the treatment may be very difficult so that the client begins to convince the practitioner that she can do it, giving her a sense of control and ownership of the process

- letting the client know that making the commitment is up to her and she can choose to participate or not, while at the same time informing her of the consequences of not choosing to participate (For example, telling her that "You can decide not to continue with therapy" while carefully acknowledging that "You may risk time in jail unless you are in therapy.")

- reminding the client of past commitments (including past commitments within therapy) that they have been able to live up to

Practitioners return to these commitment strategies as needed throughout treatment whenever the treatment appears to be reaching an impasse.

Dialogue: Gaining Commitment

Practitioner: I understand that you don't want to go to jail and that your attorney thinks that DBT might look good to the judge. I also understand you haven't felt that therapy has worked in the past and that even though DBT has good evidence behind it, you think it's a waste of time.

Rosa: Exactly.

Practitioner: And DBT isn't something you can just "mail in." It requires a willingness to do what's asked and a real desire to change, so I wonder why you'd be willing to give DBT a try.

Rosa: Well, I definitely don't want to go to jail, and if it will help me with that, it might be worth it.

Practitioner: It will mean you'll agree to come to your appointments and fill out the daily log and homework every week. Are you sure you want to commit to all that?

Rosa: That's nothing. They'd make me do a lot more than that in jail!

The practitioner lets Rosa see that she can make her own choice about attending therapy and also highlights the alternative. The practitioner discusses commitment at the same time that he validates her for feeling distrustful of treatment and the practitioner.

Daily Logs

Each client in DBT is given a thought/feeling/behavior tracking tool (Linehan, 1993a; Miller, Rathus, & Linehan, 2007) called a daily log (see page 57), which enables her to notice triggers, correlations, and patterns of behavior. The adolescent records the following pertinent information on a daily basis:

- thoughts, urges, and behaviors related to priority targets

- emotions and how strong they were on any given day

- urges (or lack of urges) to stop treatment

- skills that she used on a daily basis

Each week, the practitioner reviews the daily log with the adolescent. Daily log completion is very important to effective DBT treatment because it provides a more accurate assessment of the entire week between treatment sessions than a verbal report, and it minimizes the focus on the crisis of the moment. The information in the daily log sets the agenda for the work of the session.

Gaining Commitment to the Daily Log

The practitioner shapes compliance with the completion of the daily log by doing several things:

- explaining the importance of the daily log in helping the adolescent to track and change behaviors

- responding to hesitancy from the adolescent by initially asking only for partial completion (as in the dialogue below)

- requesting it at the beginning of every session

- looking it over thoroughly every single session and showing interest in it

- reviewing it for target behaviors, intense emotions, and behaviors that interfered with quality of life

- asking the client to fill it out in the office if it is not completed (as in the dialogue below)

Dialogue: Introducing the Daily Log to an Adolescent

Practitioner: You know, research shows that tracking our behavior is one tool that helps us make changes. Have you ever noticed that weight loss and exercise programs often include a chart or log to complete every day? The same is true when we are trying to change other behaviors. The way we do this in DBT is with the log. Let me show you what it looks like—now don't get overwhelmed! It's actually a lot easier to fill out than it looks. Let me walk you through it. Take yesterday, for example. Would you be willing to fill it out with me based on how things went yesterday? Let's look at this column—it asks if you had any urges to harm yourself yesterday. You simply put a yes or a no in the box. Now, the next column asks if you acted on any urges to kill yourself—go ahead and fill in that box with a yes or no. Nice job. Most clients tell us it takes about two or three minutes to fill this out every day. Would you be willing to do that? And it's really important to bring it with you to our appointments. It will help me see what happened during the week, and we'll use it to guide our meetings. Does that sound reasonable?

Client: I guess so…

Because of its importance to the treatment, the practitioner places a high priority on the client completing the daily log and targets it as treatment-interfering behavior if it is not completed or brought to sessions. The practitioner and the adolescent use problem-solving techniques to assess the barriers to completing the log and to find ways to ensure that the client will complete it.

It is often initially difficult for adolescents to complete the daily log. It may be just one more task for an adolescent who already feels overwhelmed, or else it may be difficult for an adolescent to admit to engaging in certain target behaviors. Some adolescents avoid the contingency of using therapy time to complete the log by completing it on the way to treatment or in the waiting room, which is initially accepted by the practitioner as a step toward shaping the behavior. At some point during the session, the practitioner will attempt to point out the importance of the daily log (client has a hard time remembering details from the week without it, and so on) and will conduct a chain analysis (see "Chain Analysis" below) of the behavior of not bringing a completed daily log to increase the chance that it will be completed the following week.

Dialogue: Responding to a Client Who Does Not Have Her Daily Log

Practitioner: Great to see you. Do you have your daily log with you?

Client: Oh, I left it at home.

Practitioner: You did? Let me give you one to fill out right now then.

Client: I really can't remember everything that happened this week, so it won't be accurate.

Practitioner: I understand. Just do the best you can, and we'll talk about it when you're done.

The client fills out the log while practitioner observes. When the log is completed, the practitioner scans the log for priority targets and resumes the session with a chain analysis of any priority target behavior, including not completing the daily log.

Dialogue: Shaping the Behavior of Completing the Daily Log

The client brings a daily log that is only partially completed. The practitioner starts by reinforcing what has been done and then goes on to problem solving.

Practitioner: Nice job on the first three days on this daily log. Tell me how you were able to remember to get it done those days.

Client: Well, I had it next to my computer, so I remembered it when I was on the computer at night.

Practitioner: That's great. You did a great job filling this out for those days. What happened on those other nights when you forgot it?

Client: I don't know, I think I must have put it in my drawer and just lost track of it.

Practitioner: You nailed this on the nights you saw it! Do you think you could think of a place you could put the daily log so you would see it every night?

Client: I guess so.

Practitioner: Or would it make more sense to fill it out at a different time of day?

The next week the client brings in a daily log with even more days filled out (although still not complete).

Practitioner: Wow! You are really moving in the right direction here! I bet you'll get it all done next week.

Practitioners underscore the importance of this tool and shape client's behavior by addressing it directly at the outset of every session. Since not bringing in a daily log is always a priority treatment target, problems with this tool tend to get resolved relatively quickly.

Practitioners continually balance a request for full compliance with the acceptance of what the client is able to do, asking for more while encouraging and supporting the attempts to comply that the adolescent makes.

Developing a Daily Log for Adolescents

There are many versions of daily logs, and we encourage practitioners to develop and individualize logs so they include the information that is most relevant for their individual clients. A template for a daily log can be found on page 57. We suggest that you use these guidelines when customizing this daily log for your clients.

- List the specific target behavior(s), which will vary depending on the problems. Target behaviors might include use of substances, stealing, aggression, not attending school, high-risk behaviors (such as driving a car under the influence of substances), bingeing and purging or restricting food intake, or behaviors related to poor judgment that might lead to danger for the adolescent (such as engaging in promiscuous sexual behavior). Include self-harm and suicidality if those are target behaviors for the adolescent. Ask your client to differentiate between thoughts ("I had a thought about wanting to hurt myself and then it went away"), urges ("I felt like I wanted to hurt myself"), and behaviors ("I cut myself").

- Include emotions that are most relevant for your client, giving the client the opportunity to rate the intensity of the emotions from 1 (lowest intensity) to 5 (highest intensity).

- Include skills from each of the DBT modules: mindfulness, distress tolerance, emotion regulation, interpersonal effectiveness, and middle path (see chapter 4). Give the adolescent the opportunity to indicate whether she tried to use the skill and whether or not it was effective in managing her emotions.

- Highlight those skills that you are working on with the client.

The daily log can be downloaded at www.newharbinger.com/27985.

DAILY LOG

NAME _____ DATE STARTED _____ Filled out daily? Yes ___ No ___

BELOW: Fill in target behaviors. Use the key at the bottom of the page to indicate the strength of the thought or urge. For the action, use Y (yes) or N (no).

T=Thought   U=Urge   A=Action

Date	Target Behaviors								Urge to quit treatment 0-5	Take prescribed medications? Y/N	Emotions 0-5								Notes
		T	U	A	T	U	A	T	U	A			Anger	Happiness	Sadness	Guilt	Shame	Fear	Anxiety	Disappointment	
Monday																					
Tuesday																					
Wednesday																					
Thursday																					
Friday																					
Saturday																					
Sunday																					

For thoughts, urges, and emotions: 0 = not at all; 1 = a little bit; 2 = somewhat; 3 = strong; 4 = very strong; 5 = extremely strong

BELOW: Note yes (Y) or no (N). You can name the specific activity you used on the back of the log.

SKILL	Monday		Tuesday		Wednesday		Thursday		Friday		Saturday		Sunday	
	Used	Helped	Used	Helped	Used	Helped	Used	Helped	Used	Helped	Used	Helped	Used	Helped
Mindfulness Practice														
Notice—one thing at a time														
Notice—nonjudgmentally														
Notice—doing what works														
Describe—one thing at a time														
Describe—nonjudgmentally														
Act—do one thing at a time														
Act—effectively														
Tolerating Distress														
Distracting activities														
Self-soothing														
Pros and cons														
Accepting reality														
Regulating Emotion														
Story of emotion														
Acting opposite														
Pleasant activities														
Did something that made me feel competent														
Wellness behaviors														
Managing Relationships														
Asking for things skillfully														
Saying no skillfully														
Focusing on relationships														
Focusing on self-respect														
Middle Path														
Self-validation														
Thinking/acting dialectically														

Exercise: Practitioner's Individual Session Planning Based on the Daily Log

You have a client who comes in late to your session. She begins talking to you almost immediately about the fight she had with her parents. When you ask for her daily log, you scan it and see that on Monday the client felt a strong urge to kill herself and told her parents that she wanted to die; on Wednesday, she cut herself on her thigh. You also note that she smoked marijuana almost daily and failed a test that she had told you was important to her.

Can you identify which behaviors are life threatening, treatment interfering, and quality of life interfering? What is the first behavior you will begin to talk about with your client? What behavior will you address next?

[The answers can be found at the end of the chapter.]

Chain Analysis

In DBT, behavioral chain analysis ("chain") is a necessary and essential tool practitioners use with the adolescent in sessions (Linehan, 1993a). A *behavioral chain analysis* is a cognitive, behavioral step-by-step exploration, guided by the practitioner and completed with the adolescent, of the thoughts, feelings, physiological sensations, and behaviors that connect a prompting event to a target behavior and then to the consequences of the behavior that may be reinforcing it.

A chain must always be done on a *specific* incident of a behavior (described in detail and including frequency, duration, and intensity), and it must be done by helping the client revisit in detail what happened to cause the behavior. If numerous behaviors have occurred, the practitioner will do a chain on the highest-priority behavior first.

The Purpose of the Behavioral Chain Analysis

The purpose of the behavioral chain analysis is for the practitioner and the adolescent to identify what causes and maintains problematic behavior and what prevents more adaptive behavior. The chain analysis looks at several aspects of behavior:

- events that may automatically elicit maladaptive behaviors (Some behaviors may be controlled by the client's conditioned responses to events.)

- behavioral deficits that may set up problematic responses

- events in either the environment or the client's past that interfere with more effective responses

- how the client arrives at her particular dysfunctional response, as well as possible alternative responses

- ways to break the links between the prompting event and the problem behavior

- ways to break the links between the problem behavior and the consequences

Collaboratively Completing a Chain Analysis

Completing a chain is a collaborative process between the practitioner and the client, often written on a large piece of paper or a white board, or sometimes done verbally. The chain is done in a nonjudgmental and validating way, with the practitioner keeping in mind how difficult it is for the adolescent to revisit behaviors that cause shame and other difficult emotions. The focus of the chain is always *the client's* thoughts, feelings, and behaviors so that the client is not able to avoid her feelings by blaming others.

One of the most important aspects of the chain analysis for the practitioner is that it minimizes assumptions about the function of the behavior and what keeps the adolescent returning to it. The practitioner makes *no* assumptions, playing the role of the naïve observer or the detective who, initially, understands nothing and questions everything. Together the practitioner and the adolescent learn the purpose of the behavior, the antecedents and consequences of the behavior, and where changes might occur. (The chart below outlines the details of how to complete a chain analysis.) The practitioner then uses the information from the chain to develop treatment goals and priorities.

How to Complete a Chain Analysis

This is a collaborative process between the practitioner and the adolescent.

Step 1. Choose the problem behavior to be chained from the various targets on the daily log. First, chain threats to life (suicide attempts, self-harm), then chain behaviors that interfere with treatment, and, finally, chain behaviors that interfere with quality of life. Even though there may be numerous instances of target behaviors, the chain must be done on one specific instance of the problem behavior at a time.

Step 2. Describe the problem/target behavior in very specific and detailed language. For example, the client might say, "I burned my right arm by placing the lit end of a cigarette against my skin for fifteen seconds."

Step 3. Describe the specific prompting event/trigger. You can start by asking when the problem began. For example, "When did you first feel upset? When did you first notice that you were feeling bad? When did you notice the urge to harm yourself?" Then identify something that triggered the rest of the chain of events. You are aiming to develop awareness of conditioned responses to triggers so they can be handled differently in the future.

Step 4. Describe what in the environment and inside the client made her *vulnerable* to the prompting events. Possibilities include physical illness, lack of sleep, stressful events, intense emotions, or use of drugs, alcohol, and so on. After the chain is completed, return to this point in the chain to assess ways to reduce or manage vulnerabilities in the future.

Step 5. Describe, in explicit detail, the links that connect the prompting event to the problem behaviors. Links in the chain can be actions, body sensations, cognitions, events in the environment, or feelings and emotions. You help the client move from one link to another by asking very specific questions to elicit specific descriptions of events, thoughts, feelings, urges and behaviors. Here are examples of questions that can help move the adolescent from link to link:

- How did you get from here to there?

- What happened next?

- What exact thought did you have at this point? What did you say to yourself?

- How intense was the feeling on a scale of 1 to 100?

- How did your body feel? Describe it.

- What time was it when the prompting event happened? What time was it when the target behavior happened? What did you do between those two events?

Step 6. Describe the specific *consequences* of the behavior. Help the adolescent define consequences that maintain, strengthen, or minimize the behaviors. Examine both the immediate effects and the long-term effects of the behavior on the adolescent and others around her. Assess what harm the behavior might have done as well as what positives might have resulted from the behavior.

Step 7. Describe in detail more skillful solutions to the problem. This is done by going back over the links and circling those where a different action might have led to a different choice of behaviors and a different ensuing chain of events. The client and practitioner explore other, more skillful behaviors that might be helpful in avoiding the problem behavior in the future.

The outline of a chain might look like this:

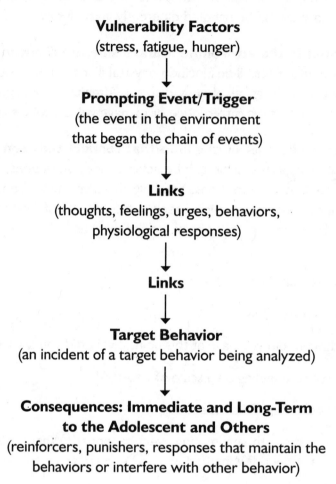

Vulnerability Factors
(stress, fatigue, hunger)

Prompting Event/Trigger
(the event in the environment
that began the chain of events)

Links
(thoughts, feelings, urges, behaviors,
physiological responses)

Links

Target Behavior
(an incident of a target behavior being analyzed)

**Consequences: Immediate and Long-Term
to the Adolescent and Others**
(reinforcers, punishers, responses that maintain the
behaviors or interfere with other behavior)

Dialogue: Explaining Chain Analysis to an Adolescent

Practitioner: One of the tools we use in DBT to help us understand the connections between thoughts, urges, feelings, and behaviors is called a chain analysis, or "chain" for short. I'll explain this to you in more detail as we move along. Let me give you an example. Today I left a little later than usual for work and I noticed that I didn't have much gas left in the car, and I also didn't have any time to stop and get gas or I would have been late. I was worried I would run out of gas. Then when I got here, I couldn't find a parking space, so I was feeling a little stressed. I noticed that my body was feeling tense and I was kind of irritable. Now, if I take the time to think about it, I can see that my stress had something to do with the things that happened this morning. These are called "links" in the chain. When we have a good understanding of the things that impact our moods, behaviors, and thoughts, we can get better control over the whole process and possibly make different choices about how we act. For example, I can give myself more time in the morning, I can do some things to calm myself down when I feel my body tensing up, or I can call in to work to tell them I'll be a few minutes late. There are lots of things I can do if I think about it. So this is the value of doing chains. We will use chains to figure out what you can do to turn things around when it feels like things are falling apart, and we'll talk about how to prevent it from happening again.

In the case of Rosa above, the practitioner will eventually chain the events that led to the DUI in order to understand what preceded Rosa's drinking, the reason why she drank, and the thinking behind her driving after drinking. Early in treatment, this will help the practitioner begin to understand Rosa and develop a relationship with her. Incidents in which she is assaultive, destructive, drinking, or not cooperating with treatment will be chained during her ongoing sessions.

The practitioner begins the chain by asking Rosa, "When did this start?" or "What happened to set this chain of events off?" to find the prompting event; then, the practitioner adds in the target behavior (in this case, breaking the window) that is being chained; and then, the practitioner continues the process by asking, "What happened next?" Some of the links in Rosa's chain might look something like this:

1. **Vulnerability:** Feeling stressed by job and recent fight with boyfriend.

↓

2. **Prompting Event/Trigger:** Called Mom to see if I could visit, found out my sister was visiting, and my mother didn't want me to come over.

↓

3. **Behavior:** Hung up the phone without saying good-bye.
Body sensation: Tension, face got red, made a fist with my hand.

↓

4. **Thought:** *I hate my mother.*
Thought: *No one cares about me.*

↓

5. **Thought:** My life is unfair, everyone hates me.
Feeling: Sadness.
Thought: My life sucks.

↓

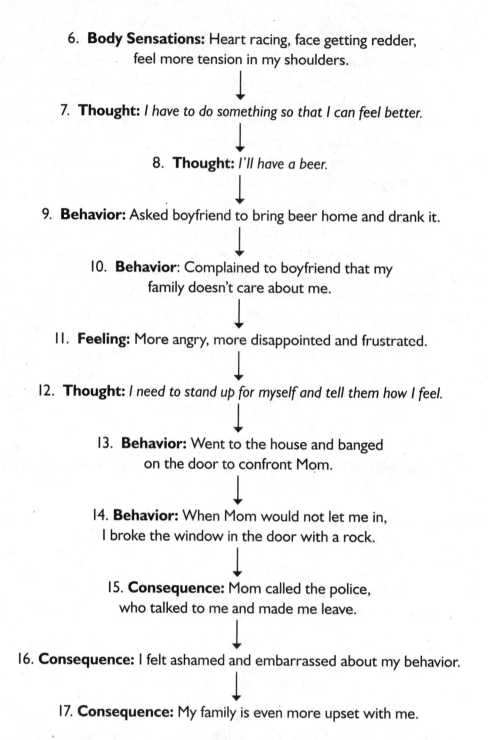

6. **Body Sensations:** Heart racing, face getting redder, feel more tension in my shoulders.

7. **Thought:** *I have to do something so that I can feel better.*

8. **Thought:** *I'll have a beer.*

9. **Behavior:** Asked boyfriend to bring beer home and drank it.

10. **Behavior:** Complained to boyfriend that my family doesn't care about me.

11. **Feeling:** More angry, more disappointed and frustrated.

12. **Thought:** *I need to stand up for myself and tell them how I feel.*

13. **Behavior:** Went to the house and banged on the door to confront Mom.

14. **Behavior:** When Mom would not let me in, I broke the window in the door with a rock.

15. **Consequence:** Mom called the police, who talked to me and made me leave.

16. **Consequence:** I felt ashamed and embarrassed about my behavior.

17. **Consequence:** My family is even more upset with me.

In analyzing the chain, the practitioner does several things:

- Notes the links on the chain where Rosa could have (a) changed thoughts to be less inflammatory (links 4, 5); (b) used skills (see chapter 4) to help soothe herself or distract herself from her thoughts and feelings (links 6, 7, 11, 14); (c) used skills to go somewhere else besides her mother's house (links 12, 13, 14).

- Helps Rosa problem solve around her vulnerabilities so that she could use a behavior or skill that might have been more pleasurable than calling her mother and that might have helped her get through the stressors she was feeling without doing something that made her feel worse.

- Points out the relevant consequences as Rosa begins to recognize that she feels worse (feels shame and embarrassment) after this behavior and has not gotten any of her needs met. She also now has additional issues that will need to be resolved.

All behaviors are caused by something, even if it is not immediately clear what the causes are. The chain analysis intervention is useful for targeting a specific behavior, and it is very helpful in working with adolescents, who frequently do not make the mental connections among thoughts, feelings, and actions or understand how behaviors are reinforced. Additionally, the systematic use of the chain analysis over time teaches the adolescent how to notice the various links in the chain, which results in more self-awareness, insight, and control over behavior. The practitioner practices patience and mindfulness with this process. The chain may need to be utilized in therapy many, many times for the same behavior before change occurs.

An example of a simplified chain analysis form for a client to complete out of the session is seen below. Some adolescents may take the chains home to look them over, and some may leave them with the practitioner. The practitioner's goal is to collaboratively complete them in the way that is most effective for each individual adolescent.

CHAIN ANALYSIS

Name _____ Date _____

Target behavior _____

- This is what prompted or triggered me:

_____

- Before this happened, I was **vulnerable** (already upset due to not getting enough sleep, being hungry, other stresses, physical illness, and so on) because

_____

- This is what I **thought** about what happened:

_____

- This is how I **felt** about what happened:

_____

- This is what I **did** (the ineffective behavior) about how I felt:

_____

- These were the **consequences** (what happened because) of my behavior:

	Immediate	Delayed
To me		
To others		

- This is what I will do the next time this happens so that the consequences are better for me and everyone else _____.

The Chain Analysis as Exposure

Adolescents usually do not want to revisit behaviors that cause them shame or guilt. Avoiding difficult and painful emotions drives many problematic behaviors; the successful avoidance of emotion through problematic behavior reinforces both the avoidance and the behavior, making them more likely to occur again. When in DBT treatment, adolescents who have been unsafe or have not followed through on treatment expectations know they will be expected to complete a chain and have the opportunity to acknowledge emotions that may be difficult. And they are thus exposed to the feelings that caused the behavior in the first place and to the shame and guilt they feel after doing the target behavior. A thorough chain can take an entire session or more, and the adolescent may experience painful emotions during this entire time. The practitioner is mindful of how difficult this process may be for the adolescent and provides validation and support while continuing to complete the chain. The practitioner may allow breaks from "chaining" to give the adolescent a chance to temporarily distract from painful emotions or use other coping skills, but she or he will always return to completing the chain. Completing a chain often allows the adolescent to practice skills to manage painful emotions and gain confidence in regulating emotions skillfully.

The Chain and Treatment Planning

The chain is one way the practitioner assesses the needs of clients and decides which change strategies will be most effective. Chains guide the ongoing treatment planning.

Focusing on the vignette above, the way in which the chain leads to change strategies and treatment planning can be seen in the chart below:

Target Behavior	Change Strategy	Impact
Rosa becomes angry when she is excluded from family events.	• dialectics • cognitive restructuring • skills training (interpersonal effectiveness skills)	Rosa understands the perspective of family members, prepares for future events, and uses skills to interact effectively, which increases the likelihood she will be invited to future events.
When Rosa gets mad, the only behavior she thinks she can do is hurt someone or something, or drink.	• skills training (distress tolerance)	Rosa learns to manage her distress more skillfully and, when necessary, to strategically distract herself from her uncomfortable feelings.

Rosa does not want to talk about the incident and does not want to complete the chain analysis.	• contingency management • exposure	Practitioner reinforces the work of the chain with praise and time to discuss other issues and enables Rosa to experience, rather than avoid, painful emotions.
Rosa says she drinks because she feels as though she has ruined her family's life and she thinks they hate her.	• dialectics • cognitive restructuring	Rosa learns to think more dialectically and accept alternative reasons for her family's behaviors.
Rosa's family is more responsive and attentive to her when she is in trouble and spends less time with her when she is doing well.	• structuring the environment • contingency management	Parents learn the principles of behavior management, which enables them to see that they inadvertently reinforce dangerous behaviors and helps them to focus on being more attentive to healthy behaviors.

Coaching in the Natural Environment

DBT practitioners understand that the skills adolescents may know, name, and be able to use in sessions or in skills training group may not be readily used when they're in their natural environment, in crisis, or emotionally dysregulated. DBT practitioners do not make the assumption that behaviors learned in one place will automatically generalize to other places. Instead, practitioners make an effort to help adolescents generalize and learn to use skills in all areas of their lives by coaching them in their various environments (Linehan, 1993a).

When an adolescent is emotionally dysregulated, the ability to think clearly is impacted and the adolescent cannot easily "access" more skillful behaviors. As a result, she may resort to past unsafe behaviors. The adolescent is thus encouraged to call, text, or otherwise reach out to the practitioner for coaching so that the practitioner can encourage the use of skills as a means for you to manage her emotions safely.

Orientation and Goals of Coaching

Clients are oriented to coaching during the very early phases of treatment because the adolescent is most at risk at this time. The practitioner focuses the coaching on the issue at the moment and does not use the time to "process" why the adolescent is upset. These are the main goals of coaching:

- assist the adolescent in using skills to help her feel better in the moment and to skillfully manage a crisis or difficult situation without making it worse

- problem solve with the client how to skillfully remain calm and get through the moment

- help the adolescent generalize the skills she learns in therapy to the rest of her life

How to Coach

Coaching phone calls or texts typically take no more than several minutes and should not be a repeat of a therapy session. When coaching, the practitioner does several things:

- assesses the safety of the adolescent

- keeps the adolescent focused on what is going on in the moment

- suggests skills that have helped the adolescent in the past

- ensures that the adolescent will follow through on suggestions

- focuses on affect and validates the adolescent's concerns

Adolescents are often driven by emotion, leading them to impulsive and rash behaviors. Having a coach available to help in these situations slows down the impulsivity and enables the adolescent to manage situations skillfully. The coach will ask the adolescent to call back if the skill suggested isn't effective and if more coaching is necessary.

If a practitioner is concerned that the adolescent is suicidal or otherwise unsafe, he may have to speak to the parents or caregivers to ensure safety. Maintaining the safety of the adolescent is the preeminent goal of coaching and takes precedence over the generalizing of skills. If an adolescent cannot commit to safety, others around the adolescent may have to become involved in helping the adolescent remain safe.

Dialogue: Introducing Phone Coaching

Practitioner: Have you ever played a sport?

Client: Yeah, I played soccer.

Practitioner: When you played soccer, you probably had practices where the coach would teach you plays, right?

Client: Yeah.

Practitioner: And then, when you played the games, the coach would be on the sidelines to give you support, guide you, and call out plays. Well, most therapy is kind of like going to the practices but not having your coach around during the games. DBT is different. I will be available by phone at critical moments—like when you have the urge to harm yourself. I want you to call me before you act on that urge. And I will coach you in that moment so that you can act skillfully and effectively.

Client: Okay.

Practitioner: Now, I mean it—you will need to call me. Let me give you my cell phone number right now, and you try calling me to make sure it works.

(Client calls practitioner while sitting in the office.)

Practitioner: Excellent! Now I have your number in my phone, so I'll know it's you when you call. Now, there are two other reasons you can call me. One is if there is something I said or did in the session that really bothered you or upset you. I'd like you to call me and bring it to my attention. The other is if you have really good news. I like to hear good news, and you can call me to share something very positive. One last thing—if you are having urges to harm yourself, you can call me any time, day or night. I may not be able to pick up your call, depending on what I'm doing, but if I can't, I will call you back as quickly as I can. And I want you to not act on your urge to self-harm while you are waiting for my call. If you are calling to share good news or to bring something to my attention about our session, I'd like you to call me between 6 a.m. and 10 p.m. That's when I'm awake. But you can call anytime if you need coaching to avoid self-harm, and I'll do my best to be available. If you can't reach me, I'm going to give you the numbers of the others on your treatment team and other community resources.

Observing Limits While Coaching

The orientation to coaching above makes it clear that the practitioner establishes expectations as well as limits. The adolescent is told when she should call the practitioner and what hours she can call. The practitioner also makes transparent that he will do the best he can to respond as quickly as possible without setting up unrealistic expectations. Finally, the practitioner differentiates between a call for help and a call to share good news, and he sets different limits on the different behaviors. This makes the entire process transparent to the adolescent. Obviously, the practitioner will take these calls when it is possible, and call back quickly if it is not. We orient our clients to the fact that we will not pick up the phone in the middle of a session (some clients see us *not* take calls on our cell phones while we are with them) or when driving, for example, but that we will call back as soon as we are able.

Evaluating the Outcome of Treatment

DBT practitioners help adolescents and their families learn more effective behaviors, and they need to evaluate whether or not their interventions are helping to promote positive behavior change. Include these questions in your evaluation:

- Is the adolescent increasing her use of more skillful and safer behaviors to manage emotions?

- Is the adolescent experiencing a decrease in dangerous behaviors and hospitalizations?

- Is the adolescent using more effective and less chaotic behaviors at home and school?

- Is the adolescent feeling less miserable and more like she is developing the life she wants?

Observing Change

Miller, Rathus, & Linehan (2007) suggest that you can observe the following changes as a way to measure client progress:

- An adolescent who rarely completed the daily log begins to bring it on a regular basis. Other changes, seen on the daily log, include a decrease in thoughts, urges, and actions related to self-harm or other target behaviors and an increase in emotions such as "happiness" or "contentment" on the daily log.

- An adolescent who rarely called for coaching now calls more often and uses the coaching to reduce self-harm.

- An adolescent has decreased therapy-interfering behaviors.

- An adolescent participates more in skills group and begins to take on a leadership role by helping orient new participants to group.

- An adolescent participates more actively in the chain analysis and is not as avoidant of facing difficult emotions.

- The family reports a decrease in aggression or unsafe behaviors at home and an increase in validation and effective communication.

It is important to monitor whether change is occurring and whether the adolescent is moving toward her goal, regardless of how slow the change may be. Change is the ultimate goal in treatment, and practitioners need to do ongoing assessment of the effectiveness of their work and strategies. If the client is not progressing, the practitioner may need to change strategies, reassess the client's commitment, or reassess the goals. Practitioners should be mindful of the importance of effectiveness, always keeping their eyes on change.

Summary

In this chapter, we discussed the basic structure and tools of individual DBT treatment, how they work together to help practitioners develop an overall treatment plan, as well as how to proceed in individual sessions. The goal is to target specific behaviors that threaten life, interfere with treatment, and impact quality of life, and to understand the function of behaviors and what maintains them. We have provided you with examples of the necessary tools so that you can begin to implement them in your own practice. You will continue to see how these tools are applied to specific problem behaviors in part 3.

Answers to the exercise on page 59:

Life-threatening behaviors: cutting her thigh, urge to kill herself, telling her parents she wanted to die.

Treatment-interfering behaviors: coming late to the session.

Quality of life–interfering behaviors: fight with parents, smoking marijuana.

The first behavior that would be discussed would be self-harm (cutting her thigh), followed by the urge to kill herself, and then her telling her parents that she wanted to die.

CHAPTER 4

DBT Skills Training

Skills training is a powerful change procedure in DBT. It focuses on teaching adolescents skills that will enable them to have the life they want by managing emotional pain *without* making situations worse (Linehan, 1993a, 1993b). This chapter begins with a discussion of the skills themselves and then proceeds to a discussion about how to teach them.

The assumption in DBT is that the adolescent lacks emotion management skills and does not have the capabilities to behave more consistently in safer, more adaptive ways. Recognizing that the adolescent's emotional intensity has interfered with learning behaviors that may come more naturally to his peers, DBT focuses on teaching skills that may not be readily available to the adolescent, or are hard to access when he is emotionally dysregulated. DBT skills training is an essential modality of DBT. The skills are usually taught in a structured group and can also be taught in separate individual sessions. When these skills are integrated, the adolescent will be able to behave in more adaptive ways by:

- managing his affect safely

- relating skillfully to those around him

- having self-awareness and awareness about those around him

- managing difficult situations without resorting to behaviors that make the situation worse or that lead to shame or guilt

- think in ways that can include alternatives

Adolescents typically respond positively to the usefulness of this aspect of the treatment, and its practical nature.

Skills Modules

There are five modules of DBT skills for adolescents (Linehan, 1993b; Miller, Rathus, & Linehan, 2007). As can be seen in the graphic representation below, mindfulness is the core module and the other four modules—emotion regulation, distress tolerance, interpersonal effectiveness, and middle path—revolve around that core.

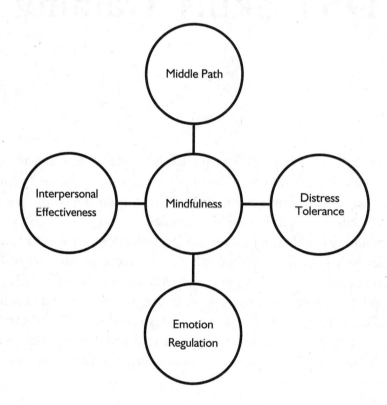

Consistent with the transparent nature of DBT practice, each module and each skill is introduced to the participants with an explanation of why this set of skills is being taught, how it can help adolescents, and why it is relevant to helping all participants create the life they want. Every session of skills training provides time for learning new skills, practicing those skills, and reinforcing previously learned skills. The ultimate goal of skills training is for participants to be able to incorporate the skills in their lives so that they can use them—on purpose and in an effective way—when they are emotionally dysregulated (Linehan, 1993a, 1993b).

DBT skills focus on decreasing challenging behaviors and increasing healthier behaviors, as seen in the chart below.

BEHAVIORS TO DECREASE	BEHAVIORS TO INCREASE
• substance abuse and dependency • physical and verbal aggression • self-injury • suicidality • disordered eating • panic attacks • avoidance of social situations • emotional outbursts • family power struggles	**MINDFULNESS SKILLS** • being aware of emotion • tolerating destructive urges • lowering emotional intensity • increasing the ability to focus and concentrate • increasing the ability to bring attention back when distracted • experiencing a sense of calm **DISTRESS TOLERANCE** • getting through difficult situations without damaging self, goals, or relationships • increasing the ability to soothe or distract effectively to manage difficult situations • accepting the reality of situations to minimize suffering and solve problems when possible **EMOTION REGULATION** • understanding the importance of emotions • being aware of vulnerabilities and triggers • recognizing and using alternative responses to emotional urges • developing a lifestyle that increases positive emotions **INTERPERSONAL EFFECTIVENESS** • skillfully asking for what one wants • maintaining healthy relationships • maintaining self-respect • using effective social skills **MIDDLE PATH** • accepting alternative possibilities • synthesizing contradictory information or emotions (dialectical thinking) • acknowledging the impact of life experiences in self and others • reinforcing skillful behaviors and not reinforcing unskillful behaviors

Information on the skills and how they are taught in DBT is widely available, and we will not repeat that in detail here. What follows is a brief overview of each module. Books and websites containing a variety of additional handouts are listed in the Resources section. New skills training materials are included at the end of the chapter

Mindfulness Skills

Mindfulness skills are considered the core skills in DBT (Linehan, 1993a) and are often taught and/ or reviewed at the beginning of each module (Miller, Rathus, & Linehan, 2007). Mindfulness skills help adolescents develop awareness of self and others by enabling them to notice and describe their experiences, and to be fully present and engaged in the moment in a nonjudgmental manner. Adolescents receive training in how to be aware when their emotions direct their behaviors, and they learn to integrate these emotions with rational and logical thought. Adolescents are taught to develop a way of thinking wisely by noticing what is around them, by describing what they observe, and by getting one hundred percent involved in what they are doing. A mindful way of thinking helps adolescents slow down their responses, which results in less impulsive behaviors. These skills are reviewed and practiced in a nonjudgmental, fully participatory, and focused way that is effective and works in the situation (Linehan, 1993b). Mindfulness leads to clearer thinking, and when adolescents learn to think this way, they are able to act in ways that help them achieve more of their goals. This awareness forms the foundation for the cognitive behavioral strategies used in other modules. For example, an adolescent notices his urges to harm himself, observes them without judgment, and responds in a safer manner. Or an adolescent who wants to yell at his parents first thinks about whether or not this will be an effective response, and uses a skillful behavior instead.

Distress Tolerance Skills

Distress tolerance skills help adolescents manage painful emotions or situations without resorting to unsafe behaviors or behaviors that make the situation worse or lead to shame or guilt. This module contains two different kinds of skills: those that help adolescents get through a difficult situation skillfully by distracting in the moment, and those that help adolescents accept painful realities that they may not be able to change so they can focus instead on problem solving (Linehan, 1993b).

Getting-Through-the-Moment Skills

Getting-through-the-moment skills, often called "coping skills," provide ways for adolescents to purposely distract themselves from painful emotions or soothe themselves until they are able to address those emotions safely and effectively. They are used deliberately and temporarily when adolescents feel overwhelmed by emotions, and they are not used to avoid or procrastinate. They briefly take the adolescent's mind off the difficult situation so that he can calm himself down and think through safe ways of resolving or getting past the moment.

These skills may appear counterintuitive to behavioral therapists; they interfere with exposure, at least temporarily. Given the potential for harm involved with at-risk adolescents, however, these skills are necessary to get through very difficult situations that otherwise might result in the adolescent resorting to behaviors that may change his life in significant ways (self-harming, drug use, criminal activity, explosive outbursts leading to fights or arrests, and so on). Increased exposure occurs later in the treatment once the high-risk behaviors have decreased and the adolescent has learned how to manage emotions and urges safely.

Often adolescents will say that their unsafe behaviors help them feel better. This statement is fairly accurate, and practitioners need to keep in mind that adolescents have actually found ways to manage their pain in the immediate moment. The skill of pros and cons (Linehan, 1993b) helps both adolescents and practitioners understand that each target behavior may have positive short-term benefits and significant negative long-term consequences. Individual practitioners and skills trainers help adolescents understand the long-term negative impact of behaviors so that they can choose to replace the unsafe behaviors they learned prior to DBT treatment with safer behaviors.

We encourage adolescents to develop—prior to a crisis—a "skills kit" that contains different things they can use depending on the intensity of emotions at the time. An adolescent may read a book, work on a puzzle, or play a videogame when he is slightly dysregulated; he may need to do something more active, like exercise, when he is even more dysregulated. Mindful awareness enables adolescents to know when they are becoming dysregulated so that they can access skills to feel better. Adolescents who phone their practitioners for coaching will be encouraged to use skills that have proven helpful in the past.

Accepting-Life-in-the-Moment Skills

Accepting-life-in-the-moment skills are predicated on the notion that suffering occurs when individuals do not accept the reality of a situation; pain is actually increased when reality is not accepted (Linehan, 1993b). Again, what initially appears counterintuitive becomes obvious; problem solving becomes more possible after a situation is accepted. For adolescents who feel that their lives are unfair, that they have been handed a "bad deal," and that life should be different than it is, it is a difficult task for them to accept their situation. They may feel that if they fight a situation, they will be able to change it, or that if they deny it, they will feel better. The opposite is true. These skills help adolescents learn how to accept the reality of their lives in this moment and to recognize that acceptance does not mean that they have "given up" or that they "like" the situation. Instead, it enables them to solve problems more effectively.

It also may seem confusing that "accepting what is" is an active process and does not just happen without effort. In fact, the skills in this module teach adolescents how to do several things:

- develop awareness of themselves and their surroundings

- relax their bodies so that they can feel more accepting

- see things in a different way

- become willing to accept painful realities (Linehan, 1993b)

The skills group itself gives the participants practice using acceptance and distress tolerance skills in vivo. Adolescents often express frustration with mindfulness activities, structure of the group, scheduling issues, and so on. Reminding participants to practice skills when these situations arise gives them the opportunity to use and improve them.

Emotion Regulation Skills

DBT hypothesizes that emotion dysregulation is the underlying cause of the problem behaviors that bring an adolescent into treatment. Therefore, the *emotion regulation* module is at the heart of DBT in that it helps clients to understand the emotions that drive so many of their behaviors and provides skills for safely managing emotions and lessening emotional suffering. Adolescents benefit from learning about emotions:

- what emotions are

- where emotions come from, whether they are primary or secondary, and why they have them

- how to recognize and name emotions

- how to manage the urges that are part of emotions

- how to reduce their vulnerability to emotion dysregulation

- how to reduce their emotional suffering (Linehan, 1993b)

Primary and Secondary Emotions

Adolescents are taught that primary emotions are hard-wired and feel automatic, while secondary emotions are caused by the way we learned to think about how we feel. *Primary emotions* are the first/initial responses to a situation or event:

- They occur in a way that feels virtually automatic.

- They are felt physiologically in your body—sometimes even before you can name the emotion.

- They serve a purpose—readying you for action, alerting you that something is happening that may need a response. (For example, if you feel threatened, your fear causes you to run or attack.)

Primary emotions include feelings like anger, fear, happiness, love, disgust, sadness, joy, interest, surprise, and guilt.

Secondary emotions are reactions to emotions—feelings about your feelings. They are based on thoughts and beliefs you have about a primary emotion that you have learned from your life experiences (for example, "People should not be afraid"). They last longer and are more under the control of your thoughts. Secondary emotions may include shame about being afraid, guilt about being angry, guilt about being happy (by thinking *I do not deserve to be happy*), or feeling depressed about being depressed.

The Story of Emotion

The *story of emotion* is a cognitive behavioral framework for explaining how emotions develop and how they are expressed. The story of emotion empowers adolescents to understand that they are not at the mercy of emotions and that they can impact how they feel and behave. By breaking down the emotion into several steps, the adolescent learns several things:

- He can protect himself from difficult circumstances if he is already feeling vulnerable.

- He is able to find alternative interpretations about events that do not lead to negative emotions.

- He can effectively manage and soothe uncomfortable body sensations (heart pounding, tightness in chest, butterflies in the stomach).

- He is able to respond in safe ways to emotions regardless of the urge to behave otherwise.

The story of emotion might lead to another story of emotion: the "outcome" or behavior at the end of one story of emotion might be the prompting event of another story. The story of emotion can also be used to orient adolescents to the chain analysis (see chapter 3), as it contains the same information used in chains. It is very important for adolescents, and others with whom they interact, to understand their own vulnerabilities, triggers, interpretations, and behavioral choices in order to change behaviors within individuals and families.

Reducing Vulnerability to Negative Emotions

Certain factors cause vulnerability and impact the way adolescents respond and react to events (Linehan, 1993a). Hunger, tiredness, hormonal cycles, having to take an exam, or participating in a major event (even if it is a happy one) can lead anyone to feel stressed, anxious, and "on edge" and may result in negative responses to situations that might not have caused a negative emotion in other circumstances.

These skills teach basic wellness and healthy lifestyle choices by encouraging adolescents to participate in activities that they enjoy and that they feel competent doing. Healthy lifestyle behaviors help adolescents feel better physically, which helps them manage their emotions more effectively (Linehan, 1993b). The Emotion Regulation Practice: Living a Healthy Lifestyle worksheet at the end of the chapter is filled out by adolescents daily to track the use of these skills.

Opposite Action Skill

Emotions have built-in and hardwired action urges. For example, the action urge to fear is to run, and the action urge to sadness is to withdraw. Adolescents often feel compelled to respond to their emotions according to their urges. The skill of *opposite action* (Linehan 1993b) helps adolescents acknowledge that they *can*, with effort, respond in opposite ways to their emotional and behavioral urges. An adolescent who approaches what he fears, spends time with others when he is sad, or does other actions that are opposite to what his emotions seem to demand finds that the intensity of his original emotion eventually lessens and he actually feels better. Adolescents learn they can change responses to situations even if the situations themselves don't change.

Interpersonal Effectiveness Skills

Adolescents who have intense emotions often have difficult interpersonal interactions. Often overcome by emotions, they do not pick up subtle cues or the lessons that other adolescents may learn through interactions with others. They may desperately want to hold on to relationships while sacrificing their own needs, or, conversely, they may be so focused on their own needs that they are not aware of the needs of others. In the *interpersonal effectiveness* module, adolescents are taught how to get their needs met, say no to requests when necessary, manage their relationships, and maintain their own self-respect. Adolescents who have emotion dysregulation need to learn how to do several things:

- balance their needs with the needs of others

- get their requests, or refusal of requests, taken seriously

- respond to others in ways that respect the other person

- respond to others in ways that increase their own self-respect (Linehan, 1993b)

Getting Needs Met Skillfully

Adolescents who want to be heard by others, have their requests taken seriously, and be respected when they say no will learn *assertiveness skills* to get their needs met. The interpersonal effectiveness skills help adolescents focus on these behaviors:

- explaining the situation that leads to their request

- asking specifically and directly for what they want and clearly stating what they do not want

- remaining focused on the request being made without becoming distracted by other issues

- asking for things or setting limits in a confident manner

- being willing to negotiate

- understanding that the environment will not always meet their needs regardless of how skillful they may be (Linehan, 1993b)

Maintaining Relationships and Self-Respect

Adolescents who have difficulty respecting the needs of others are taught skills that enable them to be sensitive to others and to take their needs into consideration when making decisions. Those adolescents who prioritize the needs of peers or family over their own or feel that their needs are not as important as those of others will learn how and when to prioritize their own needs. Adolescents can be taught to listen to others, validate them, and be calm when interacting with them. They are taught to do this while being fair, sticking to their own values without apology, and being truthful in order to maintain their own self-respect in interpersonal relationships (Linehan, 1993b).

It is also important to help adolescents understand that if they become angry or resentful, they may have gone too far to help others and have put their own needs aside. Creating balance in relationships is a goal of this module.

Interpersonal effectiveness skills lend themselves to a great deal of practice within skills groups since they are based on peer interactions. Adolescents can learn to make requests skillfully in the group. If an adolescent effectively asks for a snack using his skills, for instance, the reinforcer is readily available. Adolescents are encouraged to use these skills to resolve difficulties that occur within the group and to make requests of group leaders. Skills group facilitators can help quieter adolescents assert their needs within the group while at the same time encouraging the more dominant participants to listen to others. Skills group facilitators also model the use of these skills with their own behavior.

Middle Path

The skills in this module were originally delineated by Miller, Rathus, and Linehan (2007) specifically for adolescents and parents. The *middle path* module teaches families how to find validity in opposing perspectives and find a new way to behave that synthesizes their disparate viewpoints. In this module, adolescents are taught several skills:

- to think dialectically and diminish all-or-nothing, absolute thinking in order to accept contradictions and alternative perspectives

- to validate themselves so as to to minimize the effects of the invalidating environment that they may have internalized

- to validate others so that relationships are more reciprocal

- to understand basic behavioral principles so that they can reinforce their own positive efforts toward change while minimizing the ways in which they may be punishing themselves

- to use behavioral principles to be more skillful in influencing the behavior of others

Adolescents begin to balance their various expectations, responses, and desires—expectations of themselves, responses to limits and expectations, the desire to be independent—with their desire to still be taken care of by others. Many of these developmentally normative issues are even more difficult for adolescents with emotion dysregulation whose moods might demand one thing at certain times and the opposite at others, and who might feel like they are totally competent in some situations and totally incompetent at others. The skills in this module help adolescents move toward independence more effectively.

Several practice assignments are provided at the end of the chapter for your use with adolescents in skills training. Handouts and homework practice assignments encourage adolescents to practice the skills they are learning and to apply them in their natural environment. The importance of ongoing practice of these skills cannot be overemphasized. Adolescents report that the skills, which can be confusing when first learned, become more helpful to them the more they are practiced and used consistently in their lives. These skills are the means to enabling the adolescent to develop the life he wants.

Skills Training in Groups

Skills training is often the first DBT modality developed and implemented by practitioners. Leading a skills training group is an excellent way for practitioners to develop competency with the skills as they embark on learning more about DBT.

The Benefits of Groups

The group modality is an effective way to teach adolescents new skills and enables practitioners to teach the skills to a larger number of adolescents. Once the curriculum is mastered, practitioners find that they can use their own strengths and creativity in how they teach the skills. Group work offers several benefits:

- creates a structure within which the skills can be taught, discussed, analyzed, and practiced

- offers readily available peers for role playing, modeling, observing, resolving conflicts, and practicing the skills

- enables the peer group to reinforce the importance of skills, share ways they find the skills helpful, provide support for new members, and hold each other accountable to learning and using the skills

- minimizes stigma because other adolescents also participate

Group Rules

Practitioners develop rules and guidelines that explicitly clarify how they expect group partici-pants to behave during the group. Here are some rules, adapted from Miller, Rathus, and Linehan (2007), to consider for skills groups:

- Participants must be cooperatively participating in sessions with an individual therapist who practices or supports DBT treatment.

- Issues that are not related to skills being discussed will not be addressed in group.

- Participants are expected to come to group with a willingness and ability to learn skills; as such, they cannot attend group impaired by drugs or alcohol.

- Participants are not to self-harm during group.

- During group, participants do not share stories of self-harm unless those stories specifi-cally relate to the skills being discussed.

- Abusive or threatening language is not allowed in group.

- Participants may not discuss confidential material outside of group.

The guidelines of the group minimize the telling of stories about self-harm, suicidality, or dan-gerous behaviors because they may escalate everyone's emotions, trigger self-harming behaviors in other participants, and interfere with learning. Participants are expected to bring a binder to every group to which handouts and homework will be continually added.

Focus on Skills

Skills training groups are not process groups; they are curriculum based and focus on teaching skills, not talking about events from the previous week or how the adolescent feels at that time. Skills trainers recognize that time spent on issues not related to the skills being discussed will interfere with the goal of teaching specific skills. Participants are oriented and continually encouraged to discuss only issues related to the skills being covered in that particular group. Talking about personal issues or concerns that are not related to the skill being discussed will usually be treated as a treatment-interfering behavior, although a skills trainer might use discretion to allow some discussion to occur and then relate the discussion back to the skill being taught. Groups are often cofacilitated so that one group leader can stay focused on teaching the skills while the other group leader can manage any disruptive or crisis behaviors, if necessary.

Criteria for Participation in Group

Criteria for inclusion in group will differ among practitioners. Practitioners can consider the following factors when assessing if an adolescent can benefit from the group experience:

- The adolescent has unsafe or dangerous behaviors that result from emotion dysregulation.

- If there are psychotic symptoms, they would not significantly interfere with learning.

- The adolescent has the cognitive ability to follow the curriculum and do the homework.

- There is commitment to participate and willingness to follow the guidelines of the group.

- There is an individual practitioner who is sensitive to the importance of learning new skills, will work with the adolescent to apply the skills he learns in group to situations that occur out of group, and is willing to help and support the adolescent in completing homework assignments.

It may be useful to have separate groups for adolescents of middle school, high school, and college age; though the skills taught will be the same, the examples and issues raised will differ due to the different vulnerabilities and experiences of each developmental stage.

Group Facilitators

DBT skills group facilitators should be fluent and practiced in the skills and have personal experience applying them. The effectiveness of DBT is enhanced when the facilitators can produce evidence of how the skills have been helpful to them. Adolescents benefit from learning the skills when they understand how the skills will make their lives feel better; they are encouraged when they learn from others who have found the skills helpful.

Group Facilitator and Individual Practitioners Coordination

In DBT, the individual practitioner is responsible for coordinating the treatment of the adolescent. If a participant in skills training is having a problem with commitment, is not attending or not completing homework, or is behaving in a way that interferes with the teaching in the group, the individual practitioner will follow up on these issues.

If the adolescent participant has a problem with the individual practitioner that he shared with the skills trainer, the skills trainer encourages the adolescent to discuss this directly with his individual practitioner utilizing skills he is learning in group. Similarly, if the adolescent shares with the individual practitioner problems with the skills group or the skills group facilitator, the individual practitioner will encourage the adolescent to use skills to resolve the problems directly with the skills trainer. If the adolescent is not able to resolve the problem, practitioners may need to get more directly involved, modeling the skills for the adolescent when possible.

When the Individual Practitioner Is Also the Skills Trainer

Linehan (1993b) discussed the potential difficulties of having a skills trainer who is also the individual practitioner. She notes that it is sometimes difficult for the client to recognize that group is not the place to discuss personal difficulties, and this is made harder when the client's own practitioner is the skills trainer. In addition, the adolescent might find it difficult to share his practitioner with other adolescents.

Often, despite these concerns, the individual practitioner may also be the skills trainer. This requires that the group participants be well oriented to the expectations of groups and that the skills trainer or individual practitioner observes her own limits as well as the guidelines concerning what can and will be discussed in the group

Organizing and Facilitating Skills Training Groups

Skills groups are divided into the delivery of skills in five modules (Miller, Rathus, & Linehan, 2007), and each group session is structured to teach, review, and practice. The number of weeks that it takes to teach each module may vary. Some adolescent programs ask for four months, six months, or one year of commitment to DBT. As each practitioner develops skills groups, she considers a time frame that is viable for the population being served and should continually evaluate the effectiveness of the program and make adjustments as necessary.

Models for teaching DBT skills (Linehan 1993b; Miller, Rathus, & Linehan, 2007) allow several weeks for each of the modules and one or two weeks of mindfulness between each of the modules. Using this format, it takes about six months to be exposed to all the skills. And it may take about a year before adolescents are effectively using the skills during difficult times. Here is a sample skills group schedule:

Sample Skills Group Outline

Module	Week #	Skill
Mindfulness	1	Biosocial theory Thinking wisely DBT assumptions How to develop mindful awareness
Distress Tolerance	2–6	Introduction Getting through the moment: • pros and cons • distract and self-soothe Acceptance: • awareness exercises • accepting reality • willingness
Mindfulness	7	Biosocial theory Thinking wisely DBT assumptions How to develop mindful awareness

Emotion Regulation	8–12	Introduction
		Myths about emotions
		Theory of emotions
		• story of emotions
		• function of emotions
		Acting opposite
		Lessening vulnerability:
		• doing pleasant activities
		• appreciating the moment
		• doing what makes you feel competent
		• building a life of wellness
		Mindfulness of current emotion
Mindfulness	13	Biosocial theory
		Thinking wisely
		DBT assumptions
		How to develop mindful awareness
Interpersonal Effectiveness	14–18	Introduction
		Balancing priorities and demands
		Goals
		Myths about relationships
		Cheerleading: Supporting and encouraging one's efforts to use interpersonal effectiveness skills
		Assessing for and using effective level of intensity
		Asking for things skillfully and saying no skillfully
		Focusing on maintaining relationships
		Focusing on maintaining and building self-respect
Mindfulness	19	Biosocial theory
		Thinking wisely
		DBT assumptions
		How to develop mindful awareness

Finding the Middle Path for Adolescents and Parents	20–24	Introduction
		Dialectics and dialectical dilemmas
		What's typical for adolescents
		Validation and self-validation
		Behaviorism

The group is open-ended; some practitioners choose to have new members enter only at the beginning of a new module; others allow for the continuous incorporation of new members. The skills group is homogenous for emotion dysregulation being a core problem and heterogeneous for actual symptoms.

Therapeutic Techniques in Skills Group

Consider using the following techniques when facilitating adolescent skills groups:

- Ask a group member to prepare and lead the mindfulness practice. This allows for increased creativity and "buy-in" for mindfulness activities.

- Ask group members who have been previously exposed to a particular skill to teach the skill to the group. Teaching facilitates learning.

- Ask the group members to suggest skills or problem solve when a member reports that skills have not been effective.

- Highlight a group member who uses skills effectively by high-fiving, clapping, or otherwise recognizing success.

- Develop an incentive system by assigning points for completing homework or other target behaviors in group, and exchanging points for gift cards or self-soothing gifts (potpourri, candles, puzzles, and so on).

- Ask for repairs from the group member who has disrupted the group for others (Linehan, 1993a).

- Ask new group members to write letters to themselves to be stored by the practitioner nd read when they graduate from group.

- Maintain a graduation log in which members who are graduating can write an encouraging note to new members.

- Have a graduation ritual where members share their observations of progress in the departing member, allowing for the reinforcement of target behaviors as well as the instillation of hope in newer members.

- Laugh with the adolescents when appropriate, show your own sadness when appropriate, and maintain an overriding stance of genuineness.

- Include snacks and beverages during the break.

- Consider allowing members who have shown mastery of the skills to function as peer leaders to reinforce the skills and instill hope in members.

Priority Targets

In the same way that individual therapy uses priority targets to guide the work of the individual practitioner, skills training groups have priority targets that determine the order in which the facilitator(s) will respond to behaviors in group. Here, in order, are the priority targets of skills group (Miller, Rathus, & Linehan, 2007):

1. Treatment-destroying behaviors that pose a serious threat to the continuation of the group

2. Learning, practicing, and generalizing skills

3. Behaviors that interfere with treatment, that slow down rather than destroy treatment

Treatment-destroying behaviors. *Treatment-destroying behaviors* (Linehan, 1993a) are any behavior by a participant that makes it impossible to continue to teach the skills to others:

- violent behaviors (throwing objects, punching walls, hitting or verbally attacking other clients)

- self-harming behaviors (cutting, punching oneself)

- suicidal crisis behaviors (threatening suicide in a credible manner and then storming out of the session)

- any behavior that makes it impossible for others to focus or to hear what is going on (talking on cell phone, hysterical crying, or constantly and disruptively talking out of turn)

When a treatment-destroying behavior occurs, and if a facilitator cannot contain the disruption, the skills group facilitator stops the group, makes it clear to the participants that the behavior cannot continue, and may use the following interventions to respond to it:

- Attempt a chain analysis of the behavior.

- Reinforce cooperative behavior in others with attention, prizes, and token economy rewards.

- Set a clear limit in the group.

If there is no response, these interventions may be used:

- One group facilitator may meet with the disruptive member privately during group time to appeal for cooperation.

- A facilitator may meet with the disruptive member privately during the break to appeal for cooperation.

If there is no response and the behavior continues, these interventions may be used:

- Meet for an individual session to review goals and expectations in group, with return to group contingent upon this meeting.

- Establish clear expectations for continuing in the group and encourage effective behavior.

- Refer the behavior back to the individual therapist for further assessment and work on change.

- If necessary, "suspend" the group member until the issue has been effectively addressed in individual therapy.

- Consult with team and consider other options for targeting the behavior based on an understanding of the client and his situation.

Learning, practicing, and generalizing skills. The facilitator provides the group with handouts related to the skills to be taught that week. The facilitator ensures that the skill is taught and that there is time to discuss its relevance to the participants. Participants will also have opportunities to role-play or otherwise strengthen the skill in group while they discuss how the skills are or might be helpful to them.

Behaviors that interfere with treatment. Adolescents may show a lack of participation or otherwise appear unfocused or unwilling to participate. As long as the behavior of an adolescent does not interfere with the learning of the other participants, the facilitators may prompt more effective behavior, try to ignore the behavior, or otherwise respond in a subtle way that does not interfere with learning.

Structure of Group Sessions

Each group begins with a mindfulness practice followed by a homework review, the teaching of the new skill, and practice of the new skill. Maintaining a consistent structure is important for group members, who are reassured by knowing what to expect and by understanding the purpose and role of each section of the group experience.

Mindfulness Practice

Mindfulness practice in DBT teaches participants to focus on the present moment and refocus when they become distracted. At the beginning of each group or individual skills training session, it provides the adolescent with an opportunity to let go of distractions and begin to focus and concentrate on learning new skills. It also underscores the essential importance of this skill and the importance of ongoing practice.

Mindfulness is not to be confused with relaxation, although it may lead to greater calm. It actually requires work to focus and to remain focused. The therapeutic goals of mindfulness practice are to learn that you can control your attention and to develop awareness of the moment so that you are not at the mercy of your unpleasant thoughts and emotions (Kabat-Zinn, 2012). The goal within each session is to practice focusing one's attention so the skill becomes strengthened.

Facilitating Mindfulness Practice

Mindfulness practice begins and ends with the sound of a bell. It is a call to begin and focus, and participants may become conditioned to focus at the sound of the bell.

Breathing is often a focus of mindfulness practice as participants learn to be aware of their breath, their bodily sensations, and the thoughts that continually run through their minds. They may be given words, numbers, or sensations to concentrate on and bring their minds back to when they feel it beginning to wander. During mindfulness practice, participants are also reminded to be nonjudgmental of themselves, of others, and of the practice itself.

Each mindfulness practice is explained through a set of instructions that the mindfulness leader gives. The instructions do several things:

- give the participants a reason for the practice, focusing the group on the skill being practiced

- provide specific directions about how to proceed with the practice

- anticipate barriers and problems that the participants might experience and ways to manage those problems, including allowing adolescents to keep their eyes open during the practice

Here is a sample set of instructions for adolescents: "One of the difficulties we all face is that we sometimes become 'stuck' on a situation or an emotion, and we seem unable to move on. It may be something or someone who disappoints us. It may be a situation that causes us anxiety. Holding on makes it harder for us to stay focused in this moment. Today we are going to practice mindfulness of letting go of emotions. Get into a position that is comfortable for you. The more open your body, the more effective the practice will be. To do this practice, when you inhale, you will say to yourself, *'Mindfully breathing.'* When you exhale, you will say to yourself, *'Letting go of* _____ ' and fill in the situation or emotion you want to let go of. If you cannot think of a specific situation, simply say, *'Letting go.'* If you become distracted, gently bring your mind back to the words *'mindfully breathing, letting go.'* If you notice judgmental thoughts, simply notice them and let them go; bring your attention back to your breath. We will start and end the practice with the sound of the bell, and we will do it for three minutes."

A Mindfulness Practice for Practitioners

In order to understand how mindfulness works as well as its benefits, try the practice outlined below:

1. Get yourself into a comfortable position.

2. Develop a breathing pattern that feels comfortable to you.

3. Set a timer for three minutes (you can use timer apps or actual timers).

4. Start counting each inhale and exhale as one breath.

5. Count five breaths. Then return to one and count your next five breaths. Continue to count breaths, one through five, until the timer sounds.

6. If your mind wanders, bring it back to the counting of the breaths.

7. If you have judgmental thoughts, notice them and let them go. Do not be judgmental of the fact that you were judging.

8. If you lose track of your counting, simply return to the number one and begin again without judgment.

When you are done with the practice, notice how you feel and how you were or were not able to "bring your mind back" and stay focused. You will be able to share this experience and what you learned with group members.

Adolescents often respond most effectively to active mindfulness practices (see chart below), which provide opportunities for the adolescent to do these things:

- to remain focused in the moment

- to be aware of his distracting thoughts and bring his mind back to the practice

- to let go of judgments

- to understand how mindfulness can help him become more aware and more present

---

Active Mindfulness Practice for Adolescents

Directions:

1. Bring your attention to one thing (see below for examples).

2. When your mind wanders or begins to judge, notice it.

3. Bring your attention back to the one thing.

Examples:
- Color mandalas or pages from a coloring book.

- Make origami.

- Chew gum slowly.

- Pick an object in the room, notice it for one minute, and describe it to yourself silently for one minute.

- Make bracelets with thread or gimp.

- Have participants wear blindfolds, and then ask everyone to dance to music.

- Do yoga poses.

- Throw a ball.

- Blow bubbles.

At the end of each mindfulness practice, each participant is asked for feedback. This helps in several ways.

- It serves to maintain accountability as each adolescent expresses what worked and what did not work to all of his peers.

- It provides another opportunity for the participants to practice acceptance of each other, since mindfulness practice that works for one participant may not work for another.

- It provides information for the facilitator on which mindfulness practices are more effective in certain situations.

- It allows for more effective instructions to be developed.

Practice Assignments and Review

At the end of each group, a practice assignment (or "homework," a term often experienced as aversive by many teenagers) is distributed. The goal is to have adolescents practice and use the skills in their natural environment so that they will be better able to use the skills at times when they are emotionally dysregulated. These assignments, some of which we have included at the end of the chapter, provide essential opportunities for the adolescent to practice the skill at home.

Practice assignments should also be given if skills are being taught in individual sessions. All practices should be reviewed in the next session.

Practice review, which occurs after mindfulness, is a necessary and effective part of group:

- Practice review holds each participant accountable for completing the practice.

- It provides opportunities for the group facilitator to ensure that the skill is understood and practiced effectively.

- It provides an opportunity to continue to teach the skill from the previous week while responding to specific concerns and problems expressed by each participant.

Many adolescents report they learn more from the practice review than from the initial instruction of the skill.

Practice review needs to occur for learning and strengthening to happen. Group facilitators must build practice review into the structure of the group and ask each participant to share his practice in front of the group during every group. Without this accountability, practice may not be done and skills group will not be as effective. Practice assignments may also be reviewed in more detail by the individual practitioner, especially if the adolescent is having difficulty with a particular skill.

Practice Review and Contingency Management

For some adolescents, accountability within the group may not be enough to ensure that the out-of-session practice is completed. Keeping posted charts on who has completed the practice, praising its completion, following through with individual practitioners, and reinforcing the completion of the practice assignment can all help to ensure that the out-of-session practice is completed. If these strategies do not help adolescents complete their practice assignment (which is considered a treatment-interfering behavior), then further work on commitment with individual practitioners may be necessary.

Teaching and Practicing New Skills

Group facilitators are teachers and trainers who create a validating teaching environment in which they ensure that the specific skills of each group are taught, understood, and practiced. Facilitators arrive at group with examples and exercises intended to foster discussion about the skills among the group participants. In addition, allowing participants to express their own thoughts and feelings about the skills enables participants to become more comfortable with them. Facilitators recognize and accept that not every skill will be effective for each participant every time it is used, and some may not be effective at all for a particular adolescent.

Here are some tips for teaching skills:

- Teach them with enthusiasm, commitment, and personal examples.

- Point out when adolescents are thinking wisely or using skills during sessions.

- Use metaphors or examples from others to reinforce skills.

- Reinforce the use of distress tolerance and interpersonal effectiveness skills by encouraging their use in the group with each other and by commenting when the skills are used.

- Notice and comment on instances of dialectical thinking and validation by the group members.

- Have cofacilitators be mindful of modeling the use of skills during group, especially behavioral contingencies and interpersonal effectiveness; point out the principles behind the behaviors.

- Use a white board or flip charts to teach examples of skills and to review examples from group members.

Daily Logs

Some skills group facilitators ask to see daily logs for a quick scan during skills groups, for a variety of reasons:

- to check for active suicidality or urges to self-harm (which a facilitator will address during the break or at the end of the session to assess for safety)

- to quickly assess the emotionality of group participants

- to monitor participants who do not have DBT individual practitioners to ensure the use of the daily log

- to see what skills are being practiced outside of group

- to see what skills are *not* being practiced outside of group so troubleshooting and encouragement can occur

- to reinforce the daily log completion by showing interest in it

Facilitators focus on the skills-use section of the daily log in group and maintain a focus on use, effectiveness, and reinforcement of skills. If there is an individual practitioner who does not use the daily log or practice DBT, it is important to shape the use of the daily log by the group participants to increase self-awareness and use of skills.

Skills Training in Individual Sessions

At times, it is not possible to develop a group, or an adolescent client is not ready or is unwilling to participate in group. In these situations, a DBT practitioner might choose to teach the skills in a separate individual session or ask another practitioner to provide the skills training individually. The adolescent would then meet with the practitioner once a week to learn and practice the skills following a skills group curriculum, and would meet a second time each week for individual DBT therapy (as discussed in chapter 3). Our experience is that these two modalities (individual therapy and skills training) need to be separated, so that the skills can be taught in the didactic way that is necessary to teach them effectively and any confusion about the goals of each session is minimized. It is up to the practitioner to maintain the focus and structure of the skills training session, as adolescents will understandably try to divert attention away from the learning of skills onto the problem of the moment as they seek immediate relief from their suffering.

Graduate Groups

A participant will be ready to graduate from skills training and can choose to participate in a graduate group (Miller, Rathus, & Linehan, 2007) when he has met all of these targets:

- has completed one full cycle or more of skills training

- has been free of self-harm or suicidality for at least sixty days

- is using skills to remain in behavioral control without any treatment-interfering or severe quality of life–interfering behaviors

- is able to teach some skills (with help, if necessary) and lead mindfulness practice

Graduate groups allow adolescents to continue practicing skills, so that they can continue in turn to generalize them into their life and natural environment. An added benefit is the pressure from peers to maintain safety and behavioral control, as doing so will make it possible to join others in graduating to a new group. These groups help to prevent the isolation and stigma that these adolescents often feel and enable them to practice skills in an ongoing supportive and validating environment. The unique characteristics of the graduate group (Miller, Rathus, & Linehan, 2007) include the following:

- Members are regularly expected to lead mindfulness practice.

- Members are not required to use a daily log—instead, they remember the experiences and use of skills from the week.

- The focus of the group is on decreasing those behaviors that interfere with the participants' quality of life.

- Members will choose and often teach the skills discussed.

- Graduate groups provide more opportunity to discuss individual issues and how skills can be helpful in managing different situations that participants have experienced.

- Facilitators may take a less active role and allow members to help each other problem solve ways to resolve difficult situations.

- Group members are not required to be involved in individual therapy.

- Skills trainers may become coaches to participants who are no longer in individual therapy.

Graduate groups are an important way to provide ongoing support to adolescents, as well as a peer group that is dedicated to safe and skillful behaviors. These groups reinforce the adolescents who have worked to incorporate skills in their lives and to lessen their behavioral dyscontrol. Membership in these groups serves a goal for adolescents and a way for them to continue to receive the support and validation that helped them make the changes they have made.

Summary

DBT skills training is the modality in which adolescents with emotion dysregulation learn safer, more adaptive behaviors to replace those behaviors that create problems in their lives. Skills training (whether taught in group or individually) provides opportunities for adolescents to learn adaptive new skills and practice and strengthen them so that they can replace less adaptive behaviors. In this chapter, we discussed a variety of skills from the five DBT modules as well as unique ways to provide and enhance skills training for adolescents.

In the next chapter, we will discuss several models for teaching parents and caregivers the same DBT skills that the adolescents are learning in order to enhance the effective use of skills for all members of the family.

The following worksheets can be downloaded at www.newharbinger.com/27985.

MINDFULNESS PRACTICE

Record your experiences with mindfulness this week. Fill in each box with an example from the day.

	Sunday	Monday	Tuesday	Wednesday	Thursday	Friday	Saturday
Notice: pay attention without words							
Describe: use words to describe what you notice							
Get involved: be involved 100% in what you're doing							
Don't judge: keep it factual, and describe what you see							
Stay focused: when your mind wanders, bring it back							
Be effective: do what works in the situation							
Think wisely: use all of the above skills together							

DISTRESS TOLERANCE PRACTICE

Getting Through Difficult Moments Skillfully

Think of a situation in which you felt angry, anxious, ashamed, or sad. What happened? _____

_____

_____

Can you accept this situation as it is now? Yes _____ *No* _____

If no, can you distract or self-soothe? _____

What distract or self-soothe skill(s) can you use? _____

_____

Do you feel better? Yes _____ *No* _____

Are you able to use an accept skill? Yes _____ *No* _____

If yes, what skill can you use? _____

_____

If no, what other distract or self-soothe skill can you use? _____

_____

Are you able to accept the situation? Yes _____ *No* _____

How can you respond differently to the situation than you have in the past? _____

_____

How do you feel about the situation, about yourself, and about your life now that you have completed this worksheet? _____

_____

EMOTION REGULATION PRACTICE: LIVING A HEALTHY LIFESTYLE

Taking care of yourself helps you feel better! Keep track of the things you do this week to help you increase positive emotions in your life.

	Sunday	Monday	Tuesday	Wednesday	Thursday	Friday	Saturday
Did you exercise? What and how much?							
Did you take prescribed medication?							
How much sleep did you get?							
Were you physically ill? Did you treat it?							
What did you do to plan ahead for emotional situations?							
What did you do to increase your competency?							
Rate your overall mood for the day (0–10).							

Did you notice any patterns emerge? Did engaging in healthy activities improve your overall mood? _____

PRACTICE ACTING OPPOSITE

When Your Emotions Are Controlling Your Behaviors

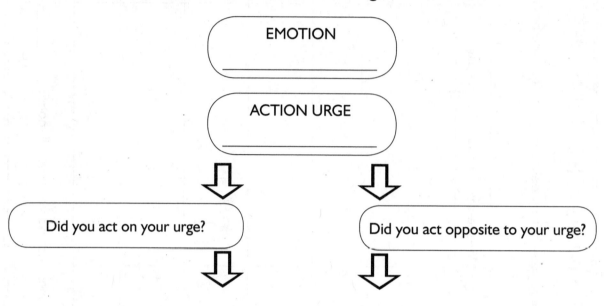

• What did you do? _____ _____	• What did you do? _____ _____
• Did your emotions increase, decrease, or stay the same in intensity? _____ _____	• Did your emotions increase, decrease, or stay the same in intensity? _____ _____
• Was this behavior effective in helping you reach your long-term goals? Yes _____ No _____ • Do you wish you had behaved differently? Yes _____ No _____	• Was this behavior effective in helping you reach your long-term goals? Yes _____ No _____ • Do you wish you had behaved differently? Yes _____ No _____

STORY OF EMOTION PRACTICE

Fill in the blanks.

VULNERABILITY FACTORS/CONTRIBUTING FACTORS—How did you feel *before* the event happened? Did you get enough sleep? Were you hungry? Were you already stressed?

PROMPTING EVENT/TRIGGER—What happened to trigger your feelings?

THOUGHTS/BELIEFS ABOUT THE EVENT—What did you *think* about what happened? Did it trigger memories or beliefs?

BODY SENSATIONS OR RESPONSES—How did your body feel? Did your heart begin to race, did you clench your fists, did you get butterflies in your stomach?

NAME YOUR EMOTION—What is the name that describes what you are feeling?

BEHAVIORS/ACTIONS—How did you act because of your feeling? Were you comfortable with your response? If not, what is another way you could have responded?

SELF-VALIDATION PRACTICE

The invalidating statement I made to myself was:

What I thought (about myself) after I told myself this was:

How I felt about myself after I told myself this was:

I am trying to hear and understand myself nonjudgmentally. I can let myself know that I am hearing, understanding, and accepting myself by making the following validating statement:

This is how I think and feel about myself after self-validating (use feeling words):

MIDDLE PATH PRACTICE

Practicing the Dialectic of Acceptance and Change

You are doing the best you can AND *you have to make changes to make your life better.*

Think of a situation in which someone wanted you to change your behavior and you wanted them to accept you just the way you are.

(Example: Your parents tell you to study and you want them to accept that you don't feel like it and will do it when you can.)

_____

_____

_____

What can you accept in yourself that would also allow you to change your behavior?

(Example: I don't feel like studying right now, which is understandable—and I have limited time to get it done, so it makes sense to start on it even though I don't feel like it.)

_____

_____

_____

_____

How do you feel when you accept yourself and also show a willingness to change?

_____

_____

_____

_____

CHAPTER 5

Working with Parents and Caregivers

It is usually parents (or caregivers) who bring the adolescent to your practice. You may find them to be somewhat dysregulated themselves as they search for answers about how to help their child. Parents often feel many conflicting emotions:

- anger at being blamed by family or friends

- shame about their own emotional reactions to their child

- guilt about what they may or may not have done to cause these problems

- grief that their child may not be able to be all that they expected and hoped for, and may not have the life they envisioned

- difficulty accepting the child they have

- feelings of being "inept" as parents despite the fact that they may have spent years trying to find the proper help for their child

- confusion because of different advice coming from various professionals

- helplessness and hopelessness about any possibility of change

By the time parents bring an adolescent to a DBT practitioner, they have already experienced years of intense emotions and behaviors at home and have already tried numerous types of treatment and therapy, which may have included residential programs, therapeutic boarding schools, wilderness programs, and/or numerous hospitalizations. Often, they have also received contradictory professional advice and guidance that has proven ineffective. Practitioners need to be sensitive to these past experiences and the desperation and fear that the parents often feel. As one parent put it, "When your daughter tries to kill herself at age sixteen, it changes everything that comes after." Parents, who often feel overwhelmed and alone, sometimes see DBT as the "last, great hope," and they are desperate for DBT to help their child.

As parents are oriented to DBT, they learn to accept that their daughter is doing the best she can do in the moment (Linehan, 1993a) as a way to lessen their emotional reactivity and begin to work on acceptance. They are also introduced to the idea that though an adolescent may not have caused all of her problems, she is the only one who can solve them (Linehan, 1993a). Parents have often been taught that it is their responsibility to take care of their child, and they believe it is their job to make their child better. It can be very painful for parents to learn that only their daughter can make changes in her life, and that she will have to be the one to choose to commit to, and make use of, treatment. Parents, who may be well-intentioned or desperate, need to learn their own limits and what they can and cannot control. Validation and sensitivity on the part of the practitioner are very important. Parents experience the power of being accepted, which is the foundation of the relationship between a practitioner and a parent. In some situations, there may be a practitioner on the treatment team who works specifically with the parents—we call this practitioner the "parent coach." Ultimately, teaching parents to respond more effectively to their adolescent's intense emotions benefits the adolescent and interrupts the escalating cycle of emotions in the family. We will see how the parent coach works with parents as we meet Paul and Diana in the vignette below and follow them through the chapter.

A Parent Vignette

Paul and Diana come to see a parent coach at the recommendation of their fifteen-year-old daughter's individual DBT practitioner. Their daughter has just returned from a non-DBT residential program to which she had gone six months earlier because of suicidal ideation and self-harming behaviors that had resulted in numerous hospitalizations. Paul and Diana express their anger and frustration that their daughter is cutting herself again, and they cannot understand why she continues to do this after they have just paid so much money for her to "get better." They are very angry that their daughter is going out with friends and not letting them know where she is; this behavior leads to a great deal of anxiety for them until she returns. Then they erupt and angrily confront their daughter. She responds with physically threatening behavior (blocking their way out of a room, or following them around the house and verbally abusing them). They have already taken away her cell phone and computer, and she has been constantly demanding that they give them back. They are very concerned about what she might be writing on her Facebook account and worried about her safety. Paul wants to give her back her access to the Internet, and Diana does not think she deserves this when she isn't following any of their rules or cooperating in the house. Her individual practitioner is concerned that their daughter is not able to contact the practitioner for coaching because she does not have her cell phone. Paul and Diana express their confusion over all the contradictory advice they have been given and how terrible it feels to them that family members blame them for their daughter's problems. During the initial session with the parent coach, Diana begins to cry, and expresses her feelings of inadequacy as a mother and her fears that her daughter will seriously or fatally harm herself or be harmed by someone else. Paul expresses his confusion about what to do as well as his frustration with his wife for enforcing rules that make their daughter angry.

The Important Role of Parents

Although parents learn that the adolescent must be responsible for changing herself, they also learn that there is a very important role they can play in structuring the environment, becoming less reactive, and helping to decrease their daughter's emotionality. Parents learn they *can* change the way they respond to their daughter, which can bring about changes in their relationship, the emotional level of their home, and their daughter as well. For example, parents have reported that the simple act of taking a walk without their child not only made them feel better, but improved their relationship with their daughter as well.

Structuring the Environment

In homes in which an adolescent has emotion dysregulation, the parents have often been conditioned by the adolescent to respond ineffectively to high-risk behaviors because they are afraid their adolescent may do something dangerous. The adolescent may threaten to harm herself if she does not get the privileges she demands or is not allowed to do what she wants, and she may have emotional outbursts that "punish" her parents. And she may also calm down and act in a more loving way when her parents do let her do what she wants, reinforcing them for this behavior. Parents often become overly lenient and conciliatory in order to lessen conflict and behavioral outbursts. Or, conversely, they may become overly authoritarian as a way to maintain control. Parents need to learn how to create an environment that is more balanced and more conducive to learning safe and skillful behaviors.

Acceptance: Creating a Validating Environment

According to the biosocial theory (see chapter 2), an invalidating environment exacerbates the emotion dysregulation of a child. When parents are able to create a more validating environment, the adolescent feels heard and better understood. This leads to more communication between the parents and adolescent, fewer emotional outbursts, and a calmer and healthier environment for the entire family (Fruzetti, 2005). The idea of validation resonates with parents who understand that their adolescent accuses them of "not getting it" or "not understanding." Validation within a family can be quite healing.

There are many reasons why it is hard for parents to validate their children. They may find it distressful to acknowledge the pain their child experiences, which is necessary to genuinely validate her. In addition, parents often want to fix problems or make them go away, especially if they are accomplished in other areas of their lives, or feel it is their responsibility to resolve their adolescent's problems. Parents may hope to minimize the pain by dismissing the problem.

Parents can become frustrated because what they see as attempts at being helpful may actually be experienced as invalidating by their adolescent and therefore ineffective, often leading to more emotional outbursts from the adolescent. Parents have to use trial and error to find ways to let their adolescent know that they are truly listening, (are trying to) understand, and are taking the concerns of the adolescent seriously. Here are some validating parental responses:

- just listening without speaking

- relating what the adolescent is feeling to what others might feel, thereby normalizing it

- repeating back what the adolescent is saying in different words

- acknowledging the affect behind the adolescent's words

Parents are sometimes hesitant to validate their child because they confuse it with agreeing with their child. It is helpful to remind parents that validating does not mean agreeing; it means genuinely acknowledging that the feelings of their adolescent make sense given the adolescent's experiences. Practitioners model validation for the parents by validating them. Parents quickly recognize how satisfying it is to be understood and acknowledge how important validating their adolescent might be to her.

Change: Using Contingency Management Effectively

Parents need to be taught and coached to use behavioral contingencies effectively to reinforce adaptive behaviors and to ignore or, if necessary, punish less adaptive and dangerous behaviors. Structuring the environment to be more positively responsive to adaptive behaviors is one of the goals of DBT (Linehan, 1993a). Helping parents learn that they might intermittently or inadvertently reinforce dangerous behaviors enables them to begin to change their responses so that they reinforce more adaptive behaviors.

Parents are often so overwhelmed by the high-risk behavior of their adolescent that they do not respond to behaviors that are adaptive. And they are so conditioned to being blamed and treated with anger and scorn that they withdraw or keep their distance even when things may be going well. Parents need to be reminded to respond positively when their adolescent behaves in normative ways, which happens more often than they expect when they are more mindfully aware of it.

Prioritizing behaviors. One aspect of contingency management includes helping parents prioritize the behaviors that they will respond to. Parents are oriented to the priority targets of DBT and encouraged to use the model to decide what behaviors to focus on. In order, the priorities are (1) safety, (2) adherence to treatment, and (3) behaviors that impair relationships, school, work, or activities. As hard as this is for parents, they are asked to pay less attention to school behaviors until their daughter is able to maintain her safety and participation in treatment. With the treatment team's support and encouragement, the parents begin to accept that emotion dysregulation may limit their adolescent until she learns the skills to help her manage her emotions and behaviors more effectively.

Responding to threats. The difficulty for parents in creating a structured environment that does not inadvertently reinforce dangerous or maladaptive behaviors is that they do not feel they can ignore threats to self-harm, so they wind up giving in to the demands of their adolescent. In DBT, parents learn how to respond to threats in effective ways that do not reinforce unproductive or dangerous behaviors. Parents have to find a way to take the adolescent's threat seriously without giving in to the adolescent's demands. Parent coaching in this regard can help the parent make the most effective decision, both immediately and for the long term.

Lessening Parental Emotional Reactivity

Parents and adolescents often become reactive, with each becoming more angry or frustrated in reaction to the other, even in typical situations. When an adolescent has emotion dysregulation, this reactivity, with its increasing spiral of emotional abuse, can become explosive and dangerous. The adolescent's anger, frustration, and disappointment are often aimed at the parents who, feeling powerless to stop the behavior of the adolescent whom they see as "disrespectful" and "out of control," react similarly. Both the parents and the adolescent may find it very difficult to step back and decide how to respond more wisely.

When parents have the opportunity to be heard and are being understood, they are less likely to be reactive to their adolescent. They are also more likely to learn more effective skills, such as those listed below, for handling difficult situations:

- understanding the function of their adolescent's behaviors so they do not take the behavior so personally

- slowing down, taking a deep breath, thinking about how to respond, and deciding on a response that will be effective in the situation—and taking "time-outs," if necessary

- being aware that they are more reactive when they think emotionally, rather than wisely

- building pleasant activities into their lives to relieve stress and vulnerability

- finding ways to self-soothe and take care of themselves so that they have the resources to take care of their adolescent

- understanding their own story of emotion and which beliefs and thoughts might lead to an increase in their emotions

- acting opposite to their emotional and behavioral urges by speaking softly when they want to yell, walking away when they are very angry, and so on

- developing effective strategies so they feel less powerless

In a DBT environment in which parents are not blamed or judged, they learn to look at their own behavior nondefensively. In this validating environment, they are accepted as doing the best they can, which enables them to make necessary changes.

Lessening Emotion Dysregulation

Parents who understand what causes their daughter to be vulnerable or become emotionally dysregulated may take active steps to lessen the reactivity. A calm and soothing home environment will help an adolescent have less intense reactions in the family. Parents can lessen their own stressful interactions with others in front of the adolescent and model ways to manage tense situations calmly and effectively. When stressful situations cannot be avoided, or when stressful events occur, it is beneficial to help the adolescent plan in advance how she will manage the situation and what she will need from her parents to be effective and safe. This kind of communication validates and empowers the adolescent at the same time.

Of course, no home environment can be calm all the time, and stress is a part of life. While the adolescent is learning how to effectively handle stress and is still emotionally dysregulated, parents can be helpful in a number of ways:

- responding in a validating, calm, and gentle manner

- encouraging their daughter to call her DBT coach

- encouraging the use of the adolescent's self-soothe toolkit

- providing an environment that is calming and restorative for their adolescent

- allowing their adolescent to take time away from stressful situations when she needs to

Parents have to understand that they are not responsible for their daughter's reactions and cannot control her behaviors. They can, however, try to create an environment that lessens emotional reactivity, and trust that this environment will be helpful to their daughter. Parents tell us that, when they become calmer and more validating, their adolescent children become calmer, and the number of emotional outbursts diminishes.

Working with Parents

Practitioners who work with adolescents quickly recognize that in order to facilitate lasting changes in their client, parents need (1) support and (2) strategies for responding effectively to their adolescent. The dilemma for the practitioner is how to provide the parents with the psychoeducation and support that they need while also developing a trusting therapeutic relationship with an adolescent who is naturally distrustful of adults, and particularly reticent to share information with someone who talks to her parents.

Difficulties in Providing Services to Parents

Parents often bring their adolescent to treatment with certain expectations of the practitioner. The parents would like the practitioner to make sure that the adolescent (1) becomes safer and less emotionally reactive, (2) meets certain expectations at home, and (3) respects their limits. The frustration that the parents have with the adolescent can easily be transferred to the practitioner if the parents feel they are not being heard or that treatment is not progressing quickly enough. Their fears and anxieties are often translated into demands and expectations of the practitioner, which may lead the practitioner to push for change too quickly and to be frustrated and/or possibly invalidating of the parents' issues. These behaviors can get in the way of effective treatment and will need to be addressed in the therapy and in the consultation team (see chapter 6). The adolescent may also be demanding confidentiality on the part of the practitioner, who is caught in the dilemma of meeting competing needs.

Family therapy, in which all members of the family meet or in which the adolescent meets with her parents, can be very difficult when the adolescent has emotion dysregulation, is emotionally reactive and sensitive to her parents, and has not yet learned ways to manage the intensity of her affect or behaviors. Parents may be similarly emotionally reactive in these situations. Parents and adolescents often trigger each other's emotions in these sessions, decreasing the effectiveness of the meeting. Family therapy can often prove emotionally intense for the practitioner as well, as she can be caught up in choosing sides, with her ability to maintain a dialectical stance sorely tested.

These dilemmas may be resolved using one or more of the following strategies:

- offering a separate parent coach/practitioner, experienced in DBT, who is specially trained in working with parents and providing immediate and strategic feedback to parents/caregivers

- scheduling strategic family meetings, rather than ongoing ones

- offering DBT skills training for parents

- orienting parents and adolescents to the guidelines and limitations of confidentiality

Parent Coaching

A separate parent coach—a practitioner trained in DBT whose focus is work with the parents or caregivers and who is a member of the DBT treatment team—can be invaluable, whenever it is possible, in supporting the parents and helping them develop effective parenting techniques. The parent coach will coordinate treatment with the adolescent's practitioner. This enables the adolescent's practitioner to stay focused on the adolescent and on advocating on her behalf. The parent coach is not burdened by the difficulties expressed by the adolescent about her parents, is more sensitive to their particular difficulties, and is better able to provide acceptance and validation for the parents. Parents who participate in DBT with a parent coach experience someone who understands and is not judgmental of them. They feel great relief in no longer feeling alone or blamed, and they may be more receptive to receiving feedback and working on change.

A parent coach is also able to do chain analyses of behavioral incidents in the home so that the parents can understand how their responses or reactions may cause their daughter to escalate her behaviors. Because these chains are done in a nonblaming way and with only the parents and the coach present, the parents are able to look with less defensiveness at their own behaviors and are more willing to make the changes necessary to minimize escalations as much as possible.

The parent coach has several goals:

- orienting the parents to DBT, biosocial theory, the concept of validation, the practice of how to think wisely, and the balance of acceptance and change. (In some practices, the individual practitioner will orient the parents as well as the adolescent to these issues, and the parent coach will reinforce what has already been told to the parents.)

- lessening the parents' reactivity to their adolescent

- providing phone, e-mail, or text coaching and support when the parents are outside the treatment office, so that they can begin to generalize the skills they are learning to interactions and situations with their child

- providing psychoeducation about normative adolescence and adolescents with emotion dysregulation

- helping parents learn how to implement effective behavioral management skills when responding to behaviors

- helping parents learn to communicate more effectively

- assisting parents in developing a more validating environment for everyone in the home

- helping parents remain focused on doing what is effective

- providing validation and supporting change

- supporting parents when their adolescent child reacts negatively to the implementation of new strategies or escalates her behavior in reaction to the parents' decisions

- helping parents focus on what their adolescent needs to do to be effective in meeting her own goals

The parent coach uses the same validation techniques to engage parents as does the adolescent's practitioner. The focus of the parent coach is always to help the parents make necessary changes in order to parent more effectively.

The Parent Coach

The practitioner who works with the parents may act just as a coach, focused solely on parenting issues, while the parents seek other practitioners to help them with their own individual or marital issues. The parent coach may also provide therapy for the parents, if necessary, helping them to understand the particular dynamics in their family and find ways to resolve the problems they experience. Parent coaches need to be sensitive to the differences between the parents and to the stress placed on the parents' relationship by a child who has at-risk behaviors. Within a DBT team, one practitioner may provide the parent coaching while another practitioner provides the adolescent therapy. In this model, the same practitioner may work with an adolescent in one family and the parents in another. The members of the team can, thus, share the work within a family and work together to provide the most effective treatment for each family.

The authors provide services to adolescents and parents with a "dedicated" parent coach, an individual whose focus is solely on parents and who is not impacted by maintaining a relationship with an adolescent. This practitioner is able to provide a nonblaming, validating environment in which the parents are the client and the practitioner is their advocate. This provides additional safety for the parents, who feel relieved that they are the focus of attention even while they recognize that they are seeing the coach in order to become more effective parents.

It is critical that the parent coach and the adolescent's individual practitioner work together, provide a consistent message, and understand each of their roles. This coordination enables the overall treatment to be most effective.

The schedule of parent coaching. Some parents benefit from one session with a coach; others come weekly or biweekly until they feel that they have learned enough strategies. Either way, they may then return on an as-needed basis. It is important to give the parents some control over how often they come and to not "pathologize" or otherwise blame them. However, if the individual practitioner or DBT team feels that the parents need additional support, more help in creating a validating environment, or more help in developing effective behavioral contingencies, they may recommend that the parents continue to work with the parent coach regularly, or ask the parent coach to reach out to the parents.

Many parents leave the first session with the parent coach and say they feel hopeful for the first time in years. They feel they have found someone who understands them, their history, and their adolescent, and who is going to teach them ways to be more effective while not blaming them. At the end of this session, there is often a palpable sense of relief that help is available and change is possible.

When a Separate Coach Is Not Available

If a separate practitioner is not available and a single practitioner works with the parents and the adolescent, the practitioner will be most effective when following the guidelines below.

- Maintain a dialectical stance in which it is understood that each participant has a valid perspective and truth is not absolute. Rather than focusing on who is "right" or "wrong," the family should remain focused on synthesizing their different perspectives and doing what is most effective.

- Provide validation for the parents as well as for the adolescent.

- Remain nonjudgmental and nonblaming to all family members.

- Maintain the confidence of the adolescent except when the adolescent is a danger to herself or others.

- Maintain the confidence of the parents, and work on having the parents and the adolescent communicate directly with each other rather than through the practitioner.

- Help the family develop reinforcing rather than punitive behavioral contracts that are agreed upon by all family members.

The importance of providing a validating, dialectical environment for all family members cannot be emphasized enough, and a practitioner who works with all family members must be mindful of her own thoughts, beliefs, and feelings as she works to provide the most effective, and very necessary, treatment for the adolescent and the parents. We can see how the parent coach provides validation in the dialogue below:

Dialogue: Validating Parents

Mom: Our daughter controls our whole house; we do not have a moment of peace.

Parent coach: That is a very difficult way to live; I can imagine how hard that is for you.

Mom: We worry constantly that she will do something to harm herself, and so we watch her all the time, we read her Facebook page, and we monitor her texts. Then we get even more angry and worried.

Parent coach: I understand that you want to do everything you can to keep your daughter safe. I see that you are doing what you can and that you have been trying to help her for a long time. I wonder if monitoring everything she does helps you feel better or makes you more anxious.

Mom: It does make me feel better to know what she is doing.

Parent coach: It is important that parents do what they can to help their kids remain safe, and also that they recognize that there are limits to what they can do. This dialectic is very painful for parents; as much as you want to help your daughter, *she* is the one who will actually have to make a commitment to change. While we work together to help you learn some strategies that you might find helpful, your daughter's practitioner will help her make a commitment to change and teach her the skills she needs to be safe..

Dad: You have no idea how many counselors, family therapists, and psychiatrists we have seen. We have tried everything they told us, and our house is still chaotic. We still don't know how to talk to her. All we do is worry all the time.

Parent coach: I can imagine how frustrating this must be for you—to have tried so hard for so long to help your daughter and to still be having so much difficulty now. This is not anyone's fault; it is the nature of emotion dysregulation. I know other parents who have similar difficulties, so you are not alone. I am here to provide support to you and to coach you when you have a hard time with your daughter. And I hope that I can help you feel more accepting of yourselves and of your daughter as time goes on.

Strategic Family Meetings

Periodic family meetings between the adolescent and the parent can occur with the permission of the adolescent if the practitioners think that there is enough emotional stability in the family to have an effective session, that does not devolve into the emotional reactivity that occurs at home. It may be many months into treatment before a family is ready for this kind of meeting. Often the individual practitioner will work with the adolescent to prepare for the meeting so that the time spent with parents can be useful. If the parents have a parent coach, they will also be working on how to remain calm and effective in the meeting. These are some of the goals of such meetings, which are often facilitated by the adolescent's individual practitioner:

- help mitigate the anxiety of the parents, whose periodic need to know what happens in the adolescent's therapy sessions can lead them to engage in behaviors that might interfere with the adolescent's treatment

- provide an opportunity for the parents to share specific concerns so that they can develop effective ways of responding to the adolescent at home

- help the adolescent advocate for herself around a specific issue and to give the family an opportunity to problem solve together.

Parent Skills Training Groups

One way that parents can learn and practice specific DBT skills is to participate in a parent DBT skills training group. The benefits of the group are the structured nature that enhances learning all the skills and the camaraderie felt among parents who have similar experiences. For some parents, this may be the first time they talk to others about their difficulties and their pain, which lessens their isolation and validates their feelings. Parents are quickly taught these foundational ideas:

- Parents will be able to benefit from learning the skills and using them in their own daily life.

- Parents model the importance of, and their commitment to, change by their willingness to learn and change themselves. This is an important message for their child.

- Parents may not be able to change their adolescent child; they will learn how to change their responses to their child, and that will provide the opportunity for her to change in response.

Adapting Skills for Parents

Parents learn the same skills that their adolescent sons and daughters learn. The focus of the skills, however, will be on how they help the parents to be more effective in communicating, interacting, and responding to their children and in de-escalating emotional situations. In the very beginning, parents are introduced to the biosocial theory (Linehan, 1993a) and the DBT assumptions (Linehan, 1993a; Miller, Rathus, & Linehan, 2007) as a way to nonjudgmentally understand their sons and daughters and themselves. Parents learn the following from each of the five modules of skills training:

Mindfulness (Linehan, 1993a). Mindful awareness enables parents to slow down their emotional reactions and allows them to respond in ways that are most effective. Mindfulness skills help parents change the automatic dysfunctional patterns in their families.

Middle path (Miller, Rathus, & Linehan, 2007). These skills are vitally important and teach parents several effective parenting behaviors:

- finding more balanced and less rigid responses

- looking for the valid aspects of their child's responses and acknowledging the very real emotional content without dismissing their child's feelings

- understanding that their responses can increase, decrease, or maintain responses from their children, and understanding that "giving in" to their child some of the time or not following through on consequences even once in a while can lead to very persistent behaviors

Distress tolerance skills (Linehan, 1993a). These skills are essential for managing the difficulties of living with high-risk adolescents. Often parents do not engage in those activities that are soothing or distracting for them because they do not have the time. It is helpful to explain to parents what flight attendants acknowledge when they admonish parents to put the oxygen mask on themselves first: you cannot take care of others effectively if you do not first take care of yourself. Parents are often relieved to be "given permission" to take time for themselves.

In this module, parents are also introduced to evaluating the positive and negative impacts of their behaviors. They learn that their initial response to their child might make the situation easier in the short run and more difficult in the long run.

Finally, parents learn the importance of accepting those aspects of their lives that they cannot change, and they learn that acceptance leads to less suffering and, paradoxically, more problem solving. Accepting "what is" becomes an invaluable skill for parents in lessening their reactivity and pain; acceptance is a skill they need to practice repeatedly until they are able to truly accept "what is" in their lives and in the life of their adolescent without feeling like they are "giving up."

Dialogue: Discussing Acceptance in Skills Group

Parent group facilitator:	Accepting life as it is in this moment is one of the skills in distress tolerance. So today we are going to talk about the importance of learning to accept in order to reduce suffering. This means that it will help you to accept that your adolescent has difficulties that make her life harder. It may mean that the life you expected for your child may not be the life she has or that she may have a harder path to getting there.
Parent 1:	I can't accept that my child will have difficulties and pain. I had so many hopes and dreams for her.
Parent group facilitator:	I understand how difficult this is. Sometimes parents whose kids have emotional difficulties actually have to mourn and grieve the child they expected to have in order to accept the child they do have. You may feel a great

deal of sadness about this, and that is understandable. The problem is that the more you deny this reality, the more you will actually suffer.

Parent 2: I feel if I accept that my daughter has difficulties, then I am giving up, and then she is doomed to a life of difficulties. How can I help her if I give up on her?

Parent group facilitator: I know this is painful for you. What I would like to emphasize is that accepting that your daughter has difficulties that make her life harder does not mean that you are giving up. It means that you will free up your emotional resources to think clearly about how to get her the most effective help and how to be most effective in your parenting.

Parent 2: It still seems too hard to accept all this. I don't want to accept it.

Parent group facilitator: This is hard. Anecdotally, parents tell me that things actually get better when they begin to accept. The paradox here is that the more you accept, the more things can actually change. I know that this is one of the most difficult concepts for parents. We will continue to wrestle with this issue, and it will continue to come up as we discuss other skills. What I hope you will begin to see is that acceptance is the path that makes forward movement and change possible.

Emotion regulation (Linehan, 1993a). Parents learn to understand their own vulnerabilities and what triggers their emotional responses to their adolescent, and they learn to be mindful of the triggers and vulnerabilities that their adolescent has. With this understanding, they are able to lessen emotional situations in their home and respond more effectively to the needs of their children. Parents also learn the importance of taking care of themselves and their children by increasing positive and competence-building activities, thereby lessening emotional reactivity. Finally, parents learn to respond to their own emotions more effectively by acting opposite to their own emotional and behavioral urges, as can be seen in the chart below:

EMOTION	ACTION URGE	ACTING OPPOSITE TO YOUR ACTION URGE
Anger	Attack physically or verbally Yell or scream Punish the adolescent	Walk away Avoid the situation Disengage from the situation Practice kindness Speak calmly and softly
Depression/Sadness (because of the difficulties of the adolescent)	Isolate Stop taking care of yourself Do not do things you enjoy	Reach out to others Participate in activities Take care of and soothe yourself Talk to other parents
Anxiety/Fear (of what might happen to the adolescent)	Prohibit the adolescent from activities Be very vigilant about all the adolescent's behaviors Restrict the adolescent's activities and freedoms	Do what is most effective for the adolescent by thinking wisely Allow the adolescent reasonable activities and freedoms Find a balanced approach to monitoring safety and accepting the limits of what a parent can do
Guilt (that your adolescent's problems are your fault)	Stop doing what you are doing Make it up to the adolescent by giving her whatever she wants	Do not make repairs unless you *intended* harm Continue to behave as you were doing Think wisely about how to respond effectively

Interpersonal effectiveness (Linehan, 1993a). This module helps parents develop and focus on the goals for their interactions with their teenagers. This results in more effectiveness and less emotional reactivity during their interactions. Parents are also asked to create a balance between what is demanded of them as parents and what priorities they have for themselves—and to understand that this balance will actually help them become more effective, less resentful, and less reactive to their adolescent son or daughter.

With these skills in mind, let's return to Paul and Diana, whom we met in the vignette earlier in this chapter. The parent coach and the parent skills group will help Paul and Diana by:

- validating their very valid fears and concerns

- explaining the biosocial theory in a nonblaming way, and helping them to see that their daughter has learned ways to manage her emotion dysregulation and can learn more adaptive behaviors in her DBT treatment, thus reassuring them that change is possible

- reminding them that they have done the best they could with a daughter who has emotion dysregulation and acknowledging their willingness to work on their own changes

- teaching them how to validate their daughter's feelings, even if she is angry at them, by explaining that validation leads to healthier family functioning and less emotional reactivity (Fruzetti, 2005) and by giving them validation practice exercises

- teaching them how to be less reactive by being mindful of their own emotions and sensitive to what their daughter might be experiencing, and by slowing down their responses and thinking wisely

- teaching them effective behavioral techniques so that they can reinforce their daughter's adaptive and cooperative behaviors, as well as allow her to have access to her cell phone, if limited, so that she can call her coach when necessary

- helping them to find a compromising path so that they can be consistent in their limits and expectations

- helping them to see what in their daughter's behavior is typical of adolescence, and to understand how to prioritize their responses to problematic behaviors based on DBT targets

- chaining incidents that result in threatening behaviors so the parents can look at how they can respond differently when their daughter escalates in order to de-escalate the situation, rather than inadvertently escalate it

- helping them to recognize when their daughter is dysregulated, and reminding them to encourage their daughter to call her coach or use her skills at those times, while they in turn lessen their demands on her

- encouraging them to add pleasant and soothing activities to their lives so they will be less vulnerable to negative emotions and have more emotional resources to effectively parent their daughter.

- listening to and validating their concerns over and over again, and providing a place where they feel accepted and less isolated

Parents often report that these skills help them with all of their children (not just those with emotion dysregulation) and that the skills are helpful in other areas of their lives as well.

Skills Groups for Parents: Various Approaches

There are several ways to provide skills training to parents in groups: independent skills groups, concurrent groups, concurrent groups with parents and adolescents joined for part of the time, monthly parent orientation groups, multifamily groups, and follow-up groups. Practitioners in adolescent programs or practices choose the approach that will be most effective for their clients and works with the professional staff they have available. A separate group is not always possible; several programs see great benefit in working with adolescents and their parents together. Each practitioner or program will assess the pros and cons of each approach to make the choice that will work most effectively.

Independent skills groups. In the independent skills group approach, a practitioner meets with parents independently in a setting free of the tension they often feel around their adolescent. The parents feel safe and learn in a relaxed and comfortable environment in which their needs come first and foremost. The goal of this approach is to offer a calm, peaceful, and validating environment where learning may occur more effectively.

This approach advocates a closed group (that is, with the same participants) that, depending on the size of the group and the availability of the skills trainer, meets for ten to twelve sessions that may last ninety minutes to two hours. In this approach, the adolescent may or may not be involved in DBT treatment; however, the parents recognize the benefit of making changes in their own behaviors. The makeup of this group includes all parents or caregivers (when possible) so that they can encourage and support each other in using the skills in their homes. Parents are oriented to the group in similar ways that the adolescents are oriented, and they learn that their group has several expectations and characteristics.

- Each member makes a commitment to attend all the sessions (with the understanding that absences may, at times, be unavoidable).

- The group follows the model developed by Linehan (1993b), which means it is didactic, not process oriented; it focuses on learning specific skills every session; it minimizes discussion of ongoing personal family problems unrelated to the skills; and it also minimizes the telling of stories about their adolescent's difficult or unsafe behaviors because doing so causes tension in all parents and detracts from learning the skills.

- Members are encouraged to use nonjudgmental language within the group.

- Parents with a pressing issue can discuss it, privately, with the facilitator, who is available before and after group.

Each session of the group focuses on particular skills (see chart below); the facilitator ensures that, in every session, homework is discussed, the group does not get distracted by personal issues, and the new skills are covered. The facilitator models nonjudgmental language, validation, and behavioral contingencies while maintaining the focus of the group on the skills that are to be learned that session.

Module	Skills
Orientation to DBT	Assumptions Biosocial framework Nonjudgmental language The dialectic of acceptance and change
Mindfulness	Noticing Describing Paying attention to one thing in the moment Thinking about their adolescent nonjudgmentally Doing what works
Middle Path	Dialectics Validation Behavioral contingencies and concepts
Distress Tolerance	Distracting and self-soothing to get through the moment Assessing the positive and negative impact of behavioral choices Actively accepting "what is," being willing
Emotion Regulation	The story of emotion Acting opposite Wellness skills
Interpersonal Effectiveness	Developing a balanced lifestyle and balancing life commitments Getting needs met skillfully Maintaining relationships skillfully Maintaining self-respect skillfully
Wrap-Up	Module reviews Review of validation Certificate of completion ceremony

The parent group parallels the structure of the adolescent skills group and follows this format:

1. Mindfulness practice, with the goal being that each participant finds a mindfulness method that works for him or her

2. Review of material from the previous week and how participants were able to use skills at home, focusing on how the skills helped them to be more effective at parenting their adolescent

3. Homework review

4. New skills presented, taught, and discussed specifically as they relate to parenting an adolescent who has emotion dysregulation

5. Assignment of homework and an ending reading that relates to the concepts being learned (See Resources for some of the books used for these readings.)

As the group progresses, participants begin to recognize and acknowledge how hard it is to change both for them and for their adolescent. They also learn the importance of acceptance—of accepting their adolescent in this moment, accepting the difficulties she faces, and accepting that she is doing the best she can. And parents struggle with, and eventually accept, the following dialectic: that they can provide an environment that reinforces healthy choices *and* that their adolescent ultimately has to make the necessary changes in her own life.

The parents are encouraged to seek out or accept individualized parent coaching in order to effectively use the skills and develop new strategies for the problems they face at home. This mirrors the experience of the adolescent and contributes to mutual respect for everyone's efforts to change.

Separate concurrent groups. This approach asks parents to attend their own separate group while their adolescent attends skills group. The adolescents and parents work on the same module and might have the same or similar homework assignments. This model ensures parent involvement and increases the possibility that the parent and adolescent will discuss the skills, practice them together, and support one another's learning. This group proceeds in a manner similar to the adolescent group: parent participants enter when their adolescent enters group, and there is an ongoing rotation of the skills. Thus, the parents and adolescents attend as long as necessary to learn the skills. This model follows the group structure presented above.

Concurrent groups—parents and adolescents joined part of the time. This approach provides the opportunity for the parents and adolescents to spend time learning together—doing mindfulness and/or sharing the didactic portion of the group—so that they can practice their skills together and resolve difficulties in using the skills with the help and influence of the group facilitator. In this approach, during part of the group time, one facilitator meets with the parents and the other facilitator meets separately with the adolescents to practice and discuss skills and/or homework. The separate component of this model provides opportunities for participants to discuss difficulties with the skills without worry about blame, guilt, or frustration.

Monthly parents orientation groups. When it is difficult for practitioners to facilitate an ongoing independent or concurrent parent group, it may be helpful to meet with parents of adolescents in skills group at the beginning of each module to orient the parents to the skills that will be taught. This parent group begins with mindfulness. Parents also receive the handouts that the adolescents receive. The goal is to help the parents understand the skills and feel more connected to the adolescents' work. The meeting can be entirely focused on orienting the parents to the skills or can include some time for the parents to share concerns about the use of skills at home. The facilitator should remain focused on the task of orienting to the skills and not be distracted by the immediate needs and concerns of the parents. Parents who need more DBT guidance can be referred for individualized parent coaching.

Multifamily groups. This skills training approach (Miller, Rathus, & Linehan, 2007) combines adolescents and parents in a multifamily group; the entire group time is spent together. It is mandatory that adolescents and parents participate together in the group for all sessions—learning, discussing, and practicing the skills together. Given the large number of participants, coleaders may split the group to review homework, or they may limit homework review in the interest of time.

Follow-up groups. Parent participants sometimes struggle when the group ends because they find the support of the other members to be so valuable. There are a number of ways to follow up and provide other opportunities for the parents to learn and review their skills. These include "graduate" groups for parents or periodic refresher groups in which participants can review the skills that they have learned.

Providing Skills Groups for Parents: Which Model to Use

The most effective way to provide skills groups for parents can be assessed using the information in the following chart:

Question	If yes, then use the model(s) below:	If no, then use the model below:
Do you expect parents whose adolescents are in DBT treatment to attend a group?	• concurrent group with or without parents and adolescents together, or • multifamily group	• orientation group for each module • parents group (voluntary attendance)
Do you want to emphasize that parents have a group in which they are free from potential judgments from their child and can feel safe to express their feelings and concerns?	• independent parent skills group • separate concurrent group	• concurrent groups with or without parents and adolescents joined part of the time • multifamily skills group
Do you want to emphasize that the parents and adolescent learn the skills together?	• multi-family group • concurrent group in which parents and adolescents do some learning together	• independent skills group • separate concurrent group
Do you have enough space and practitioner time to provide separate parent groups?	• independent skills group • concurrent group with or without parents and adolescents together	• multifamily skills group

Handouts and homework practice sheets that are modified for parents are provided to them, and they are also encouraged to keep a DBT binder. Worksheets that are included in chapter 4 may also be used with parents. For worksheets explicitly for parents, see the end of this chapter.

Confidentiality

Adolescents and parents are oriented to the rules of confidentiality as well as its limits. If the adolescent is willing to allow the practitioner to speak with parents and authorizes the release of information (state laws vary on the age at which the adolescent is entitled to confidentiality with differently licensed professionals), the practitioner is able to share information about major issues without revealing specific details that are discussed in therapy. In these instances, the practitioner should still discuss with the adolescent what information will be shared. In addition, parents should be told that some of the information they share with the practitioner will also be shared with the adolescent, and they can be asked to let the adolescent know what they are sharing through such means as copying the adolescent on e-mails or other correspondence. This open and transparent communication helps adolescents feel that their relationship with the practitioner is not being compromised and leads to greater communication between parent and child.

If the adolescent's individual practitioner does not have authorization to talk to parents, depending on state law, she will not be able to share information. This may be difficult for the parents to accept and requires that the parents prioritize the relationship between the practitioner and the adolescent before their own needs. This is a situation in which the parents will need validation and support, and possibly their own parent coach. Whether the practitioner has an authorization to release information or not, the adolescent and the parents know that information about potentially dangerous behaviors or threats to self or others will be shared, in order to ensure the safety of the adolescent and others.

Helping Parents Respond to Threats

One of the most difficult areas of concern for parents and practitioners is threats an adolescent makes to self-harm or suicide. While both self-harm and suicidal threats may relieve pain in adolescents and need to be taken seriously, they may necessitate different responses from parents.

Parents face the dialectic of trying to provide safety for the adolescent while also recognizing that they cannot control all of her behavior or watch her all the time. The practitioner faces the dilemma of trying to keep the adolescent in the community and making sure that she is safe.

Parents may begin to "give in" to the adolescent in order to eliminate the threat of self-harm. This reinforces the efficacy of the threat and almost always increases the likelihood that the threats will continue. Other parents may ignore the threats and refuse to "give in." They may then find that the adolescent becomes further dysregulated and her behaviors more out of control, resulting in guilt on the part of the parent. Parental guilt, which often is present in either scenario, makes it harder for parents to respond in effective ways. Parent coaches help the parents minimize their own guilt so that they can respond effectively—which may, at times, involve calling for mental health assistance—to the threats from their adolescent.

The adolescent's practitioner will continually be assessing for suicidality and will work together with the parents to ensure safety. This will be discussed further in chapter 7.

Responding to Self-Harm

An adolescent may self-harm or threaten to self-harm without there being a need to take her to the hospital unless medical treatment is necessary. Parents should focus on creating a safe environment to the extent that they can. And parents should alert the practitioner to self-harm even if the practitioner is not able to communicate to the parents. Self-harm will be addressed in therapy, and it is a matter best left between the adolescent and her treatment providers. It is not typically effective for parents to attend to it or spend time discussing it, as doing so may reinforce the behavior or lead to further dysregulation. This is best left to the adolescent and her treatment providers. However, when their adolescent self-harms, it is helpful for the parents to receive support from their parent coach or the person who is involved in family work with them, to help them cope with the sense of helplessness that can result.

Responding to Suicide Threats

Consider the following steps for parents to follow when an adolescent threatens suicide:

- Have the adolescent contact her practitioner or skills coach for assessment and coaching.

- Remain calm and validating and encourage the use of skills.

- Make sure the house is safe and that means of suicide are not readily available.

- Ask if the adolescent has a plan and, if so, take her to the hospital for assessment.

- If the adolescent is suicidal, unresponsive to de-escalation techniques, and unwilling to speak with her DBT practitioner or use skills, take her to the emergency room or crisis center, or call emergency personnel for further evaluation.

Parents need to take their adolescent's threats seriously and respond in a way that ensures safety and does not cause the behavior to escalate further. This behavior will also be addressed by the practitioner during their next session.

Summary

In this chapter, we discussed the importance of family work and the critical role of parents in helping to structure the natural environment of the adolescent. In order to lessen judgments toward parents and to enable practitioners to become more validating, work with parents was placed in the context of understanding the difficulties that parents face. We discussed various approaches for working with parents, including coaching and skills training, and gave examples of how each addresses the issues of parents and leads to more effective parenting.

The following worksheets can be downloaded at www.newharbinger.com/27985.

THINKING AND COMMUNICATING IN A *NONJUDGMENTAL* MANNER

Parent Worksheet

Think about your adolescent at times when you are angry, disappointed, frustrated, or hopeless. What judgmental thoughts are you having? Notice thoughts that include "should," "shouldn't," "must," "appropriate," or "s/he is doing this because…"

Write down your judgmental thoughts:

_____

_____

_____

_____

_____

Use skills to think of your adolescent nonjudgmentally. Be aware of and then let go of evaluations. Do not make assumptions. You will know that you have been effective when you have fewer negative feelings. Describe your child nonjudgmentally:

_____

_____

_____

_____

_____

Notice judgments and let them go.

Do not judge your judging.

Remember to describe, describe, describe in order to be nonjudgmental.

SEARCHING FOR WHAT IS VALID
TO YOUR ADOLESCENT

What is valid and real in the experience of your child?

What is the music when you ignore the lyrics?

What emotion might lie behind what your child says?

How does your child experience his or her life?

Look for the difficulty in the task at hand, the importance of the situation/problem to your child, the amount of pain your child experiences, and/or the wisdom in the ultimate goal that your child is trying to attain.

When your adolescent child says:	Think about what is valid:
You had me (or chose to adopt me), so you have to deal with me.	
My problems are your fault, not my fault.	
You need to learn better parenting skills.	
You don't understand me.	
I don't know why you are upset with me.	
I don't care what you say; I am doing what I want to do anyway.	
You never do anything I want you to do. Or: you never let me do anything I want to do.	

PRACTICE: EVALUATING CONSEQUENCES OF PARENTS' ACTIONS OR RESPONSES

Focusing on Positive and Negative Impacts of Parent Responses

Select one event/situation/interaction in which you had to decide how to respond and in which there were a number of possible responses.

Situation I was faced with:

_____

_____

_____

Fill in the boxes below using two possible responses: (1) the way that you usually responded in the past or the way you react emotionally, or (2) a response that is different or possibly opposite to your usual response. Describe how each response makes you feel and the potential impact on your child in the boxes below, beneath the examples given.

Response	Positive Impact	Negative Impact
1. Typical response: _____ _____	Example: I feel more comfortable responding the way I usually do. _____ _____	Example: There is no change in my child. _____ _____
2. Responding using DBT skills/ thinking-through responses: _____ _____	Example: There is a possibility of change in my child. _____ _____	Example: I feel anxiety about my child's response to this change in my behavior. _____ _____

Which response will be more effective in reaching your overall goal of long-term change in your adolescent?

_____

Think about skills that will help you to use a more effective behavior in challenging situations like you described above. Below list the skills that can help you to be more effective. (Example: use mindfulness, use self-soothing, change my thinking, and so on):

_____

BEHAVIORISM PRACTICE EXERCISE

You have the opportunity to reinforce adaptive behaviors in your adolescent child and thus increase the possibility that those behaviors will occur more often.

WHAT BEHAVIOR DO YOU WANT TO CHANGE?

Describe the behavior specifically. How often does it occur?

Do you want to increase a behavior or decrease a behavior?

WHAT CONSEQUENCES USUALLY FOLLOW THE BEHAVIOR?

How do you generally respond to the behavior?

What other consequences occur after the behavior?

Are there long-term consequences?

If you want to increase a behavior, what reinforcer will you use?	If you want to decrease a behavior, what behavior can you increase in its place? Would punishment be effective?
Remember: Choose a reinforcer that is available and that you can give yourself or get from others consistently.	What reinforcer will you use to reinforce the new behavior? What "punishment"?

WHAT IS THE IMMEDIATE RESPONSE TO THE CONSEQUENCE?

How do you and your child feel?

Is the behavior changing?

WHAT IS THE LONGER-TERM CONSEQUENCE?

VALIDATION PRACTICE FOR PARENTS

Situation I am facing (list your observations and/or describe what your child is doing):

_____

_____

_____

My thoughts and feelings about this situation are:

_____

_____

_____

I am working on understanding my adolescent child in nonjudgmental ways. I am searching for what is valid for my child. What is valid is:

_____

_____

_____

My adolescent child is doing the best he or she can. I can acknowledge that I hear and understand my child in the context of his or her life by saying:

_____

_____

_____

The outcome of this situation is:

_____

_____

I feel:

_____

_____

CHAPTER 6

Consultation Team and Coordinating Treatment

The consultation team is the DBT modality that meets the goal of providing support, consultation, and ongoing training for practitioners. It is expected, and invaluable, for anyone providing DBT treatment to participate in a consultation team as a way to maintain a DBT focus in treatment, to receive ongoing training, and to lessen vulnerability to burnout when working with such a high-risk population (Linehan, 1993a).

The Goals of the Consultation Team

Many factors—maintaining a nonjudgmental stance, balancing conflicting and contradictory perspectives, trying to engage adolescents in the hard work of treatment when they don't think they have a problem, and the fear that an adolescent may do something harmful to himself—may lead to frustration, exhaustion, and burnout for the practitioner. To combat practitioner fatigue in working with this challenging population and to enhance treatment effectiveness, a consultation team provides the practitioner with several types of support as well as guidance about providing effective treatment:

- accountability for remaining consistent with the DBT philosophies and interventions

- peer reinforcement for implementing the challenging and difficult tasks of DBT (Adolescents may resist DBT interventions and, without support, it can be easy to give in to this resistance.)

- a nonjudgmental and validating place to discuss difficulties and concerns about clients without fear of being evaluated negatively by peers

- an organized and structured environment in which there is a focus on maintaining a nonpejorative stance toward clients and their families

- an opportunity for practitioners to develop awareness of thoughts and feelings that may interfere with providing effective practice

- guidance on providing the most effective way to conduct treatment and the most effective strategies to use with particular clients

- a community of other DBT practitioners to help the practitioner maintain a dialectical stance, which is practiced within the team and toward clients through recognizing and synthesizing alternative and contradictory perspectives

- an opportunity for the DBT practitioner to enhance his or her learning and improve therapeutic skills.

- support in maintaining his or her own limits

The consultation team helps the practitioner remain nonjudgmental and accepting while still focused on change. Participation in the team enables the practitioner to remain hopeful, supported, and committed to the treatment despite the natural and inevitable highs and lows of working with high-risk adolescents.

Consultation Teams and Confidentiality

Consultation team members benefit greatly from being able to discuss difficulties in their clinical work. It is therefore important that clients know that what they discuss with the practitioner will be shared within the consultation team so that the practitioner can provide the most effective treatment. When the client is an adolescent, both the adolescent and his parents are oriented to the consultation team and asked to authorize this release of information so that clinical information can be discussed within team meetings.

The Consultation Team and Risk Assessment

Practitioners who work with high-risk, suicidal, or self-harming adolescents find the support and safety of the consultation team invaluable as they assess risk and manage safety concerns. Practitioners may consult with the team when considering how to manage a particularly unsafe adolescent in outpatient care, or deciding whether hospitalization or residential care may be necessary for an adolescent. Often the consultation team will serve as the outside observer or make the risk assessment when the practitioner is too close to make it. And the notes from the consultation team are an invaluable documentation of the supervision received and reflect the shared liability the team holds for the clinical outcome (Koerner, 2012).

Postsuicide (Attempt) Assessment

A practitioner has the support of the team after a client has made a suicide attempt or completed suicide. In this situation, the team provides invaluable support and validation to the practitioner. In addition, the team helps the practitioner to chain recent events and interventions to assess what was done effectively, what might have been missed, and what might be done more effectively in the future. The team also helps the practitioner develop a treatment plan going forward, if the client is still engaged in treatment. The nonjudgmental atmosphere of the consultation team helps all members learn from difficult and painful client situations how to become even more effective practitioners.

Developing a Consultation Team

Developing a consultation team is an essential part of implementing DBT. When beginning to offer DBT, the consultation team can provide the training for the practitioners in the philosophy and skills of DBT and provide ongoing orientation to the DBT framework. If the practice or organization already offers DBT, the consultation team provides ongoing support and guidance in following a DBT stance. It is thus imperative that a consultation team be developed to support a practitioner of DBT.

Two options enable a solo practitioner to fulfill the requirement of participation in a consultation team. First, the practitioner may join an already existing consultation team or a peer supervision group that is willing to adopt the DBT philosophy. Second, the practitioner may develop a consultation team by bringing together DBT practitioners from independent practices who meet regularly to discuss clinical material, evaluate DBT practices, and seek ways to make each practice more effective. This consultation team also allows practitioners to coordinate treatment for clients who may be seen in separate practices for individual therapy, skills training, and parent work. This can be accomplished through ongoing phone or computer conferences if the distance between DBT practitioners makes it prohibitive to meet in person. Consultation teams, regardless of the form they take, may consider hiring a DBT consultant to help the team remain consistent and effective.

Consultation Team Agreements

The trusting, nonjudgmental, and accepting environment that is necessary for an effective consultation team is developed and maintained by a series of "agreements" that guide the work of the team and provide a DBT framework within the team. This framework is similar to the one that guides clinical work (Linehan, 1993a). Every participant agrees to abide by the guidelines, which are reviewed regularly by the team, and help to resolve disagreements or contradictions when they inevitably occur. These principles, adapted from Miller, Rathus, and Linehan (2007), help practitioners apply DBT within the consultation team.

- Accept that there are different perspectives and that team members should search for a way to integrate and synthesize contradictory perspectives rather than search for the "truth."

- Understand that disagreements are inevitable, and recognize opportunities to practice skills in order to resolve or accept differences and conflicts.

- Recognize that consistency within the team is not always necessary and that inconsistencies among practitioners provide clients who experience those inconsistencies with opportunities to use skills to resolve real-world contradictions. (Clients may have to find the validity within each practitioner's perspective even if they are not all in agreement.)

- Observe personal and professional limits without judgment from other team members and without self-judgment.

- Accept that other team members will provide validation *and* problem solving if a team member's behaviors interfere with treatment.

- Create a nonjudgmental environment in which members agree to search for a nonjudgmental understanding of the client, agree to hold each other nonjudgmentally to the DBT framework, and accept feedback from other members when they use judgmental thinking or language while having their feelings and concerns validated.

- Accept that all practitioners can make mistakes and should be treated nonjudgmentally while also being given feedback on more effective DBT ways to help clients and provide effective services.

The consultation team increases fidelity to the DBT model, and provides an environment in which participants are able to practice the skills that their clients are being taught and to experience some of the feelings their clients have in group treatment. Practitioners may need to develop insight into their own reactions to clients and to assess what gets in the way of effective work. In this way, the members of the team may practice therapeutic skills such as validation, behavior analysis, and problem solving on the practitioner (Koerner, 2012). Practitioners thus learn about themselves as well as develop insights into what their clients experience in DBT treatment, enhancing the sensitivity and effectiveness of all members of the team.

Responding to Problems Within the Team

Disagreement within a team is inevitable and is important in helping the team practice a dialectical stance. DBT principles and skills provide ways to problem solve and resolve disagreements within the team. In addition, some consultation teams use an observer to alert team members when they are not following the DBT agreements. The observer may comment if members become judgmental, neglect to validate each other, avoid commenting on therapy-interfering behaviors on the part of other members, get into power struggles in a search for the "truth," or otherwise disregard a DBT framework during the team meeting.

Teams need to learn how to work together effectively according to DBT guidelines. These contingencies within a meeting may help to move the team toward more effective work:

- Expect a repair when a member has disrupted the meeting either by arriving late, taking a phone call, or otherwise distracting other members.

- Do a chain analysis if a member consistently disrupts the group.

- Reinforce the group for effective work, attendance, coming on time, following the DBT guidelines, and so on.

A consultation team provides a parallel process for practitioners who use the same skills with other team members that make their work with adolescents effective. The philosophy of DBT encourages practitioners to be validating and accepting of each other while also maintaining a focus on helping each team member provide the most effective treatment for all of their clients.

Initial Decisions

Creating an effective team takes planning and preparation. Some initial decisions that you will make in developing your team include meeting frequency and duration, team membership, facilitation, and whether your team will be open or closed. We take a closer look at each of these decisions below.

Meeting Frequency and Duration

Many teams meet weekly (for an hour to an hour and a half), while others may meet for a longer period (perhaps two hours) every other week. Meeting frequency depends on the availability of the team members and the level of clinical need. Teams meet long enough that every member has, at a minimum, about twenty minutes of clinical consultation every other week (Swenson, 2012). The amount of time you have may determine the number of participants you are able to accomodate.

Team Membership

We recommend between four and eight team members—enough to provide divergent views and feedback from a number of perspectives, and not so many that the needs of each member to discuss clients and other issues cannot be met.

Everyone on the team is treated equally, according to the guidelines discussed above, even when supervisors and supervisees, employees, bosses, or associates participate on the same consultation team. Information gained from the team should not be used outside the team in a way that is punitive for participants. If these agreements are followed, all DBT practitioners in a practice or program should be able to work together on a consultation team. If an issue comes up in the team that is problematic within an organization, it may be discussed with the participant outside of the team if necessary (similar to addressing certain behaviors with clients outside of group).

Facilitation

Different teams choose different forms of facilitating the team meeting. Some rotate the role of group facilitator from meeting to meeting, empowering all members to take a leadership role and responsibility for the team. Others may have a dedicated facilitator—often the member who has more DBT experience, or has more experience leading the team.

The role of the facilitator is to establish an agenda for the meeting, prioritize agenda items, and manage time to ensure that everyone's needs are met. Every team chooses the form of facilitation that meets its needs most effectively.

Open Team vs. Closed Team

Should the consultation team be open (and accept new members on a continual basis) or closed (with the same members)? In an organizational setting or within a private practice, all practitioners who work with the adolescents will be on the consultation team, which means that the team is open and continually accepts new practitioners. For solo practitioners who form a team with other practitioners, they may decide if and when to accept new members. New members to teams can bring new ideas and new perspectives; they may also threaten the comfort of the others. Members of teams may find safety in a closed group in which they have developed trust *and* they also may recognize the importance of change. It may be helpful for team members to step out of their comfort zone, as they ask their clients to do, and use skills to manage any feelings they have about new members or changes in the team.

The Structure of a Team Meeting

The agenda for each consultation team meeting adheres to a consistent structure. Some teams have members send their questions and concerns prior to the meeting, while others have participants express their needs at the beginning of the meeting. Each consultation team meeting should include the following elements addressed in the order shown (Miller, Rathus, & Linehan, 2007):

1. Mindfulness and follow-up discussion to help participants get focused in the moment, learn and practice new mindfulness exercises, and receive feedback on effective instructions for exercises.

2. Review of consultation team agreements (see "Consultation Team Agreements" above).

3. Clinical consultation about clients to help practitioners conceptualize the client in DBT theoretical terms. Priority is given to the same targets that guide the clinical session. Practitioners will present specific questions related to clients in the following order:

   a. behaviors that threaten life or physical safety

   b. behaviors on the part of the client, family member, or practitioner that get in the way of providing effective treatment

   c. behaviors that interfere with the client establishing the life he or she wants

4. Discussion of skills training groups and any behaviors that interfere with treatment in groups (if the team is coordinating treatment between skills trainers and individual practitioners).

5. Good news about practitioners or clients and updates about effective treatment.

6. Discussion of any organizational issues that may be interfering with treatment or that need a team synthesis.

7. Ongoing training: review of skills being learned in skills groups or review of literature related to DBT treatment.

The consultation team meeting provides the support that practitioners need to maintain a balanced approach to an emotionally challenging and high-risk population. As members of our own consultation team and facilitators of other teams, we can attest to how invaluable these meetings are in providing effective DBT treatment; how much members look forward to the acceptance, validation, and camaraderie they experience; how reassuring it is to know that there is an opportunity to discuss difficult issues, concerns, or judgments about clients; and how the meetings encourage participants to continue to seek ways to provide ever more effective treatment to their clients.

Coordinating Treatment

Adolescents remain dependent on adults despite their desire for independence and control over their lives. While consultation to the client and teaching the client to self-advocate is always a DBT goal, it is also necessary for practitioners who work with adolescents to coordinate their treatment so that the adolescent and his parents are not receiving contradictory information or conflicting advice, and so that treatment can be as effective as possible.

An adolescent often has several members in his treatment team and even more professionals who may be helping him in different areas of his life (school, work, home, extended family, medical, sports, and so on). While not every professional working with the adolescent will need to know all the difficulties the adolescent experiences, those individuals who may be responsible for the at-risk adolescent at different times (especially at school) should be aware of the need for safety, validation, and the reinforcement of adaptive behaviors.

Coordinating treatment also minimizes the potential confusion and disagreement when the adolescent presents different information to different members of the team, or behaves differently depending on his emotional state at certain times. Ongoing communication and coordination enables all professionals working with the adolescent to remain effectively engaged in the task of helping the adolescent without the barrier of miscommunication or the potential conflicts it can create.

Coordination Within the Treatment Team

Adolescents will often have several practitioners within a DBT team who are involved in their treatment. An adolescent who is in individual therapy, and a skills group (possibly with two coleaders) and whose parents are involved in family work can have up to four different members of the team working with him. In some practices, a psychiatrist may also be a member of the team and may have one or more roles. While it is not necessary that there be absolute consistency among the treatment providers (see "Consultation Team Agreements" above), it is important that all members of the team share a similar theoretical understanding of the adolescent and have consistent information about the broad (although not necessarily the specific) details of the adolescent's life.

Within the DBT treatment team, the individual practitioner is responsible for coordinating the treatment and for keeping other members informed of important information. Sharing of information needs to be done with the knowledge, understanding, and permission of the adolescent and the parents. Practitioners sharing information must also be sensitive to the difference between information that is "need to know"—necessary to keep the adolescent safe and to develop and maintain a validating environment—and confidential information and insights, which may be personal and private to the adolescent and do not add any new information to understanding or parenting him. Unsafe or life-threatening behaviors will always be shared as a way to maintain safety for the adolescent, which is always the priority of DBT. The individual practitioner balances helping the team develop the most effective treatment plan with maintaining the trust and relationship he or she has with the adolescent.

If there is a separate parent coach, that practitioner orients the parents to the importance of working with the team and gets permission from the family to share information. This sharing is also done with sensitivity to what is important for the team to know (important events that may impact the adolescent, family changes, fears about life-threatening behaviors, treatment-interfering behaviors) and what the parents may want to keep confidential. Parents are usually pleased to know about this team approach and welcome the parent coach's work with the team to develop a consistent and effective approach to helping their adolescent.

Coordinating with Outside Providers

Within the DBT framework, it is the adolescent's individual practitioner who will coordinate treatment with other professionals (school personnel, psychiatrists) so that all professionals have information necessary to maintain safety, provide effective treatment, and increase the possibility that the adolescent will receive consistent messages from all treatment providers. Practitioners should remember the dialectical stance in working with other professionals; they should be willing to accept alternative perspectives, remember that they do not have the only valid ideas, and work toward a synthesis of varying ideas. The DBT practitioner will also maintain a nonjudgmental and validating stance toward the adolescent and his family, and help others to understand the adolescent within the nonblaming DBT framework.

While it is more effective for the adolescent to have a DBT individual practitioner, coordination of treatment is necessary even when this is not possible. If the adolescent is in a DBT skills group and receives individual therapy from a non-DBT clinician (or a clinician outside the team), the skills group facilitator will keep the practitioner up-to-date on the adolescent's experience and behaviors in skills group:

- the skills being learned in group, so that they can be reinforced in individual therapy

- treatment-interfering issues that can be addressed by the individual practitioner as well as by the skills trainer

- commitment issues that may arise and will need to be addressed by the individual practitioner

- positive behavior changes seen in the group, so that the individual practitioner can provide additional reinforcement for effective changes

This information can be shared by e-mail or phone call between the skills trainer and the individual practitioner or psychiatrist. An effective way to provide this information in a timely way is by sending an e-mail (with permission from the adolescent) to other professionals and parents following skills group, and copying the adolescent. This e-mail can include information about the mindfulness exercise, the new skills that were learned and practiced, and whether or not the adolescent brought in his homework or actively participated. When this information is sent in a positive, nonjudgmental, and validating way, it enables ongoing coordination of treatment and assessment of progress.

If a non-DBT individual practitioner is interfering with the treatment (not addressing commitment or noncompliance with homework or daily logs, not doing chains, and so on), the DBT consultation team will need to discuss an effective strategy to decrease this interference and increase reasonable cooperation. We have found that providing skills group to adolescents receiving non-DBT individual therapy can be problematic unless the practitioner has agreed in advance to do specific tasks in the individual sessions.

Coordinating treatment with other professionals is invaluable even if those professionals are not providing DBT treatment. It is comforting to share responsibility for high-risk adolescents, to be able to talk to others, and to develop an effective synthesis from different perspectives.

Summary

In this chapter, we discussed the importance of the consultation team and ways to coordinate treatment across providers. We discussed several ways to develop a consultation team, the guidelines and agenda for the team meetings, and the ways in which the team can provide necessary validation for the team members. If you are not in a consultation team, we recommend that you find a way to develop one or to receive ongoing support from other practitioners who understand the DBT philosophy. This will allow you to offer ever more effective treatment, and will provide you with invaluable support and camaraderie as you continue to work with high-risk adolescents.

PART 3

DBT Treatment for Specific Behavioral Problems in Adolescents

CHAPTER 7

Self-Harming and Suicidal Behaviors

DBT was originally developed to help adults whose emotional pain led them either to hurt them-selves to relieve the pain and feel better or to try to kill themselves to escape the pain permanently (Linehan, 1993a). Adolescents are particularly prone to searching for ways to get rid of emotional pain, because they lack the life experience to know that pain will not go on forever and can be managed in less drastic ways. They cannot see beyond the immediacy of their pain and seek imme-diate relief, sometimes in dangerous ways. The message of DBT is a hopeful one—that adolescents *can* find a life worth living despite the emotional pain and desperation that they feel in this moment. This was the experience of DBT developer Marsha Linehan (Carey, 2011). As such, DBT is not an antisuicide treatment; rather, it is a treatment that helps adolescents to find reasons for living and to develop the life they would like to have (Linehan, 1993a).

Suicide is the third leading cause of death among adolescents; DBT is effective with suicidal adolescents (Miller, Rathus, & Linehan, 2007), and as a result a DBT practitioner will typically treat adolescents who have self-harming and/or suicidal behaviors. Referrals may come from hospitals, residential treatment programs, schools, or other therapists who are not prepared to handle the dangerous and risky behaviors of these clients. A practitioner may be seeing an adolescent who has been self-harming for some time without any suicide attempts, or an adolescent who has just made her first suicide attempt, which comes as a surprise to family members. The parents, seen at intake, are most likely scared, overwhelmed, angry, defeated, or very sad, depending on how long the behavior has been going on. The practitioner will be asked to make the adolescent better and safer, and to lessen suicidal and self-harming behaviors.

To do this, the practitioner will have to balance his own tolerance for risk, knowledge of the client, and recognition that change will occur slowly with the imperative to gain commitment to life and safety from the adolescent as quickly as possible. This chapter will address how to structure therapeutic work to address this dialectic and to be most effective in helping the adolescent move from misery and desperation to a life she wants to live.

Assessment of Unsafe Behaviors

In order to be effective in helping to manage unsafe behaviors, the practitioner uses data from clinical interviews, structured self-reports, and assessments from other practitioners (Miller, Rathus, & Linehan, 2007). Together these assessments give the practitioner the following information about the adolescent's level of risk:

- the lethality of the self-harming and suicidal behavior

- risk factors for suicide, such as prior attempts, history of family suicide, sexual promiscuity (Kim, Moon, & Kim, 2011), or the presence of mental illness in the adolescent or family members

- adolescent's intention to die versus reasons for living

- the function of the self-harming or suicidal behavior, its antecedents, and the contingencies that maintain it

- diagnosis of comorbid conditions

As the therapeutic relationship progresses, the practitioner will gain a deeper and more complete understanding of the adolescent and her behaviors. This will provide additional data to guide interventions.

Assessing Suicidality

When assessing for suicidality, the practitioner will note the risk factors listed above and also assess the risk from stressful life circumstances, abuse, difficulties at school, issues with sexuality or gender identity, contagion effect from other suicides, and access to suicidal means. An adolescent who has past suicidal behaviors is more at risk and will need to be assessed very carefully for future suicidality (Miller, Rathus, & Linehan, 2007).

Self-Harming Behavior vs. Suicidal Behavior

Self-harming behaviors, parasuicide, or nonsuicidal self-harming behavior are deliberate acts in which there is no intent to die. They include a wide variety of behaviors that cause some physical damage to the adolescent with the function being to regulate emotions. Behaviors such as cutting, burning, or purging relieve and distract from pain and stimulate a pain-relief response within the body. Suicidal behaviors, in contrast, will include those behaviors in which there is at least an ambivalent, if not a certain, intent to die (Miller, Rathus, & Linehan, 2007).

While some self-harming behaviors may not appear dangerous (superficial scratching of the arm with a paper clip, for example), they are considered life threatening in DBT because they may *lead to* serious unintentional injury or death, and they are often predictors of eventual suicide (Miller, Rathus, & Linehan, 2007). Practitioners need to take all instances of self-harming behaviors seriously.

The practitioner will experience the dialectic of needing to attend to all self-harm and assess the intent and safety of the adolescent while neither reinforcing the behavior with attention or increased treatment nor reacting automatically with hospitalizations. The practitioner maintains a nonjudgmental stance toward self-harming and suicidal behaviors, understanding that they are attempts to regulate pain and may also be inadvertently reinforced by the environment. At the same time, the practitioner will seek a commitment from the adolescent to stop these behaviors.

Chronic Suicidal Ideation

Some adolescents present with ongoing suicidal thinking without immediate intention to act. They may continue to have those thoughts to remind themselves that there is a way out of what feels like relentless pain. This thinking will be targeted and chained.

Hospitalizations and Inpatient Treatment

One of the difficult dilemmas faced by practitioners who work with suicidal or self-harming adolescents is trying to keep them out of the hospital so that they can learn to live their life and use their skills, while also ensuring that they are safe at times when they are not able to use their skills. Parents often face this dilemma as well as they wrestle with trying to keep an adolescent safe who is unwilling, at times, to keep herself safe. Keeping an adolescent alive is the primary goal of any intervention. The practitioner will assess the adolescent for suicidality in every encounter. If the adolescent is unable to commit to safety, if she has a lethal plan, or when her high impulsivity leads the practitioner to believe that she poses a risk to herself, hospitalization must be considered until the adolescent can maintain her commitment to life.

When the adolescent is in the hospital, the practitioner serves as her consultant (Linehan, 1993a). The practitioner does not usually intervene directly on her behalf with the hospital staff, other than to provide relevant clinical and treatment information. The practitioner takes the position that she will coach the adolescent on techniques and skills that will get her out of the hospital, assuming that she wants to leave.

When an adolescent wants to be in the hospital (for a variety of possible reasons, including the safety and security experienced there and the escape from problems outside the hospital), the practitioner guides the parents to inform the hospital staff of the reinforcing quality of the hospital so the clinical staff can make efforts to not inadvertently reinforce the behavior they want to decrease. Hospitalizations may become treatment interfering if the adolescent misses appointments because of hospital stays. The practitioner will chain the behavior that resulted in hospitalization, as well as the desire to be in the hospital, when the adolescent returns to treatment.

We will illustrate how to work with adolescents who have self-harming behaviors and/or suicidal ideation by discussing Gabriella, who is introduced in the vignette below:

Eighteen-year-old Gabriella attended college out of state. After her boyfriend broke up with her, she jumped out of her fourth-floor dormitory window, severely injuring herself. While recovering in the hospital, she told the clinician that she wanted to die. She added that the relationship with her boyfriend had been very conflicted, and she felt criticized by him. Despite her outstanding grades, active social life, and performance on the school debate team in both high school and college, she felt worthless and hopeless. Gabriella had been treated for depression in high school and had a history of cutting herself when upset, which remitted before she went to college, while working with a practitioner for two years. Prior to going to college, she had thought about suicide as an option if she didn't get into her top-choice school; but when she did get into that school, the thought disappeared. She had gone to the college counseling center a couple of times but didn't connect with the counselor and had not been receiving treatment for two months prior to the suicide attempt. Gabriella has a history of frequent sexual encounters with many males and says these helped her feel loved, although each encounter was followed by shame and disgust with herself. She thought things were actually going better in college because she had a boyfriend. Her parents are very worried about her ability to remain safe, as is her college. She has returned home to focus on her mental health needs, and her plans for her education are on hold.

Theoretical Dialectics

In the case of self-harm and suicidality, DBT acknowledges that there is a desperate desire to end the pain and suffering and, at the same time, a desire to keep living. The very fact that the client comes to your office underscores the desire to live. The synthesis in DBT is that life does bring suffering and pain *and* clients can learn to manage this effectively and keep living (Linehan, 1993a): both terrible pain and a commitment to life can exist at the same time. The practitioner maintains this position and aims for the client to integrate this dialectical synthesis during treatment.

Parents may find themselves polarized when managing adolescents with self-harming behaviors. One task of the parent coach on the DBT team is to help them find the synthesis between permissive and lenient parenting, which seeks to avoid struggles, and authoritarian and controlling parenting that seeks to minimize parental anxiety by protecting the adolescent. The parent coach recognizes and validates the desire of each parent to protect his or her child and/or minimize conflict. The parent coach helps parents support one another and focus on what will be most effective in keeping their adolescent safe and encouraging him or her to make safe behavioral choices. This can be particularly challenging given the contagious and escalating nature of emotion dysregulation, and it will need to be addressed consistently and with a gentle and validating touch by the parent coach.

Case Conceptualization and Goal Setting

Self-harming is reinforced by its consequences, which may include the management of painful emotions, self-punishment, the ability to "feel" something, increased social acceptance, validation of pain, and/or an end to dissociative episodes (Klonsky & Muehlenkamp, 2007). The unique combination of factors influencing a particular adolescent's self-harm will be discovered in therapy.

Adolescents often hide the fact that they engage in self-harm and only eventually confess that the intent of the self-harm is to lessen the intense pain they feel despite apparent competence in many areas of their lives. Some people in the adolescents' lives believe that gaining attention is the reason for the self-harming behaviors. In actuality, though the attention may be a consequence of self-harm, that does not mean it was the intention of the behavior. This is often confusing for practitioners, family members, and others who define self-harm as "attention seeking" or "manipulative," especially when adolescents later threaten to harm themselves if they don't get what they want. Self-harm can become habituated by how it makes the adolescent feel, making it a reinforcing (yet potentially fatal) technique for managing distress. The adolescent is reinforced for this behavior, not necessarily by attention but by the relief of pain, or distraction from it.

Suicidal ideation and behavior is, likewise, not viewed as attention seeking in DBT. It is seen as a reaction to extreme emotional pain and the belief that the pain will never end. Suicide is seen as a way out of the pain and deep darkness that feel endless to adolescents. Parents who have never experienced this sort of emotional pain cannot understand how an adolescent who seems to have everything can want to end her life. The practitioner (or parent coach) helps parents understand that the adolescent is searching desperately for ways to end the pain she feels, even while the practitioner searches for ways to help the adolescent end her misery safely and keep her alive until she can discover the life she wants to have.

The chart below can help practitioners and others understand the function of self-harming behavior and the difficulties inherent in giving it up. An adolescent who gives up self-harming will have to learn how to manage the pain she continues to experience with other, safer means that may not be quite as effective, at least initially. The practitioner who understands this will be more effective in validating the adolescent and in helping her make a commitment to giving up self-harming.

Behavior	Positive Impact	Negative Impact
Engaging in self-harm	• feeling immediate relief; escape from painful thoughts and feelings • focusing attention away from pain and onto the act and consequences of the self-harm • feeling some control	• risking serious injury or death • facing possible hospitalization • creating permanent scarring • losing freedom and trust from parents
Using safe skills to manage pain	• minimizing serious injury risk • gaining more freedom and trust from others • remaining out of the hospital	• minimizing scars • facing problems and difficulties without escape • feeling emotional pain with less effective relief

Validation and Acceptance

The practitioner shows acceptance and understanding of the adolescent by taking the adolescent's description of her emotional experiences seriously. The practitioner will validate thoughts, feelings, and behaviors of the adolescent through awareness of the following realities:

- She is in tremendous pain.

- She finds it helpful to self-harm and may not want to give it up.

- She has not been or felt understood by others in her life.

- She feels miserable despite appearing successful and competent to others.

- She cannot find a way to get out of the misery she feels.

- She may not like the idea of talking about her self-harming to others, including the practitioner, because of the shame she feels about it.

While the practitioner validates the adolescent, he is also aware of the dialectic that necessitates that the practitioner demand a commitment to life and safety in order to engage in treatment.

Gaining Commitment

A practitioner who works with a self-harming or suicidal adolescent will ask for a commitment to life and safe behaviors, and will work with the adolescent to develop a safety plan to ensure life. If an adolescent is not ready to commit to staying alive while in treatment, the practitioner will use commitment strategies to obtain a commitment to staying alive for a month or until the next appointment. (If the practitioner is unable to gain a commitment for any length of time, the adolescent may not be ready for outpatient treatment.) The practitioner will also ask for a commitment from the adolescent to call him prior to any self-harming behavior.

The practitioner will also discuss with the adolescent the reasons why she has not had a commitment to treatment in the past or has stopped treatment with other providers. It is important for the practitioner to gain a commitment from the adolescent to engage in the hard work of treatment and to address issues of mistrust and lack of collaboration immediately. The practitioner also validates the concerns of the adolescent about the treatment process and being in therapy, in order to minimize possible and potential treatment-interfering behaviors. We met Gabriella earlier in the chapter. Now we can see how her practitioner talks with her about commitment.

Dialogue: Commitment in Beginning Treatment with a Suicidal Adolescent

Practitioner: I understand the tough situation you're in. You want to return to school and get on with your life, and at the same time the school and your parents require you to get treatment before you return. You feel that keeping you out of school is going to make you more depressed.

Gabriella: Exactly! They are making a big mistake. I'll be better when I get back to school.

Practitioner: So, in order to get back to school, you need to have treatment, and I'm willing to see you if you're interested. DBT has been very helpful to others who have attempted suicide; it has good research behind it. Would you like to hear more about it?

Gabriella: I guess I don't have a choice.

Practitioner: Well, let me give you more information, and then you can decide if it's right for you.

Gabriella: Okay.

Practitioner: Now, one of the things that this treatment puts a lot of emphasis on is staying alive. We will both be working hard to make things better for you, and you'll need to be alive in order to come in and do that work so you can return to school. I'd like you to commit to staying alive while you are in therapy with me. Would you be willing to make that commitment?

Gabriella: I really don't think I can promise that…I mean, what if I don't end up going back to school at all? I think I'll just throw in the towel at that point.

Practitioner: I know that's a lot to ask. Would you be willing to make a commitment to staying alive for the next six months? You won't know about school until after that anyway.

Gabriella: I guess I could do that.

Practitioner: Now, that also means you commit to not self-harming.

Gabriella: What?! I can't do that.

Practitioner: That's a lot to commit to.

Gabriella: I mean, I stopped that already, but I can't promise on that one.

Practitioner: Would you be willing to commit to not self-harming until our next meeting, and we can talk more about it then?

Gabriella: Yeah, I can do that.

Practitioner: Great. Let me tell you more about how this treatment works…

The practitioner dialectically asks for and expects a commitment to no self-harm, and at the same time accepts that episodes of self-harm may recur. The practitioner will follow up on these occurrences without judgment and with the goal of having the client learn how to prevent subsequent occurrences over time.

Priority Targets and Goal Setting

When a practitioner begins work with an adolescent who self-harms or is suicidal, the highest-priority target will be decreasing suicide and self-harming behaviors (reducing life-threatening behaviors) and increasing behavioral control and commitment to life (Linehan, 1993a).

The second priority of maintaining a connection and commitment to treatment will be addressed concurrently, in order to keep the adolescent in therapy. And the practitioner will address the third priority, quality-of-life issues that are important to the adolescent, while maintaining a primary focus on eliminating dangerous behaviors. Gabriella, for example, may be focused on the goal of getting back to school; the practitioner will link developing a commitment to safety and the acquisition and use of skills when dysregulated as ways to get there.

Here are examples of priority targets from the vignette about Gabriella:

Treatment Priority	Specific Behaviors
Life-threatening behaviors	Suicidal behavior
	Suicidal ideation
	Cutting
Treatment-interfering behaviors	Stopping treatment prematurely
	Not talking to practitioner prior to suicide attempt or self-harming
	Not "connecting" to practitioner
Quality of life–interfering behaviors	Arguing with parents
	Unsafe reactions to disappointment
	Conflicted relationships with boyfriends
	Risky sexual activity

The practitioner will work with the suicidal adolescent to define her goals. We can see in the dialogue below how Gabriella's practitioner approaches setting goals with her.

Dialogue: Helping the Adolescent Define Goals

Practitioner: Can I ask you something, Gabriella? You said a moment ago that things will be better when you get back to college. What else will change when things are better?

Gabriella: That's pretty much it. I just need to get back to school.

Practitioner: I want to know what your life will look like when you are living the kind of life you want to live. So, what do you want life to look like? What will make you want to stay alive?

Gabriella: Besides being back in school? I guess my parents will back off and let me live my life. And in a perfect world, I'd like a boyfriend who doesn't treat me like shit.

Practitioner: Okay, that all makes a lot of sense. What else?

Gabriella: That's it, really.

Practitioner: You didn't mention anything about hurting or killing yourself.

Gabriella: Yeah, that too. If everything is going well, I won't have those kinds of thoughts.

Practitioner: Hmmm...I bet you're right. I'm also thinking that those kinds of thoughts do pass through people's minds at times, and it would be really great if, when those thoughts arise, you have an effective system for getting through those times safely.

Gabriella: That would be good. I mean, look at the mess it's created for me.

The practitioner clearly establishes what a "life worth living" (Linehan, 1993a) looks like. He also establishes an explicit goal of eliminating self-harm or suicide.

Client Goals

When Gabriella enters treatment, she and the practitioner will discuss her concerns and what she would like to see change in her life. She lists her goals:

- to return to school

- to get her parents to stop worrying about her so she can do what she wants to do

- to find a boyfriend who treats her better than her last boyfriend

Practitioner Goals

The practitioner will link safe behaviors to these goals by explaining that she will be able to have more freedoms and return to college when she has developed safer ways of managing her pain and her emotions. The practitioner's priority goals are openly shared with Gabriella, in the following order:

1. eliminating suicidal behaviors

2. decreasing self-harming behaviors

3. using skills to manage painful emotions

4. letting the practitioner know when she feels suicidal or intends to hurt herself

5. reducing risky sexual behavior

The practitioner knows that when Gabriella is able to meet these measurable goals, she will be more likely to meet her stated ones. The target behaviors concerning safety are related to both life-threatening and quality of life—interfering behaviors: when she can maintain her safety, she can return to school and the life she wants to have. Knowing that these behaviors are interrelated allows the practitioner multiple entry points for discussing successes and problems in the therapy sessions.

Confidentiality

An additional dilemma for the practitioner is the dialectic of maintaining a productive, trusting relationship with the adolescent by observing confidentiality in the treatment *and* the importance of protecting the adolescent from her own behaviors. Practitioners need to carefully consider which episodes of self-harm will result in disclosure to parents and discuss what behaviors will be shared with parents. While not all occurrences of self-harm will cross the threshold of disclosure, increases in the frequency or severity of self-harm will prompt a careful consideration of notifying parents or caregivers (Miller, Rathus, & Linehan, 2007).

If the adolescent is suicidal or in the practitioner's judgment poses a serious threat to herself, the practitioner will notify her parents. He will always make every effort to include the adolescent in the process.

Ongoing Assessment Tools and Strategies

The following behavior analysis and change strategies will be balanced with the validation strategies noted above. While validation is necessary, the DBT practitioner will also constantly focus on helping the adolescent make changes in her life that will increase her safety.

Daily Log

The log filled out by the adolescent daily and brought to the practitioner weekly will help the adolescent develop awareness of her emotions, thoughts, and urges and the relationships between them, and it will enable her practitioner to focus on the priority targets in the session. A log for Gabriella will include priority targets for suicidal ideation and urges and for self-harming. It will also include arguing with parents and risky sexual activity as additional targets. The log will be reviewed at the beginning of every therapy session, and the therapy session will follow the priority targets outlined in chapter 3.

Chain Analysis

The practitioner conducts a chain analysis of the suicidal or self-harming behavior that brings the adolescent into treatment, to gain insights into antecedents of the behavior (thoughts, feelings, and triggers), contingencies that maintain the behavior, and the vulnerabilities that the adolescent brings to the situation. Ongoing chain analysis of incidents of self-harm, suicidal ideation, or suicidal behaviors will increase understanding of the causes of the behaviors and the consequences that maintain it. A chain analysis of Gabriella's suicide attempt might look like this:

I didn't get much sleep because I was so upset about my boyfriend
and worried about the test I was not able to study for.

↓

I was stressed out because my boyfriend and I were fighting and he was criticizing me.

↓

I thought I was worthless and would never have a good relationship with a boyfriend.

↓

I was feeling sad and depressed and did not want to go to classes.

↓

I called my boyfriend and told him how I was feeling.
He told me I should get over it, which made me feel worse.

↓

I went over to his dorm room so that I could feel better.
He told me he wanted to break up.

↓

I couldn't breathe as I ran from his room.
My heart was pounding. I thought, *My life is over.*

↓

I thought, *Everyone will be better off if I'm dead.*
None of my friends were around, and I felt so alone.

↓

I ran to my room, thinking about how much I hurt.

↓

I thought, *How nice would it be to not feel this pain anymore.*
I could barely breathe.

↓

I stared out the window.
I felt like I was in a daze.
I thought about ending the pain.
I jumped out the window.

↓

I woke up in the hospital and was sorry I was still alive.

↓

Now everyone is worried about me, and I can't go back to school.
I miss my friends and my life in school, and I hate that my parents are so upset.

Every step in the chain brings with it a possible intervention for averting a repeat of the behavior. From this chain, the practitioner recognizes that stress and a sense of worthlessness were the vulnerability factors preceding the suicide attempt. Rejection by her boyfriend triggered the attempt. Impaired decision making is associated with suicidal behaviors in adolescents (Bridge et al., 2012), and doing the chain analysis allows Gabriella to improve decision-making ability by becoming aware of the thoughts and feelings that lead to her suicidality, reviewing other choices she can make to effectively manage these thoughts and feelings in the future, and recognizing that her desire to escape had numerous unintended consequences. The chain allows Gabriella and the practitioner to examine the suicide attempt with the perspective that time brings, allowing for the opportunity to learn from experience. This initial chain identifies a variety of skills to teach and therapeutic interventions that may be used:

- mindfulness skills to help Gabriella develop self-awareness about her vulnerabilities

- planning ahead to reduce vulnerabilities

- distracting and self-soothing skills to use strategically when Gabriella feels overwhelmed and dysregulated

- cognitive restructuring with Gabriella's thoughts about being worthless

- interpersonal effectiveness skills to teach Gabriella how to balance her own needs and self-respect with the needs and demands of those around her

- careful exposure to painful emotions to help Gabriella learn that she can tolerate them without seeking ways to escape them

Change Strategies

When the practitioner and the adolescent have identified areas for behavioral and cognitive change, the practitioner chooses from the various DBT change strategies: cognitive restructuring, exposure, contingency management through structuring the environment, and skills training.

Cognitive Restructuring

In the vignette above, the practitioner works with Gabriella on replacing her beliefs that success is dependent upon attendance at a particular college and that her self-esteem is influenced by sexual attention from males. The practitioner will patiently challenge Gabriella's thoughts and encourage her to consider other perspectives using established cognitive therapy techniques.

Exposure

Gabriella feels that she is inadequate and a failure without the "name brand" school and the attention of a male. The practitioner might encourage Gabriella to take classes at a local community college while she is at home, partly to maintain exposure to some academic stress and partly to expose herself to other kinds of schools and the feelings they arouse in her, and he will explain this reasoning fully to Gabriella. The practitioner might also encourage Gabriella to take a break from dating so she can learn to manage the feelings associated with not having encounters with males. The practitioner will balance this exposure and teach skills to manage these feelings with recognition of the urges she will feel to return to the behaviors that she has relied on in the past.

Contingency Management Through Structuring the Environment

When an adolescent tries to kill herself, parents have a number of reactions and conflicting emotions. These reactions and emotions, which may include those listed below, can change over time:

- anger at the adolescent for "throwing away all she has been given"

- overwhelming feelings of worry, which lead to not leaving the adolescent by herself at any time and to monitoring all of her communications with others

- frustration that their adolescent has returned home from college, which impacts their plans for her and for themselves

- embarrassment that their adolescent is not following through on the cultural expectations of going to college and moving on to a career

- feeling that this is somehow their fault and they have not been effective parents

- feeling very sad and grieving that their dreams for their daughter may not come to be

Parents who were first angry may become very sad when they recognize and accept that their adolescent is in emotional pain. In Gabriella's case, she has often been very effective at masking her pain, and her parents were surprised to find out about the internal and private experience of their child. They may have to shift their entire understanding of their child, and this can be a slow and painful process.

Validating Parents

The practitioner or parent coach will recognize and acknowledge the pain and confusion of the parents. Practitioners will validate the efforts and feelings of the parents by confirming that:

- They have done the best they could with what they understood about their daughter and about parenting prior to the suicide attempt.

- They are scared and worried about what will happen to their daughter.

- They feel isolated, embarrassed, and worried about what others will think.

- They are sad that their life is not turning out the way they hoped.

- They may be mourning the child they expected.

- They need to work on accepting the adolescent they have.

Parent Goals

The validation that the parents experience will help them effectively structure the environment by thinking wisely and less emotionally. The parents will face the dialectic of trying to keep their daughter safe and recognizing that they cannot control every aspect of her life. They will work on minimizing their own emotional reactivity so that their emotions do not overwhelm them or their daughter. The goals of the parents will align with the priority targets of the practitioner: maintaining safety, encouraging and supporting their daughter's participation in treatment, and then focusing on getting her back to school or encouraging her social life. The parents will work on structuring the environment in the ways outlined below:

- They will try to provide as much safety as possible so that means for suicide or self-harm are not readily available.

- They will increase their validation of their daughter (including her desire to return to school) and listen to her concerns and her pain without judgment or blame.

- They will encourage and support their daughter in using distracting and self-soothing techniques to manage difficult times.

- They will encourage her to speak with her practitioner rather than talking at length about distressing situations (which may trigger more emotions rather than diminish them).

- They will try to not be overly intrusive in her life, which she may experience as invalidating of her needs and concerns, and try instead to find a middle ground, being alert to self-harm while respecting her autonomy.

- They will strategically minimize reactivity or attention to self-harming behaviors.

- They will spend more time with their daughter when she behaves in safe and adaptive ways.

Skills Training

Adolescents who self-harm or have suicidal behaviors are referred to skills training groups to learn the skills necessary to understand and safely manage their painful emotions. The skills group leader will quickly review the daily log to assess safety in the group and will discourage any discussion of self-harm in the past week. Cofacilitators are very helpful when there are participants in group who have had recent suicidal behaviors. If the adolescent leaves the group in distress, the cofacilitator may accompany the adolescent in order to ensure safety. The cofacilitator will be careful not to give attention to the adolescent beyond assessing for safety and trying to get the adolescent back into the group, so as not to inadvertently reinforce leaving the group. The skills facilitator will work on reinforcing adaptive behaviors and maintaining safety.

All of the skills in DBT (Linehan, 1993b) have value for adolescents with self-harming or suicidal behaviors, as can be seen in the chart below:

Skill Set	Relevance to self-harming or suicidal behavior
Mindfulness	• teaches adolescents to experience emotion without acting on it, which enables skills development • builds in a delay to counter impulsive self-injury
Distress Tolerance	• teaches alternatives to self-harm and suicidality • enables adolescents to tolerate the difficult moments without self-harming • is self-reinforced, making the skills easily learned by adolescents
Emotion Regulation	• enables understanding of the purpose and value of emotions • increases understanding of the chain of events that precedes and follows the urges to self-harm • makes possible increased control over emotions • assists in management of triggers through planning ahead, responding safely, and acting opposite when necessary
Middle Path (Miller, Rathus, & Linehan, 2007)	• teaches that things are not all good or all bad • emphasizes that change, and therefore hope, is always possible • teaches that there are alternative perspectives • promotes acceptance of self and others
Interpersonal Effectiveness Skills	• teaches adolescents how to get their needs met more skillfully, thus reducing stress and isolation • encourages adolescents to behave in ways that promote self-respect, thereby minimizing feelings of worthlessness

Two additional skills initially developed for children with suicidal ideation and useful with adolescents may be taught in either group or individual skills training. STOP (Stahl & Goldstein, 2010; Perepletchikova et al., 2011) is a critical distress-tolerance skill, given the relationship between impulsivity and self-harming behavior:

- Stop! Don't move. Interrupt the chain of events.

- Take a step back. Allow yourself some perspective.

- Observe what is going on. Nonjudgmentally, pay attention to the facts, your thoughts, and your feelings.

- Proceed mindfully. Stay focused on your long-term goals and consider what will make things better in the long run.

The second skill is called LAUGH (Perepletchikova et. al., 2011). It is an emotion regulation skill that focuses on building a life worth living and enjoying it:

- Let go of worries.

- Apply yourself.

- Use coping skills.

- Set Goals.

- Have fun!

Assigning Out-of-Session Practice

The practitioner may assign specific tasks to the adolescent between sessions. In Gabriella's case, she identified lack of sleep as a vulnerability factor, so the practitioner may ask Gabriella to keep a sleep diary to track the impact of lack of sleep on her mood.

The practitioner might also encourage Gabriella to practice a specific distress tolerance skill every day between sessions. Gabriella might also be encouraged to practice mindfulness daily to increase her ability to develop awareness and focus on the present. These assignments will be idiosyncratic and will reinforce specific skills taught in skills training.

Phone Coaching

With suicidal and self-harming adolescents, phone coaching will ideally be available twenty-four hours a day. Adolescents should be provided with several other phone numbers to call if they are unable to reach the practitioner. There are national and local hotlines for suicidal adolescents (see Resources), and these may be backups for the practitioners on the DBT team. At the start of treatment, phone coaching is often not utilized by adolescents consistently; adequately orienting adolescents to phone coaching and shaping the behavior is important and necessary.

A practitioner assesses for suicidality when the adolescent calls, and takes whatever actions are necessary to keep the adolescent safe (including contacting parents). The goal, however, is to coach the adolescent to use skills to get through the moment safely, without making the situation worse. If necessary, the practitioner will get a commitment to safety and a commitment to call back if the adolescent again begins to feel pressure to self-harm or commit suicide.

Summary

In this chapter, we addressed how a DBT practitioner provides treatment when the adolescent presents with suicidal and self-harming behaviors. From a thorough assessment to chain analysis and daily logs, the practitioner seeks an understanding of the function and intention of the behaviors while also using change strategies (cognitive restructuring, exposure, contingency management through structuring the environment, and skills training) and phone coaching to help the client maintain safety and develop the life she wants. We have addressed some of the very difficult dialectics presented by these adolescents, and provided guidance that enables the practitioner to maintain the focus on balancing both acceptance and change while prioritizing safety at all times.

CHAPTER 8

Substance Abuse Behaviors

Difficulties with impulsivity and managing emotions contribute to substance abuse (Bornovalova, Lejuez, Daughters, Rosenthal, & Lynch, 2005; Davenport, Bore, & Campbell, 2010), which is widespread among adolescents. It makes sense, then, that a treatment developed for emotion dysregulation would have particular usefulness for substance abuse disorders in adolescents.

When substance abuse—the use of substances that negatively affects quality of life—is one of the presenting problems for an adolescent, the goal for the parents or caregivers is usually to end the substance abuse. This is usually *not* the goal of the adolescent, whose substance abuse is often reinforced by peers and the immediate, though temporary, relief of emotional pain provided by the substance. The DBT practitioner focuses attention on the function of the behavior while engaging the adolescent by addressing issues that are relevant to him. At the same time, the practitioner constantly looks for opportunities to address the emotional and problem-solving needs that may lead to the use of substances. It is important for the practitioner to withhold judgments and assumptions, to search for an understanding of the problem directly with the adolescent, and, at the same time, to work on change.

Practitioners will note the difference between an adolescent who experimentally uses substances as part of normative adolescent development and those who use it to manage difficult and painful emotions. DBT is a dual (or triple, or more) diagnosis treatment, and an adolescent substance abuser with an underlying mood, anxiety, or personality disorder will be most responsive to DBT. The practitioner will want to consider less costly and less intensive treatments before implementing DBT, if they have not been previously attempted, or if pervasive emotion dysregulation is not a factor in the substance abuse.

To illustrate how DBT can be effective with adolescents who have substance abuse behaviors, we will look at James in the vignette below and follow his treatment through this chapter.

Fifteen-year-old James was adopted internationally at thirty months and had experienced significant neglect and possible abuse prior to the adoption. James has been using marijuana daily for over a year, and he reports that it helps him "chill." His grades have deteriorated rapidly, and he spends time with other boys who skip classes and do poorly in school. His parents report great concerns about his poor school performance; they also note that they have had liquor and money disappear from their home, and they found marijuana in James's room. James denies taking things from the home and gets angry with his parents at these accusations. He says that his marijuana and alcohol use is not a problem and that he'll stop if it ever gets out of hand. While he says he has no problems, he does express some concern about the drop in his grades and how this might impact his plan to attend college in two years. His parents enrolled him in a local outpatient drug treatment program, and he was discharged for continuing to use. They have said that if he doesn't stop using drugs, they plan to send him away, and James says he will run away if this happens.

Theoretical Dialectics

DBT is unique in that it encourages a synthesis of opposing viewpoints. This is particularly true in substance abuse treatment. The DBT practitioner asks for abstinence and nonjudgmentally accepts relapse as a natural part of recovery. Some substance abusers may not require abstinence to be functional; however, this is initially the goal. At the same time, relapse prevention is addressed through chain analyses when the adolescent inevitably uses.

Harm reduction represents the middle path in substance abuse treatment (Blume, 2012). This approach accepts that practitioners may not be effective in eliminating use of substances entirely, and it supports work toward safer and decreased use of substances so that use no longer interferes with attaining goals or quality of life. While this approach is not explicitly embraced in DBT, the DBT practitioner will take what changes she can get, while always maintaining a focus on abstinence.

Drug users are said to be in "addict mind"; their thoughts, feelings, and behaviors are controlled by the drugs. With abstinence, the young person develops "clean mind"; he appears confident and is not using, while at the same time he is still vulnerable to triggers, not having developed coping strategies and an awareness of the cunning nature of abuse and addiction. An adolescent in clean mind is especially vulnerable to a return to using substances. DBT sees the dialectical synthesis of "addict mind" and "clean mind" as "clear mind." In clear mind, the adolescent is abstinent and at the same time fully alert and aware of the high risk for relapse; he also has learned skills to manage distress effectively (Dimeff, Koerner, & Linehan, 2008).

Case Conceptualization and Goal Setting

The DBT formulation of substance abuse is that an adolescent who has emotion dysregulation and a high sensitivity to emotional situations is likely to be abusing substances as a way to manage or avoid difficult emotions or thoughts. Using drugs and alcohol helps adolescents to manage emotions by providing short-term relief, though it does not ultimately solve the problem that leads to the painful emotions in the first place. However, while others may define the substance abuse as yet another problem, the adolescent feels as though he is managing the first problem, that of painful emotions, quite well.

In the diagram below, we see that James's emotion dysregulation (the cause of the problem), substance abuse (the problem that causes most of the behavior difficulties and most of the negative consequences in James's life), and school problems and family tension (the problems James identifies as the most pressing and immediate) interact in a dynamic way, with each increasing the other and all playing a part in the difficulties that James experiences. The practitioner will need to keep each in mind as she continues to help James make changes.

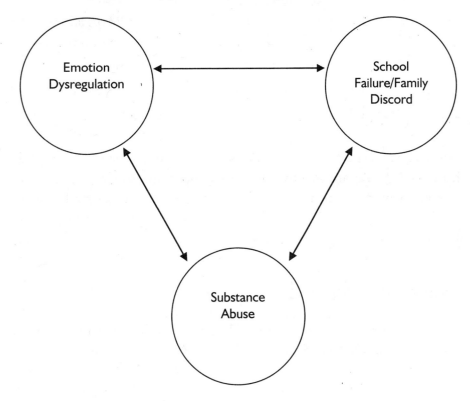

The chart below helps the practitioner understand and be sensitive to how effective these substance abuse behaviors are for the adolescent, why he will not want to give them up, and the difficulties inherent in becoming and staying sober:

Behavior	Positive Impact	Negative Impact
Using Substances	• allows adolescent to feel relief and escape from painful thoughts and feelings • lessens social inhibition • increases socialization, enables more activity with peer group	• compounds problems at home; heightens lack of trust from parents, leading to increased monitoring and less freedom • contributes to problems at school, such as poor grades and behavioral difficulties • increases risk of legal problems
Abstinence from Substances	• eliminates legal problems • lessens problems at home, resulting in more trust from parents • facilitates ability to do better in school	• requires facing problems and difficulties without escape • leaves adolescent to feel emotional pain • potentially creates more difficulties with current peer group

Practitioners will be most effective with adolescents who use substances when they recognize and accept that the substances are effective for the adolescent in lessening his pain, and, as a result, he is likely to resist changing the behavior. The practitioner will begin with the adolescent's goals for treatment and collaboratively help the adolescent to connect meeting those goals with lessening his use of substances.

Validation and Acceptance

When she validates him, the practitioner lets the adolescent know that she takes him seriously and accepts him. She acknowledges the following feelings and experiences:

- He feels misunderstood.

- He may feel anger about others' attempts to change his behavior.

- He may have difficulty with intense emotions.

- He experiences good feelings when he uses substances, and may like getting high.

- He likes the friends he has, even if his parents disapprove of them.

- His goals may conflict with those of his parents.

- He may not like that he has to meet with a practitioner.

When talking with James, the practitioner will validate him in this way:

Practitioner: I can see that, from your perspective, smoking weed is a good time. You hang out with your buddies and get away from your parents' nagging about school.

James: Yup.

Practitioner: And you feel that since you haven't ever been in trouble with the police, you have things under control.

James: Uh huh.

Practitioner: What's the downside of alcohol and weed?

James: Nothing, really…just having to come here.

Practitioner: So it's enjoyable on one level, *and* it results in conflict at home and having to come to therapy.

The practitioner begins to highlight the positive and negative impacts of James's behaviors. She will later highlight further impact of the drug use, but only after the relationship has been established and James's defensiveness about use has begun to dissipate.

Priority Targets and Goal Setting

The practitioner works on establishing goals for treatment after the initial assessment. The practitioner immediately undertakes the task of understanding, accepting, and clarifying the client's goals, as they will guide the treatment.

In the vignette above, the practitioner recognizes that James does not have life-threatening behaviors (unless he uses substances and then drives or gets into other life-threatening situations). The practitioner will be alert to the opportunity to complete chains on substance abuse to underscore the central role the practitioner places on the ongoing use and its impact on functioning.

The practitioner will ask for as much abstinence as the adolescent feels he can commit to, even if it is just the therapy hour, and will shape abstinence as the treatment progresses. In DBT, staying in treatment is not contingent on abstinence, as in some substance abuse programs. If an adolescent comes to a session under the influence of substances, the practitioner will note that this is a therapy-interfering behavior because it makes it harder to focus on the work of treatment. The adolescent will be warned about this behavior continuing, and a chain analysis will be done. If the adolescent returns to a subsequent session under the influence, it will be up to the discretion of the practitioner to decide if the adolescent is too impaired to do any work. If this is the case, the practitioner might end the session early (but only if this will not reinforce the use by allowing the adolescent to avoid therapy). For the most part, the practitioner will continue with the relentless pursuit of change by validating the adolescent while completing chains of the therapy-interfering behavior.

Quality of life–interfering targets, which are those behaviors that get in the way of James leading the life he and his parents would like him to have, will include these behaviors:

- having illegal substances in his room

- getting poor grades

- stealing from his parents

When practitioners work with adolescents who have substance-abusing behaviors, priority targets, as they relate mostly to therapy-interfering and quality of life–interfering behaviors, will be addressed according to DBT protocols. It is critical for the practitioner to maintain a respectful and accepting attitude in order to effectively establish and address the target behaviors.

Dialogue: Helping the Adolescent Define Goals

Practitioner: So what I'm hearing is that your parents think the drinking and pot use is a problem and you don't.

James: (Nods)

Practitioner: And your parents say that if you don't stop the drugs and alcohol, they plan to send you away.

James: They'll be sorry if they do that—I'll run away and never come back.

Practitioner: And that you would like to get back on track in school…get your grades back to where they used to be.

James: Yeah, that's the main thing. I need to get my grades back up.

Practitioner: So let me ask you a question: when things somehow change and the problems that bring you to therapy are solved, you would probably notice that you were doing some things differently, right?

James: I guess so.

Practitioner: What would you notice? What will you be doing differently when your problems are solved?

James: Hmm…I guess I won't be fighting so much with my parents.

Practitioner: Really? What will you be doing instead?

James: Getting along with them, having good times together, like when we watch TV.

Practitioner: Okay, what else will you be doing?

James: Probably a little more school work.

Practitioner: And what else? *(Dialogue would continue as James states the changes he would like to see in his life.)*

Client Goals

As the practitioner and James work together to assess how he can make his life feel better, James lists these goals:

- getting better grades

- getting along better with his parents

- making sure his parents don't send him away

- getting his parents to trust him more so they leave him alone

Practitioner Goal

The practitioner will, at this point, add the goal of abstinence from drug use to the goals list. She will identify it as the practitioner's goal if James does not show a willingness to work on it, as we see in the dialogue below.

Dialogue: Adding Goal of Abstaining from Substance Use

Practitioner: James, these are really well-stated goals. I can see you want things to get better. I want to also let you know that based on the things you have told me, you use alcohol and marijuana more than is typical and you meet criteria for substance abuse (or dependency). The drugs make the situation at school and home worse, and those situations make you want to use more. I recommend that you quit. What do you think?

James: No way. You're crazy if you think I'm going to give up weed.

Practitioner: I think things will eventually get better when you do, and I also understand that's not on your list of goals right now. I'd like to add it to the list of goals, and I'll note that I added it, not you. Is that okay?

Practitioner Dialectics

A dialectic for the DBT practitioner is that an eventual goal of treatment will be eliminating substance abuse and the adolescent might disengage from treatment if the practitioner advances this goal before the adolescent is ready to commit to it. Because the other problems in James's life interact transactionally with the substance abuse, a change in the other problem areas may result in a change in the substance abuse over time. The practitioner will balance accepting the goals that are important to the adolescent with looking for opportunities to link the adolescent's goals with eliminating substances (by talking about how his grades and family interaction may be affected by his use of substances and vice versa). Over time, James and the practitioner will link the use of substances with how using substances impacts his long-term goals.

It is important for the practitioner to state the obvious—that the substance abuse is a problem—and to do so in a validating and nonjudgmental manner. In order to do this effectively, the practitioner will spend considerable time engaging James in the treatment. She might consider easing into the substance abuse discussions by doing only brief chains initially; making an effort to accommodate James by meeting with him in the community (at a coffee shop, for example) if he is hesitant or resistant to meeting in the practitioner's office; adapting the length of the therapy session to better suit him; reaching out to him when he misses appointments; and generally showing a commitment to James and the relationship (McMain, Fayrs, Dimeff, & Linehan, 2007).

Gaining Commitment

Once the goals are established, the practitioner will want to engage James in a treatment that will be collaborative and cooperative.

Practitioner: James, you know what's interesting? People typically use drugs for the same reasons they come to counseling: they want to feel better, think differently, or change their behavior.

James: Okaaaay…

Practitioner: Drugs usually accomplish this in the short run, but in order to keep the changes going, the drug use continues. In therapy, the goal is to solve the same problems, and to do it in a more permanent way.

James: Yeeeaaah…?

Practitioner: So I wonder if you'd be willing to give this therapy a try?

Bornovalova and Daughters (2007) proposed that three factors predict treatment dropout among substance abusers in DBT:

- low motivation to make a change

- inadequate therapeutic alliance

- inability to tolerate distress

The effective DBT practitioner addresses the variables above simultaneously by using a range of DBT commitment and change strategies to engage the young person in treatment (Linehan, 1993a), including highlighting the freedom to choose whether or not to be in treatment and also highlighting the absence of alternatives (jail, boarding school, or residential treatment) and generating hope for the young person. Generating hope refers to remaining stubbornly optimistic and relentlessly focused on a better life for the adolescent.

Ongoing Assessment Tools and Strategies

The practitioner will use the daily log and chain analysis to gain insight into and understanding of target behaviors. The information from these tools will also be used to guide the ongoing treatment.

Daily Log

The daily log can be adapted for substance-abusing adolescents. Specific columns are added for thoughts, urges, and use of the drugs of choice. The adolescent tracks his use, and the practitioner has a record of the use from week to week. For adolescents who are fearful that the daily log will be read by parents and result in punishment, the practitioner reinforces for the parents that the daily log is private and is shared only at the discretion of the adolescent.

Chain Analysis

In the scenario above, James does not have any life-threatening target behaviors. The practitioner will thus target therapy-interfering behaviors, if any, and then behaviors that interfere with his quality of life. Any instance of substance abuse, stealing, lying, aggression, or other behaviors that interfere with his ability to live at home or maintain passing grades will be chained as quality of life—interfering behavior. The practitioner will always be on the lookout for opportunities to chain events.

In the circumstance chained below, James initially resisted doing a chain on the marijuana use recorded on his daily log, so the practitioner suggested they chain the test failure recorded there instead. The practitioner realizes that engaging in a power struggle will be counterproductive to the therapy and looks for ways to link the test failure to the substance abuse, assuming they are transactionally related. The chain below illustrates the connections between the adolescent's use of substances and how it will interfere with his goals while also providing relief from his pain:

Problem Behavior: Failed a Test

My friends were going out to party and wanted me to attend.

↓

I told my parents I was leaving and they told me that I needed to study and couldn't go.

↓

I thought that my parents had no right to control my life.

↓

I thought, *They don't understand me.*

↓

I got angry at my parents for pressuring me and I became worried about the exam.

↓

I thought about my friends and that I would not be invited to other parties if I didn't go.

↓

I felt anxious, my heart began to race and I wanted to run.

↓

I left the house, called my friends and had them pick me up.

↓

I smoked at the party.

↓

I felt much more relaxed and enjoyed myself.

↓

I failed the test and felt embarrassed and ashamed of myself.

↓

My parents got mad and threatened to send me away.

↓

I felt even more anxious, guilty and angry.

↓

I wanted to use weed again to feel better.

This chain identifies a variety of issues, and continued instances of chaining behaviors will underscore the patterns, issues, and necessary change strategies for James's treatment. This particular chain identifies the skills that will be important for James to learn in therapy:

- mindfulness skills to increase effective behavior

- assertiveness skills to use with friends and parents

- cognitive restructuring to help him understand possible reasons why his parents do not understand or his friends may react as they do

- emotion regulation and distress tolerance skills for anxiety management

- skills to help him plan ahead for situations when he will face conflicting demands

- learning to understand the difference between primary and secondary emotions

- behavioral concepts to help him understand how drug use is self-perpetuating and self-reinforcing

The role of the parents in James's chains can also guide the practitioner or parent coach in helping the parents to structure the environment differently. This chain is an example, and it is important to keep in mind that every adolescent has an idiosyncratic set of links in every chain.

Change Strategies

The practitioner will use the behavioral analysis and assessment in choosing change strategies to encourage James and his family to more skillfully manage the problems that lead to substance abuse. It will be through these change strategies that James will learn to use more skillful ways of managing his emotions and responding to difficulties.

Contingency Management Through Structuring the Environment

It may be most effective for James's parents to have a separate parent coach. This enables the parents to be validated for their very real concerns and also helps them create a structure that reinforces studying and effective behavior while minimizing reactivity and threats of punishment. The parents will work with the coach to make the following changes in their own behaviors and thoughts so that they can be more effective when they interact with their son:

- accepting and validating that James "is doing the best he can" at this time with the emotion dysregulation that he experiences

- recognizing that he will need encouragement and support in making the changes he needs to make

- developing specific guidelines about how to structure a more reinforcing and less threatening home

- allowing natural consequences to occur when James makes ineffective choices and decisions

- taking care of their own needs and building in pleasant activities so they are less vulnerable to James's emotions and behaviors

- noticing their own reactions and when they need to walk away until they can have more effective communications with their son

- accepting that James is responsible for his own behavior and for the consequences of his behaviors, and that there is a limit to how much they can control

- recognizing that they do not have to respond immediately, and that taking time to think and talk together often helps them to develop more effective responses

The parent coach will also help the parents develop strategies for structuring the environment. A number of behavioral changes and strategies may be utilized:

- creating a contract that consistently reinforces James for studying and doing well with additional privileges and freedoms, rather than one that punishes poor grades by taking away privileges

- incentivizing his participation in treatment

- providing validation for James's desire to be with his friends and understanding his disappointment when he cannot do what he wants

- building in time for James to do soothing and pleasant activities that enable him to manage difficult emotions and build a sense of competency

- encouraging and enabling him to take time to settle himself when necessary or to call his practitioner/coach

- working with James and the school to ensure that he has a course load that is not too overwhelming, and that he can manage without additional anxiety

- acknowledging and minimizing additional activities that cause James more anxiety

Some parents wonder if they should drug test their adolescents. If the parents are reinforcing sobriety, they may need an objective way to assess this. However, adolescents have numerous ways to "beat the test" that often render the testing ineffective. It is usually more effective to focus on other behaviors, such as lessening anger and doing better in school, and to reinforce them, rather than drug testing an adolescent.

Practitioner Contingencies

The practitioner will attempt to create contingencies that reinforce behaviors that are consistent with abstinence or decreases in use. This might include privileges at home, gift cards, prizes, certificates, or other tokens of accomplishment in skills group, or extra warm responses in therapy. The practitioner reinforces abstinence by allowing James more time to talk about the school and family issues that are important to him when he has not used.

Skills Training

Skills training will introduce an adolescent who is engaged in substance abuse to all of the DBT skills. The individual practitioner will focus on applying the skills that are most relevant and helpful.

Deficits in distress tolerance correlate with increased use of alcohol and other drugs (Howell, Leyro, Hogan, Buckner, & Zvolensky, 2010; Buckner, Keough, & Schmidt, 2007); therefore, the distress tolerance skills are given particular emphasis. James will need to focus on being mindful of thoughts and feelings that lead to urges to use substances, as well as on how to use distress tolerance skills to manage his anxiety, anger, and urges. James will work on developing and accepting behavioral contingencies so that he can build in his own discipline and reinforcers for school success and clean days. He'll also work on understanding how the pressure he puts on himself leads to vulnerability and intense emotions, by looking at his story of emotions. James will learn the value of evaluating the positive and negative impact of his behaviors when triggered. Over time, James will learn to make decisions that are more effective in helping him find the life he wants.

Mindfulness skills are critical to substance abuse treatment. Mindfulness teaches adolescents to notice their thoughts, feelings, and urges without engaging with them; this allows for increased exposure to thoughts, urges, and feelings that previously were followed very quickly by the abuse of a substance. In this way, mindfulness allows for greater exposure, and eventual habituation, to these experiences—which lessens their strength as triggers for the previously subsequent substance abuse.

Several additional skills are taught to substance abusers in DBT (Dimeff & Koerner 2007):

- **Urge surfing.** Clients are taught to notice urges and then step back and observe them without acting on them. This can be practiced by noticing urges to move, scratch an itch, look around, and so on without acting on them. The skill is based on mindfulness and allows for practicing self-control. The adolescent learns that if he does not act on or attend to an urge immediately, it usually drifts away.

- **Alternate rebellion.** Adolescents frequently rebel against the status quo and substance use meets this need. Adolescent substance abusers are taught to consider alternatives to using substances by "rebelling" in other ways such as making clothing choices that their parents might not approve of, responding directly (not necessarily politely) when someone asks how they are, playing music very loudly, and so on.

- **Avoiding cues to use.** Triggers are identified in chains, and the practitioner works on engaging the adolescent in a willingness to avoid these triggers (referred to as "people, places, and things" in 12-step programs).

- **Burning bridges.** This is a coping-ahead skill, also used in 12-step programs. The adolescent is encouraged to erase phone numbers for dealers from his phone, throwing away the "stash" in his room, and so on.

The use of skills group can be a powerful influence on adolescents who are ambivalent or resistant to stopping their abuse of substances. Exposure to peers who are more motivated to change and who take a leadership role in teaching skills exploits the adolescent susceptibility to peer pressure in the service of growth. An adolescent substance abuser will thus benefit from skills training group even if it is not exclusively for substance abusers.

Cognitive Restructuring

James may have thoughts like *I can't afford to miss a party—my friends will have fun without me and stop inviting me, My parents don't care about my happiness,* or *I can't cope without weed.* He will be encouraged to challenge these beliefs, test the evidence, and consider alternate perspectives using cognitive techniques. The practitioner will validate how James might arrive at these conclusions, even as she relentlessly challenges them.

Dialogue: Cognitive Restructuring

Practitioner: It makes sense to me that you believe you'll drop off the radar with your friends if you miss too many events, and at the same time I wonder if that's really the case. Do you have any evidence to support that belief?

James: Not really, it's just a feeling.

Practitioner: You have a thought that your friends will move on and forget about you, and that leads to you feeling worried if you miss a party, right? *(Practitioner clarifies the difference between thoughts and feelings.)*

James: Uh huh.

Practitioner: I wonder if you'd be willing to test that thought out. (This will lead to the practitioner prescribing a therapeutic task to test the evidence for the belief.)

Exposure

Ultimately, DBT relies heavily on exposure treatment. James has an urge to use drugs or drink that is very similar to (or may actually be) a compulsion. The practitioner will look for opportunities to explain the model of reinforcement and extinction, such as the strategic removal of rewards to change behaviors; and she will make efforts to support James in behaving counter to the urge longer than he typically does, to give him the opportunity to manage his emotions using skills.

When an adolescent has emotion dysregulation, substance abuse is a very effective way to avoid and escape painful emotions. In therapy, he may change the subject away from topics that make him anxious, like discussing school, his future, or his drug use. He may focus his attention on how his parents do not understand him and may have more difficulty facing his own concerns about the choices he makes. The therapy itself is an exposure tool, enabling the practitioner to do several things:

- validate the adolescent's concerns as they come up and gently guide him to talk about those issues that cause him to become dysregulated

- encourage the adolescent to "sit with" the feelings rather than coming up with "quick fix" answers that allow him to quickly feel better when he is anxious, angry, or sad, thus increasing tolerance for uncomfortable feelings

- help the adolescent become mindful of what his body feels and what he thinks, as a way to become more aware of these cues, help him learn that he can manage his emotions, and help him recognize the impact of bodily sensations on moods and urges

- help the adolescent use skills that he is learning in skills training to help him soothe himself and then return to his emotions

As the adolescent learns that he can manage his emotions safely and without escaping, he will be encouraged to apply those skills when he has the urge to use. This is successful when the practitioner explains the process fully and openly to the client.

Phone Coaching

Phone coaching (calling one's sponsor or friends in the program) has long been utilized by 12-step programs as an effective tool in preventing relapses. DBT recognizes that an adolescent may be overwhelmed in the natural environment and encourages him to call the practitioner for coaching when he is triggered to use. There are a number of coaching applications for smartphones (PTSD Coach, DBT Coach, and so on), and a pilot study showed the use of DBT Coach in particular reduced emotional intensity and urges to use substances (Rizvi, Dimeff, Skutch, Carroll, & Linehan, 2011).

Finally, the availability of phone coaching, even if it is rarely used by an adolescent, demonstrates the practitioner's commitment to the client, and it may also contribute to the development of hope and the connection with the practitioner.

Adjunctive Services

The focus in DBT is always on doing what is effective to help the adolescent. It is important to consider other services that may be helpful to the adolescent.

12-Step Programs

Alcoholics Anonymous, Narcotics Anonymous, Marijuana Anonymous, and other 12-step programs are particularly effective with users who are ready to make a change. Many adolescents who have invested in these programs have made remarkable progress. Many of the tenets of 12-step programs overlap with DBT skills and concepts (radical acceptance, willingness, repairs, mindfulness, managing urges, building a support network, coping ahead, identifying triggers, distraction, contributing, and so on). While many adolescents connect quickly to these programs, many do not. We encourage and reinforce exposure to these programs and accept the adolescent's response—positive, negative, or neutral.

Medications

Alternative medications are often used for young people with dependencies on stimulants, narcotics, or anxiolytics. The goal is to manage medically, while adolescents engage in treatment, the symptoms that they have been addressing through drug abuse. The replacement drug can be tapered as treatment progresses, and the goal is to do this when the adolescent has been successful with skills and the overall treatment.

Summary

This chapter addressed the use of DBT when the adolescent presents with substance abuse that is serving the purpose of helping him to regulate or escape painful emotions. We have presented ways that the practitioner can validate the adolescent even if the adolescent denies that his substance abuse is a problem. The practitioner's acceptance of the adolescent in the stage he is in and acknowledgment of the goals that he initially sets enables the adolescent to become engaged in the treatment process. And it is the adolescent's engagement in the process and his trust that the practitioner "gets him" that will increase the likelihood that he will be able to acknowledge the negative impact of the substance abuse, link his use to problems in his life, and make the decision to replace it with more adaptive behaviors.

CHAPTER 9

Anxiety-Driven Behaviors

Anxiety is prevalent among adolescents, and though the symptoms may differ, the physiological and emotional intensity of the emotions felt by the adolescent is the common theme. Adolescents with anxiety that manifests in behaviors such as constantly worrying or being afraid, having specific fears that lead to avoidance of specific situations, constant vigilance or nightmares, or obsessive or compulsive behaviors are often treated with cognitive behavioral therapy techniques. However, when standard CBT or other evidence-based approaches have not been effective, an adolescent may be referred for DBT for its emphasis on developing mindfulness, distress tolerance, and other skills, and because of its success with multiple diagnoses. DBT is a validating exposure-based approach; it helps adolescents understand, respond to, and ultimately manage their anxiety effectively. The DBT emphasis on balancing acceptance with change makes DBT an effective treatment for adolescents with anxiety disorders.

The adolescent who has anxiety-driven behaviors often experiences the same intense emotional reactions and desires to escape or avoid those uncomfortable feelings as individuals for whom DBT was initially developed. When an adolescent has anxiety-driven behaviors, the escape or avoidance itself may be the symptom, and the adolescent may not resort to harmful or dangerous behaviors. She may instead avoid or overattend to situations that might produce the intense emotion, thereby limiting her activities and her ability to fully experience her life. DBT will help the adolescent learn how to manage her anxiety so that she can experience the activities that enable her to have the life she desires.

In addition, the lives of adolescents who have anxiety-driven behaviors may be significantly impaired or restricted by their anxiety, and they may be so filled with shame and embarrassment that trusting a practitioner or staying in treatment is often a challenge. DBT strategies that prioritize treatment-interfering and quality of life–interfering behaviors help these adolescents make a commitment to treatment and to making positive changes in their lives.

In some adolescents, the nature of anxiety and the avoidance that results from it make it less apparent to those around them. Adolescents are able to hide their anxiety through obsessive thoughts, compulsive rituals, and high expectations of themselves, and by finding what seem to be reasonable excuses for avoiding or ending situations that cause anxiety. It may be that the level of anxiety is not noticed until an adolescent reaches a certain point:

- experiences a disappointment that is emotionally unacceptable to her and that she is not able to tolerate in a healthy, adaptive manner

- is unable to live up to her own expectations

- is so consumed by rituals that she becomes disruptive in the home or school

- stops activities that were important to her

Other adolescents may have shown signs of anxiety, difficulty adjusting to new situations, or compulsive or avoidant behaviors for much of their lives. Whether the adolescent has shown outward signs of anxiety for a long time or only recently, these behaviors may bewilder parents, teachers, and others who may recommend treatment. Such was the case with Sonia.

Sonia is fifteen years old. Her parents are concerned because she misses about two to three days of school with stomachaches every week. This began happening after she had the flu three months ago and was out of school for a week. She had what appears to have been a panic attack at school around the time she returned from her illness and has not attended consistently since then. Her medical team has ruled out physical illness. She has a history of giving up and withdrawing from activities (Girl Scouts, clubs, and sports) and has a history of transient compulsive behaviors, including hair pulling, nail biting, and perfectionism. She has one close friend. Her parents report that she has always been shy and that it takes her a long time to warm up to new situations and people. She had not responded to therapy with her previous therapist and was referred to DBT when she began to react to her anxiety with increasing verbal aggression and abuse when asked to go to school.

Theoretical Dialectics

Anxiety is a necessary and useful emotion; it alerts adolescents to potential danger and allows their brains and bodies to react quickly and appropriately to protect themselves. Anxiety tends to result either in a conscientious effort to solve a problem—to study for a test, be on time for an activity, and so on—or an effective avoidance of a problem: avoiding dangerous places, driving carefully, and so on. Both problem solving *and* avoidance are effective and necessary in certain situations. However, some adolescents experience threat where none or very little exists. They may misperceive or misinterpret a situation and react with obsessions, compulsions, or avoidance, and these symptoms get in the way of their abilities to live the life they want to live. The dialectic with anxiety is that there *is* threat in the world, and at the same time, avoidance of all threat results in increasing isolation, narrowing of activities, and impairment in functioning. Exposure to threat and avoidance of threat are both valid at times. When adolescents seek therapy for anxiety-driven behaviors, they typically exhibit one of the two behavioral patterns below:

1. The *adolescent avoids situations* when exposure is required (not attending school, not preparing for a test), which reinforces itself and results in the development of other problems (school failure, isolation, substance abuse, and so on). The adolescent seeks treatment when these *other* problems become overwhelming. This cycle can be seen in the diagram below:

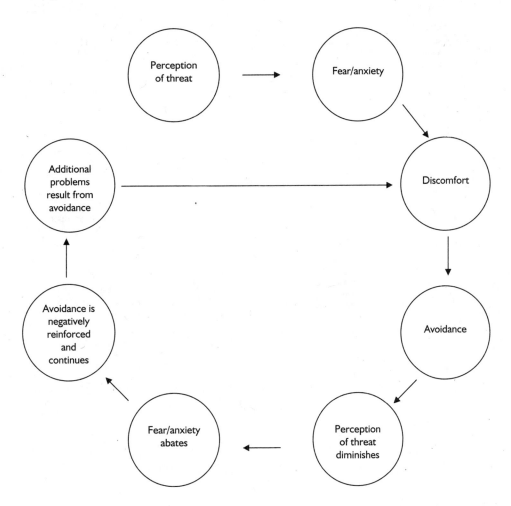

2. The *adolescent confronts the trigger* when avoiding or distracting would be more effective (for example, obsessing about a peer interaction and demanding reassurance). Responding in an intense manner is often not effective at solving the original problem, and results in ongoing anxiety. At other times, the problem *is* solved by responding intensely (for example, sending multiple text messages to elicit a reassuring response from a peer) and as a result the behavior is reinforced (when the peer responds) and continues, creating

additional problems (in the future when peers are annoyed by these behaviors). This cycle can be seen in the diagram below:

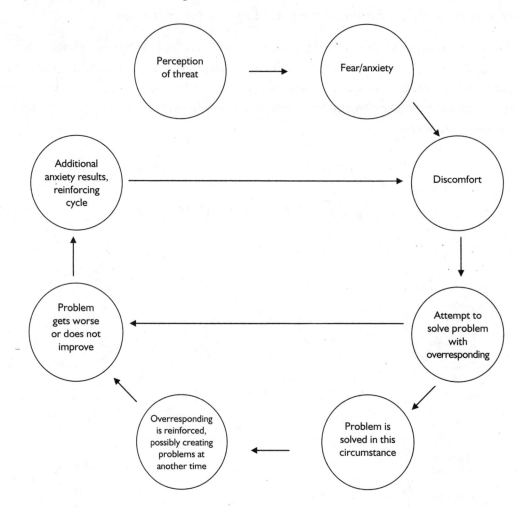

The dialectic is that both avoidance and exposure can be valid. It is necessary to find the most effective balance between them in any given situation.

Case Conceptualization and Goal Setting

The adolescent who experiences extreme anxiety may find ways to escape from painful situations or to avoid any situation that *may* cause anxiety. Escape may be sought in compulsive behaviors, dissociation, ending activities, or the externalization of anxiety in aggressive behaviors, while avoidance can eventually paralyze the adolescent, whose fear of *possible* anxiety causes her to severely limit her activities. This means that the adolescent is not only limiting her life, she is also not allowing herself to experience situations in which she may learn to manage her emotions. And yet the adolescent is calmed by not having to face anxiety-provoking situations, which is reinforcing. Her world continues to shrink in size and experience. She does not know that her anxiety can be managed because she does not allow herself to fully experience the emotion in the first place, as can be seen in the dialogue below:

Dialogue: Introduction to Treatment for Anxiety

Practitioner: Sonia, I would like to teach you a little about how anxiety works. When our brain experiences something threatening, it goes on autopilot and does a number of things to protect us. Some of these automatic reactions are increased heartbeat, sweating, rapid breathing, and other symptoms that can be uncomfortable and even scary. They help us either get away from a threat or fight it off. A problem occurs when these signals and experiences are misinterpreted—the brain senses danger where there is no real danger, as in a panic attack or a phobia, or when we avoid something that we should face head on.

Sonia: So what do I do to change it?

Practitioner: Luckily, anxiety has been well researched, and there is very good treatment for it. The treatment can be uncomfortable though, because, even though we will be careful and provide a lot of support, it still requires you to actually face your fears. When you do this regularly, there's a very good chance that your anxiety will go down.

Sonia: I don't know…

Practitioner: I understand. It can be hard. Remember that things are usually difficult when you first learn them, and they become easier with time. That's true of this treatment as well. Would you like to hear more about it?

Positive and Negative Impacts of Avoidance and Escape

The DBT practitioner working with an adolescent who has anxiety-driven behaviors will need to provide a very safe environment if the adolescent is going to be able to attend treatment at all. There will need to be an emphasis on validation until the adolescent is willing to participate in treatment, share her experiences, and commit to making changes. The chart below will help the adolescent and the practitioner understand the dialectic that avoidance at certain times can be effective and necessary and that, at other times, experiencing anxiety can be just as important.

Behavior	Positive Impact	Negative Impact
Avoiding or escaping activities	• experiences freedom from fear and anxiety • does not experience overwhelming emotions • feels safe • feels some control	• misses out on activities and life • does not learn that anxiety can be managed • withdraws from friends and family, which results in loneliness
Engaging in anxiety-provoking activities	• participates with friends and family • recognizes the ability to survive and manage emotional experiences • enhances social connections • results in more fulfilling life	• experiences the anxiety • feels overwhelmed • fears that emotions cannot be managed • gives up the comfort of avoidance

Validation and Acceptance

The DBT practitioner will show acceptance of the adolescent who has anxiety by recognizing the reality of her current situation and explicitly validating her experience:

- Emotions can be paralyzing and overwhelming.

- Rituals and avoidance can be comforting.

- She is ashamed of her behaviors.

- Her life feels uncomfortable.

- She feels bewildered by the fact that things that seem so easy to others are so painfully hard for her.

- Others may not accept or understand the level of her anxiety or may blame her for avoiding things.

The DBT practitioner will focus on validating the experience of the adolescent in order to engage her in treatment. While the behaviors of the adolescent with anxiety may be disruptive to her life, they are not as likely to be self-harming or dangerous to others. This gives the practitioner more time to build a trusting relationship, without worrying about threats to the adolescent's life, while gaining commitment to change.

Priority Targets and Goal Setting

While the practitioner develops a trusting therapeutic relationship and a commitment to change, he also develops those target behaviors that are based on the DBT framework. The target behaviors for Sonia would look like this:

Treatment Priority	Specific Behaviors
Life-threatening behaviors	None known at this time
Treatment-interfering behaviors	Not relating to therapist
	Difficulty engaging in therapy
	Not completing treatment activities
Quality of life–interfering behaviors	Missing school
	Frequent stomachaches/somatic complaints
	Panic attacks
	Compulsive behaviors
	Not completing activities
	Verbal aggression

Even though Sonia may not, at this time, have any life-threatening behaviors, she is a candidate for DBT because of her mood intensity and the significant ways in which her anxiety symptoms impact her ability to live the life she wants, and because previous treatments have proven ineffective.

Client Goals

The practitioner helps to link the adolescent's goals to her anxiety, as can be seen in the dialogue below:

Dialogue: Helping the Adolescent Define Goals

Practitioner: So, Sonia, let's talk about what you would like things to be like. When things are better, and this anxiety is under control, what will be different?

Sonia: I guess I won't have panic attacks in school anymore.

Practitioner: And when the panic attacks aren't happening in school, what will you be doing?

Sonia: Going to class, hanging out with my friends…

Practitioner: Will anything else be different?

Sonia: My parents will lighten up, and we can have good times at home again.

When Sonia meets with the DBT practitioner, they will discuss her goals, which will generally be related to the positive consequences of reducing her anxiety. Her goals emerged from the above dialogue:

- return to school consistently

- reduce panic attacks and stomachaches (which she may see as medical issues)

- have more time with friends

- get her parents to pressure her less and leave her alone

Practitioner Goals

The practitioner will work with Sonia on her goals while at the same time beginning to address reducing anxiety through exposure to certain emotions. The practitioner will gradually link the anxiety that Sonia feels with its impact on meeting her goals. The practitioner establishes his own goals:

- reduce anxiety

- increase mindfulness to emotions, body sensations, and thoughts

- help Sonia live in the present moment to reduce worry and anticipatory anxiety (Chapman, Gratz, Tull, & Keane, 2011)

- increase use of self-soothing activities to manage overwhelming anxiety

- increase Sonia's ability to express her emotions and needs in words rather than through physical symptoms

- increase her active attempts to take care of her physical well-being as a way to minimize vulnerability to overwhelming emotions

The practitioner will articulate these goals, and will work to link Sonia's goals with the necessity of learning how to manage painful emotions skillfully without avoidance and escape. And he will make it clear to her that doing so will help her achieve her stated goals.

Gaining Commitment

The initial goal of treatment with an adolescent who has anxiety-driven behaviors is to engage her in treatment and help her develop a commitment to change. She will be ambivalent about giving up the avoidance (and the safety it provides). The treatment will enable her to see that experiencing anxiety-provoking situations will not only allow her to have positive life experiences but also reduce her anxiety in the long run.

Therapy is seen by the adolescent as an unknown situation and, as such, increases anxiety in and of itself. The adolescent may not readily engage in therapy, and the practitioner will need to work on engaging her with a combination of validation, understanding, and letting her see that life can improve. Psychoeducation about anxiety, the self-reinforcing role of avoidance, and the benefits of carefully planned exposure are helpful in engaging adolescents in treatment. Just as adolescents find the biosocial theory of emotion dysregulation validating, they are similarly reassured by learning about anxiety, how it develops, and its function, and by the nonblaming understanding of the emotion. The practitioner will need to be patient and supportive in providing this psychoeducation. Many adolescents find the nonjudgmental explanation and normalization of anxiety to be helpful in reducing the secondary emotions of shame and guilt associated with avoidance or rituals.

Ongoing Assessment Tools and Strategies

When working with adolescents who have anxiety-driven behaviors, the practitioner will use DBT tools to assess what triggers the behaviors and what consequences maintain them. The practitioner will look for conditioned responses as well as behaviors that are maintained by the responses that follow.

Daily Log

The daily log for an adolescent with anxiety disorders will minimize the target behaviors of self-harm and suicidality unless the adolescent (or family) has indicated that this is an issue. The daily log will be customized by targeting any instance of school absence, stomachaches or other somatic issues, verbal aggression, panic attacks, or other significant anxiety symptoms.

Chain Analysis

A chain analysis of Sonia's avoidant behavior might look like this:

I was worried about a test I was having.

↓

I was absent from school a lot, so I was sure
I was going to fail it and not get an A+.

↓

I had trouble sleeping, thinking about the test.

↓

When I woke up, my stomach hurt.

↓

I wanted to go to the doctor. My mother said I had to go to school.

↓

I thought, *Nobody understands how much my stomach hurts.
Everyone thinks I'm faking it but it's real.*

↓

I began to tremble and my head began to hurt.

↓

I said to myself, "Oh no, here we go again."
I knew I couldn't go to school because I felt so sick.

↓

I screamed at my mother that if she loved me,
she wouldn't make me go to school.

↓

I stayed in bed all day. I worried about when I would
be able to take a make-up exam.

↓

I felt ashamed and guilty, and my stomach still hurt.

From this chain, the practitioner recognizes several places where change strategies can be used to intervene and change the chain's outcome:

- Cognitive restructuring and dialectical thinking will help Sonia address her need to be perfect or risk feeling like a failure.

- Exposure will help Sonia realize that she can manage difficult and stressful situations.

- Skills training includes the teaching of distress tolerance skills, which can help Sonia learn to calm herself when she wakes up anxious or distressed; and mindfulness, enabling her to stay in the present so that she can sleep without worrying about the next day.

The chain underscores the relationship among thoughts, feelings, and behaviors. It highlights that changing one part of the chain can influence the outcome of the situation.

Change Strategies

When an adolescent has anxiety-driven behaviors, one of the major change strategies will be exposure to emotions to lessen the reinforced responses of avoidance or escape. In order to practice exposure, the adolescent will need all of the skills in skills training and will also need assistance with cognitive restructuring. It is equally important that parents and family members do not seek to "save" the adolescent from feeling anxious, since this actually reinforces the use of avoidance.

Exposure

The most powerful therapeutic tools for anxiety are exposure-based interventions. These interventions directly address avoidance, have tremendous impact on problematic beliefs, and often completely eliminate the adolescent's fear. These can be some of the most difficult strategies to implement, given that exposure only works if the adolescent allows her anxiety to increase long enough for her to experience the eventual decrease in the symptoms. It is important for the practitioner to thoroughly orient the adolescent and ensure that she understands the following concepts and components of the treatment:

- the exposure process

- the importance of practice between sessions

- the paradox that she may feel an increase in her anxiety before the treatment begins to decrease her anxiety

- the importance of *not* using distress tolerance skills during planned exposure, since they are a form of the avoidance that she is working to eliminate

- the importance of using mindfulness skills to manage the discomfort she will experience

The goal of exposure-based interventions is for the adolescent to have experiences that challenge her beliefs, leading to a decrease in avoidance behaviors. Adolescents who complete an exposure protocol are likely to have significant improvement in their anxiety symptoms (Nakamura, Pestle, & Chorpita, 2009).

Adolescents are encouraged to develop an exposure lifestyle, one in which they make an effort to consistently recognize when anxiety impacts their behavior and to approach, not avoid, as necessary to the circumstances, when they feel anxiety. DBT integrates both exposure (acting opposite, planning ahead, assertiveness skills) *and* avoidance (distraction and self-soothing). For exposure to be effective, the practitioner needs to use effective strategies and sensitivity in helping the adolescent to balance this dialectic.

Skills Training

Difficulties with emotion regulation impact ability to manage anxiety and are associated with increases in obsessions (Cougle, Timpano, & Goetz, 2012). Therefore, emotion regulation and distress tolerance skills are of particular relevance to adolescents who have anxiety-driven behaviors, while mindfulness skills teach the awareness and focus that are necessary to use them.

Mindfulness

Mindfulness skills are useful for slowing down responses and tolerating affect long enough for exposure to be effective. They also give the adolescent a framework for becoming aware of her anxiety, observing it or describing it, and noticing the wave-like manner in which it comes and goes when no action is taken to avoid or escape from it.

Distress Tolerance

Distress tolerance skills (Linehan, 1993b) teach adolescents to accept feelings, or to distract from them when necessary. While distraction/avoidance is an effective method for managing anxiety in the short run (taking a break from studying when becoming too stressed), it does not effectively resolve the problems that lead to anxiety in the long run, and it does not give the adolescent the experience of learning to manage anxiety in more effective ways. At the same time, because of its effectiveness in reducing anxiety, distraction/avoidance often becomes a learned response to anxiety. Distraction and self-soothing skills for anxiety must be used judiciously and briefly. Otherwise, the adolescent is not adequately exposed to the feeling and does not learn to employ other skills to manage it.

Emotion Regulation

Adolescents in DBT learn the purpose and value of anxiety. The skill of acting opposite teaches young people to strategically expose themselves to the discomfort rather than avoid it. Exercise, adequate sleep, taking care of illnesses, and the other skills associated with reducing emotional vulnerability are also useful for managing anxiety symptoms. The story of emotion helps adolescents recognize the triggers for anxiety, the reinforcing impact of avoidance or overattention, as well as the consequences of these behaviors (Linehan, 1993a). It also helps the adolescent to reframe the thoughts about the triggers that cause the anxiety.

Validation and Dialectics

Validation is very useful for reducing emotional intensity and is critical when conducting exposure. It also helps an adolescent who desires perfection to be more accepting of herself.

Adolescents with anxiety tend to see the world in a nondialectical, either/or way that leads to fear of failure, criticism, or not being "right." These fears in turn lead to an inability to take risks, learn through mistakes, or try things that may be difficult. Learning how to think dialectically—to accept that you can make mistakes and not be a "failure," and that it is not the end of the world to be "wrong"—can help free an adolescent to learn, grow, and live more comfortably with herself and in her world with others (Miller, Rathus, & Linehan, 2007).

Interpersonal Effectiveness

Interpersonal effectiveness skills (Linehan, 1993b) are valuable for adolescents with anxiety. They help the adolescent approach situations that they may seek to avoid by giving them the skills to manage their feelings in those situations:

- skills to communicate feelings of anxiety effectively so the adolescent can get the support she wants

- assertiveness skills that are useful for adolescents with social anxiety

- skills to get needs met in effective rather than overly aggressive or passive interpersonal ways when she is anxious

The use of these skills allows the adolescent to expose herself to feared interpersonal interactions. These skills help adolescents find the assertive middle ground between avoidance and attack.

Cognitive Restructuring

Anxiety frequently results from overestimating the risk in a given situation or fearing any form of "failure." These overestimations and fears will emerge in chain analyses and in therapeutic conversation. The skilled DBT practitioner uses techniques for challenging the adolescent's beliefs while continuing to validate her feelings and fears.

Sonia has beliefs and fears about the likelihood of another panic attack occurring when she returns to school, her lack of ability to manage a panic attack when it occurs, and the reactions of others when they observe a panic attack. The practitioner's goals are to challenge these thoughts while validating the very real fear Sonia has about them, and to educate her about the connections among thoughts, feelings, and behaviors and the reinforcing nature of avoidance. Interventions include these (Barlow et. al. 2010):

- educating Sonia about the common "cognitive distortions" (catastrophizing and increased fear based on overestimating risk and probability of failure/danger)

- teaching Sonia methods for assessing the accuracy of her beliefs

- providing techniques for recognizing obsessions and challenging Sonia's interpretation of their meaning

Contingency Management Through Structuring the Environment

Parents who have an adolescent who experiences anxiety try to help their adolescent by minimizing stressful situations or by telling the adolescent that, of course, he or she can manage or go to school or do well on a test, are inadvertently invalidating her very real emotions. Despite the adolescent's apparent success at school, she is very fearful that the next test will result in failure; there is a very real sense in which the adolescent believes she is not truly competent and is only fooling the people around her. The adolescent's absolute thinking also causes her to believe that anything less than perfection is a failure. If the parents do not understand this, they will inadvertently invalidate the adolescent's experience and cause her to feel even more anxiety and frustration as she tries to prove to others that her fears are real and her feelings are overwhelming.

For the parents to be effective, they also need to be validated for their own feelings:

- frustration that their daughter is not doing expected tasks like going to school

- anxiety about their own failings and worry about what others think when they are not able to get their daughter to meet basic expectations

- anxiety about wanting to be helpful and supportive and not always knowing how to do this effectively

- sadness about how difficult and painful life is for their daughter

- fears that their daughter will not have the life they anticipated for her

- pain that their child is different from their friends' children even though she looks, and can act, just like every other adolescent

A separate parent coach can help parents understand the dilemmas faced by their adolescent while the adolescent's individual therapist works to develop a trusting relationship. The parent coach will help the parents with these tasks:

- understanding the very real feelings of their daughter and the nature of emotion dys-regulation and anxiety-driven behaviors

- providing a validating environment for their daughter's feelings without "giving in" to their daughter's behavioral avoidance

- understanding that their role is not to create a nonstressful environment or protect their daughter from difficult circumstances; it is to support their daughter through her feelings of pain and anxiety when she experiences difficult situations

- reinforcing adaptive behaviors and ignoring less-than-adaptive behaviors (Sonia's parents might give her privileges *only* when she attends school)

- avoiding power struggles with Sonia (because, eventually Sonia may experience some difficult natural consequences, and it is more effective to have her learn through her own life experiences than through her parents' struggles with her)

- accepting that their role as parents may be different than they expected because they cannot protect her from all the things that are difficult for her

- recognizing that Sonia will need to make some changes in her life that they, in turn, will need to support and reinforce

- accepting that they may need to accept fewer academic successes while focusing on Sonia's ability to have more life experiences

It is often quite difficult to develop contingencies and structure the environment when an adolescent avoids or escapes from difficult situations. Parents will need to reinforce their daughter when she faces difficult circumstances and not enable the avoidance or escape that the treatment targets. It is very important that parents understand the concepts of behavioral management so that they understand why they are structuring an environment in ways that may, initially, be very difficult for their adolescent to manage and themselves to maintain.

Summary

In this chapter, we addressed why DBT treatment can be helpful if a practitioner is working with an adolescent who has anxiety-driven behaviors. We discussed the importance of recognizing and validating the overwhelming nature of the emotion of anxiety and how it significantly impairs an adolescent's ability to have the life she wants. We pointed out that DBT's focus on the dialectic of acceptance and change is as vitally important in engaging an adolescent with anxiety-driven behaviors as it is with an adolescent who self-harms. Finally, we discussed the importance of all of the DBT skills and change procedures in helping an adolescent become aware of her anxiety, accept it, and learn how to manage it without avoiding the things that cause it.

CHAPTER 10

Disordered Eating

An adolescent may present to a practitioner with disordered eating that is either the primary behavioral concern, or occurs alongside other behavioral issues that are related to emotion dysregulation. When an adolescent exhibits disordered eating, there is usually a great deal of anxiety about her health. This symptom of emotion dysregulation presents a complexity of concerns for parents, who naturally just want their adolescent to be healthy and eat in healthy ways. DBT is a structured behavioral treatment; it helps the adolescent replace disordered behaviors with safer ones that are more effective in the long run.

There is an evidence-based treatment for extreme restricting behaviors (family-based treatment for anorexia nervosa, sometimes referred to as the Maudsley approach). Therefore, this chapter will focus only on bingeing and purging behaviors that are used by the adolescent as one of several problematic behaviors to regulate painful emotions, consistent with DBT's effectiveness for treating adolescents who have multiple behaviors that are causing problems. DBT may also be effective when integrated into traditional treatment approaches for disordered eating with adolescents who do not respond to or comply with those approaches. DBT can also be used to help parents whose adolescents are involved in traditional treatment to respond effectively and non-judgmentally to their adolescents.

The underlying assumption in DBT treatment is that the adolescent, even when appearing outwardly competent in many areas, feels chaos and pain internally and requires validation and acceptance before she will be able to make significant changes. The DBT practitioner provides this nonjudgmental and validating environment, which will help to decrease the power struggles that are often inherent in work with adolescents with disordered eating. The practitioner will focus the adolescent on replacing dangerous behaviors with healthier choices so that she can develop a life that minimizes the ongoing crises and struggles that she currently experiences, as can be seen in the vignette below:

Jenni, sixteen years old, was referred for DBT by her previous practitioner after the practitioner became aware that, in addition to her disordered eating, Jenni was getting increasingly angry and aggressive with her parents when they tried to monitor or supervise her eating or other behaviors. She was also stealing from the home and outside of it and lying to her parents. Her parents were concerned about Jenni's angry responses whenever they addressed her eating, and they were frustrated by having to lock up their valuables in their own home. Her parents worry that the situation at home is increasingly out of control. The previous practitioner felt uncomfortable managing Jenni's anger and increasingly disordered eating and didn't feel she had expertise in these areas. For the past six months, Jenni's pattern has included binge eating when upset, followed by guilt and purging, followed by shame. She does not like to eat in front of others, and her parents have become concerned about her poor nutrition. Her body mass index indicates she is slightly overweight, and her medical condition is stable, according to her pediatrician. She has several friends, and none of them know about her eating issues. Jenni's parents continue to worry about her health, and they are beginning to give up hope that any of these behaviors can change. Jenni does not want to discuss her eating in therapy and prefers to talk about the conflict between her and her parents.

DBT for adolescents with disordered eating is a multidisciplinary team effort. In addition to the individual practitioner and skills group leader, the team includes a pediatrician to monitor ongoing health, a nutritionist to teach healthy eating skills, and a parent therapist/coach to help the parents lessen their own reactivity and decrease behaviors that may trigger emotional dysregulation in their adolescent. The DBT practitioner focuses on engaging the adolescent while always assessing health concerns and physical safety.

Theoretical Dialectics

The practitioner who works with an adolescent who has disordered eating will balance the goal of healthy eating with the acceptance that the adolescent is doing the best she can, given the pain she feels and the emotional chaos she experiences. Some of these adolescents may hide their emotions, while trying to take care of their problems on their own. It sometimes comes as a surprise to parents and others when seemingly controlled adolescents become upset or otherwise begin to outwardly express their emotions. Other parents are surprised to discover their adolescent is vomiting in the bathroom following meals. The DBT practitioner helps the adolescent and her family balance new understandings of how the adolescent feels with the hope that change is possible.

The practitioner working with adolescents who have disordered eating will face a number of inherent dialectics. These dialectics will challenge the practitioner and the adolescent as they seek a synthesis that the adolescent will be able to accept.

Health and Safety and Disordered Eating

One inherent dialectic is balancing a focus on safety and health with an understanding that the adolescent may not yet be willing or have the skills necessary to give up unhealthy eating. The practitioner asks the adolescent to commit to abstaining from disordered eating at the same time that the practitioner recognizes that the adolescent has found that this behavior has worked in some ways to manage emotions and she may have a hard time making this commitment. The practitioner may also recognize and accept that, once a commitment is made, the adolescent may lapse and the commitment may weaken at times. The practitioner looks for ways to link disordered eating with concerns that are important to the adolescent so that they can work together to regain a healthy approach to eating. The synthesis of this dialectic is that the DBT practitioner will always work toward behavior change while accepting that the adolescent satisfies emotional needs through the disordered eating behavior and is ambivalent, unwilling, or unable to change it at the present time.

Competency and Limitations

Adolescents who have disordered eating may appear quite competent to those around them. They may do well academically, be athletic, and have friends. They may have high expectations of themselves and have a difficult time when they are not able to live up to their exceptionally high goals. Their black-and-white thinking makes it hard for them to accept less than what they think they are capable of doing; and, because they may not have had many experiences with failure, they may not have learned how to manage a lack of success. At the same time, they do not have the ability or the skills to manage intense emotions effectively, resulting in a great deal of shame or guilt, or the feeling that they have failed. At these times, they are not acting competently and are so overwhelmed that they are not able to complete tasks that have appeared so easy for them in the past. They are, therefore, unlikely to reach out for help. The dialectic here is one of competency in some areas (such as academics, social life, or athletics) and a lack of competency in others (such as emotion regulation). The synthesis of this dialectic is to help the adolescent and her parents recognize and accept areas of both competency and limitations. A validating DBT practitioner will help the adolescent recognize that accepting help from others can be a strength and is not a sign of failure. The adolescent and the practitioner accept that the adolescent can feel competent in some areas while other areas of her life provide challenges.

Rigid Adherence to and Complete Disregard of Eating "Rules"

An adolescent who perceives a loss of control in eating or who is unable to follow her own eating rules may exhibit extreme responses of either bingeing or restricting as a way to self-regulate. The synthesis of this dialectic of either rigidly following eating "rules" or completely disregarding them is balanced, effective eating and effective emotional management, which will include these elements:

- being aware of emotional needs and healthy responses to those needs

- recognizing the feelings of hunger and fullness

- eating when hungry

- not eating when full

- recognizing that there are times for "fun foods" and that ingesting these foods within an overall balanced eating routine does not signal the onset of binge eating

- being aware that overeating is common in certain situations (holidays, parties, special occasions, and so on) and does not signify a complete loss of balanced eating

No Eating Routine and Rigid Eating Routine

Other adolescents, at times, may not have any eating routine at all and at other times may exhibit rigid, rule-driven eating behaviors (Wisniewski & Kelly, 2003). They may binge, diet, or restrict, and do so based on their emotional triggers rather than their nutritional needs. Their disrupted eating cycle interferes with cognitive function, which in turn impacts emotion regulation (see diagram below). This results in more disordered eating and further dysregulation. The synthesis of this dialectic is the development of a sound eating plan that allows for pleasure in eating without guilt or shame.

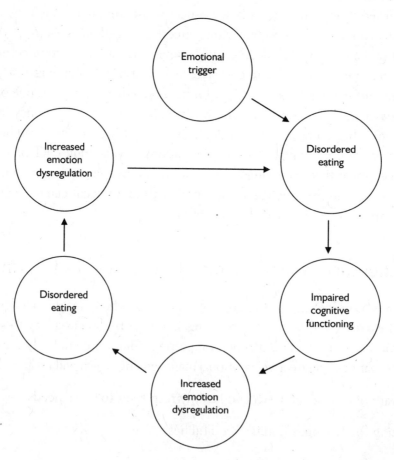

The practitioner for such a client is often faced with helping an adolescent who feels like a failure if she is not perfect to accept her imperfections. Helping the adolescent to accept both black and white in order to develop dialectical thinking is a major focus of the overall treatment.

Case Conceptualization and Goal Setting

DBT views disordered eating as behavior that adolescents developed to help themselves feel better when overwhelmed with emotions that they do not understand and do not know how to manage effectively. Linehan's biosocial theory (1993a) proposes that adolescents whose internal experiences and intense emotions may have been denied, dismissed, or trivialized develop effective yet problematic ways to manage emotions. It is hypothesized that in addition to this *emotional* vulnerability, some adolescents may have a *nutrition-related* vulnerability that impacts the ability to know when one is hungry or full and which may lead to or be the result of disordered eating (Wisniewski & Kelly, 2003). Practitioners will need to communicate an understanding of the adolescent's experience in order to develop a treatment alliance.

The relationship between emotion dysregulation and binge eating can be seen in the diagram below.

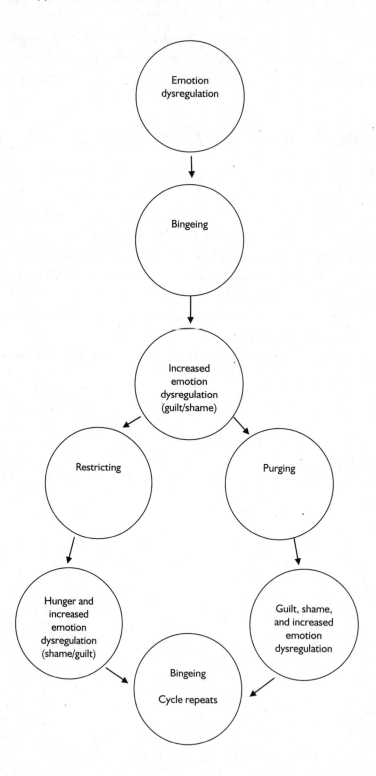

The DBT practitioner understands, and can increase sensitivity to, the behavior of the adolescent by assessing both the positive and negative impact of disordered eating behaviors. See the charts below:

Bingeing Behaviors

Behavior	Positive Impact	Negative Impact
Bingeing	• feelings of relief, escape from painful thoughts and feelings • feelings of being soothed and comforted by the pleasure of eating the food	• problems at home; parents constantly focused on what is being eaten • health problems • fear of gaining weight • not feeling well and not being able to focus on school work. • shame and guilt
Abstinence from bingeing	• fewer health problems • fewer problems with parents • feeling better and having greater ability to focus	• facing problems and difficulties without being able to soothe and comfort herself • emotional pain

Purging Behaviors

Behavior	Positive Impact	Negative Impact
Purging	• feelings of relief, escape from painful or uncomfortable thoughts and emotions • perception that she will not gain weight	• problems at home; parents constantly focused on what is being eaten • health problems • feeling unwell and being unable to focus on school work • shame and guilt
Abstinence from purging	• fewer health problems • fewer problems with parents • feeling better and having greater ability to focus	• facing problems and difficulties without being able to soothe and comfort herself • fear of gaining weight • not feeling good about herself

Validation and Acceptance

The practitioner provides validation for the adolescent by accepting the adolescent's feelings and experiences. The practitioner will acknowledge that the adolescent may experience emotions and thoughts such as:

- anger at everyone for being so focused on food

- not feeling or wanting to acknowledge that she has such a big problem

- feeling that her parents are "in her face" and she cannot get them to leave her alone

- wanting to be left alone to manage by herself and feeling that she needs to manage on her own

- feeling inadequate and unable to manage her own emotions and behavior, while also feeling ashamed of admitting this to others

- shame and guilt about her behaviors and not knowing how to manage those emotions without outward displays of anger toward others

- not wanting to address changing her behaviors unless or until others change their behaviors

The practitioner will validate all of this and how it impacts the adolescent's reluctance to change. At the same time, the practitioner will encourage change, avoiding power struggles about it.

Priority Targets and Goal Setting

The practitioner will engage the adolescent around issues and concerns that are important to her while continuing to focus on health and wellness. These issues will be prioritized in the ways we explain below.

The DBT target hierarchy (Linehan, 1993a) is followed. Life-threatening behaviors are always targeted first, including eating behaviors that are imminently life threatening as well as other self-harming behaviors (cutting, suicide attempts, and so on). Behaviors that interfere with therapy are targeted second, with the practitioner collaboratively doing chain analyses and problem solving for not completing logs, not doing homework, or other behavior (such as throwing up in the office bathroom, lying to the practitioner, refusing medical care, refusing to be weighed, and so on) that impacts the ability of the practitioner to provide treatment in a caring and committed manner. Behaviors that interfere with quality of life will then be targeted. In Jenni's case, this will include stealing, bingeing or purging (unless it is life threatening, in which case it becomes the first priority), other behavioral issues that may arise (substance abuse, legal problems, academic issues, and so on), and lack of skillful behavior when dysregulated.

The practitioner will need to give thought to the order in which to address these targets. In Jenni's case, it is possible that her stealing leads to emotion dysregulation, which in turn may lead to disordered eating. Or it may be that emotion dysregulation leads to stealing. Triggers and causes for each behavior will become clear as treatment progresses and chain analyses are performed. The practitioner will strategically choose the order in which targets are addressed within this category with an awareness that problems interact with one another, often in complex and reinforcing ways.

Feedback from medical personnel helps the DBT practitioner to be aware of and focus on the highest-priority behavior. The practitioner will use this feedback to determine how to prioritize treatment targets:

- If the medical practitioner on the team says that the adolescent is physically stable and there are no acute health concerns, the DBT practitioner can proceed by focusing on the goals of the adolescent and will prioritize the symptoms of the disordered eating as quality of life—interfering behaviors.

- If the disordered eating causes life-threatening health concerns such as arrthymia or electrolyte abnormalities, or if there is chronic ipecac or laxative abuse, the practitioner will necessarily prioritize the disordered eating as a life-threatening behavior and may need to facilitate medical intervention or hospitalization (Wisniewski, 2012). The inclusion of a medical practitioner on the team is critical, given these potential medical concerns.

Client Goals

The practitioner will take great care to establish goals collaboratively with the adolescent, focusing on a life worth living (Linehan, 1993a). It is these goals that will allow the treatment to proceed when inevitable challenges arise. The practitioner knows that the client's stated goals will likely be related to the problem eating in one way or another, and will be mindfully aware of times when these connections can be made, as we see in the dialogue below:

Dialogue: Helping the Adolescent Define Goals

Practitioner: Jenni, I wonder what you would like to see change. What could you do differently that would make your life the way you want it to be?

Jenni: That's easy—my parents will back off and let me live my own life.

Practitioner: I wonder what you might do differently that would increase the likelihood of that happening.

Jenni: I guess I won't be stealing their stuff anymore. They really get upset about that.

Practitioner: What else?

Jenni: Well, I think they'll back off more if they think I'm more in control of myself.

Practitioner: You know, I would like to get your commitment to work with me on eating as well. I'd like to figure out how it may or may not be related to the other things going on in your life. Would that be okay?

Jenni: I don't know about that one…I think I have that under control.

Practitioner: Okay, I will note that you don't feel that is important.

The practitioner works on establishing goals that the adolescent will agree to work on, and accepts that her stated goals may not initially include changes in eating behaviors. In Jenni's case, increasing her self-control when she is dysregulated will initially be addressed by talking about stealing and her anger. The practitioner will link this to eating at every opportunity. Treatment will highlight for the adolescent the role that balanced eating plays in emotion regulation (we all have had the experience of being more irritable when hungry) and will attempt to engage her around changing the ways that she manages emotions as the treatment progresses. The practitioner uses pros and cons (Linehan, 1993a) to help the adolescent assess the consequences of her behavioral choices, and links current behaviors with their likely outcome, connecting them to the long-term goals of the adolescent.

Practitioner Goals

The practitioner clearly states to the adolescent that the disordered eating is also a focus of the treatment, while not insisting on change unless the behavior is life threatening. The practitioner, nutritionist, and pediatrician will all provide psychoeducation about the consequences of disordered eating. Many adolescents are unaware of the impact of eating on mood and behaviors, and it is important that this information be made explicit. The practitioner works toward the goal of the adolescent eating three meals and two snacks a day with nutritionally balanced food choices overall. This building of structure into eating habits anchors the adolescent in a routine that lessens vulnerability factors and increases emotional control.

The following chart summarizes the common behavioral targets that are the focus of treatment when an adolescent has disordered eating:

Behaviors to Increase	Behaviors to Decrease
• healthy eating routines • nutritionally balanced food intake • awareness of hunger and fullness • use of skills to manage emotion dysregulation	• behaviors used to compensate for eating (excessive exercise, purging, using diuretics) • focus on body weight and shape • use of disordered eating to regulate painful emotions

A Word About Weight Loss

Adolescents frequently add weight loss to their goals for treatment, and this needs to be addressed carefully by the practitioner. Modest weight loss is usually achievable, more likely to result in improved health outcomes, and more likely to be maintained than the extreme weight loss the adolescent may desire and which is encouraged through youth culture. The practitioner will typically support the goal of weight loss if the BMI is in the overweight range, while helping the adolescent change behaviors that will result in a healthy and safe weight, such as appropriate levels of exercise, development of an eating plan rather than a diet, and so on (Wisniewski, Safer, & Chen, 2007). If the BMI is within normal range, the practitioner will support the adolescent in maintaining a healthy weight and a healthy lifestyle.

Gaining Commitment

The practitioner works carefully to obtain commitment from the adolescent for some behavioral change at the outset of treatment, and will ask for a commitment to a change in eating behaviors if they interfere with quality of life. At the same time, the practitioner will accept that the adolescent initially may not be ready to commit to changing eating behaviors and/or may have trouble maintaining such a commitment. The practitioner will continue to use various commitment strategies, and keep returning to them, so as to encourage the adolescent to work, eventually, on healthier eating behaviors as a way to improve her overall quality of life.

Ongoing Assessment Tools and Strategies

DBT treatment with adolescents who have disordered eating issues will use the same assessment tools and strategies as are used in DBT with any adolescent with life-threatening, treatment-interfering, or quality of life–interfering problem behaviors. Because of the medical concerns related to this population, additional assessment tools will be utilized as well.

Daily Logs and Food Logs

In the early stages of treatment or until adherence to a meal plan has been established, the daily log may be supplemented with the food log. A template of the log is below; a downloadable version can be found at www.newharbinger.com/27985.

	Sunday	Monday	Tuesday	Wednesday	Thursday	Friday	Saturday
Breakfast							
Snack							
Lunch							
Snack							
Dinner							
Binge? Y/N							
Purge? Y/N							
Exercise? Describe							

List food eaten

This log is used in the early stages of treatment to track what is eaten and when. And, used in conjunction with the daily log, it reveals how eating or restricting impacts mood. It promotes adherence to a meal plan (eating three times a day and having two snacks or, if a meal includes more food than usual, compensating by eating less at the next meal or by skipping a snack). It also links emotions and skills use to eating, hunger, and fullness, helping the adolescent and the practitioner understand the relationship among emotions, food, and eating. This log will provide useful information for chain analyses and problem solving during therapy. It helps the adolescent remember specific information that might otherwise be forgotten, and, as with any tracking tool, its completion is correlated with behavior change. Not completing the food log is targeted as therapy-interfering behavior.

Once an eating plan has been established and the adolescent is following the plan, the food log can be eliminated and the standard daily log will be modified to include the behaviors being targeted or tracked for the adolescent. Here are some examples of target behaviors:

- urges to binge and bingeing behavior

- urges to vomit and vomiting

- amount of exercise

- use of diuretics

- following meal plans

- any other behavior (such as aggression or illegal activities) that significantly impair the life of the adolescent

Chain Analysis

Chain analysis is used for any target behavior in the food log or daily log (for example, bingeing, restricting, purging, not cooperating with medical assessments, or not following the nutritionist's plan), choosing the highest-priority target to chain in each session.

A chain analysis of Jenni's behaviors might look like this:

I was tired and stressed because I was studying for some exams.

↓

My mother reminded me that I had to eat the breakfast
that the stupid nutritionist she makes me go to said I have to eat.

↓

I thought, *She has no idea what I'm going through.*
She doesn't understand that I have other things on my mind
and I don't want to eat what someone tells me to eat.

↓

I began to feel a tightening in my stomach.

↓

I thought, *I hate myself and I hate my body.*
I can't stand this anymore. I was angry and sad.

↓

I began to eat some chips I had hidden in my room.

↓

I ate the whole bag.

↓

I felt disgusted with myself and ashamed of myself.

↓

I went into the bathroom and threw up.

↓

Then my father came in and talked to me about what I did.
I liked that he was talking to me.

↓

My mother heard me throwing up.
She came upstairs and was very upset with me.

In this chain, a number of issues become clear and several change strategies can be developed. Here are the issues identified:

- Jenni already feels vulnerable because of the exam that she is studying for and that she is very anxious about.

- Jenni is triggered by her mother's reminders about eating.

- Jenni feels that others do not understand what she is going through.

- Jenni uses food to comfort herself and will need to learn healthier distress tolerance techniques.

- Jenni's shame leads her to purge.

- Jenni's father was more comforting after Jenni threw up, which may inadvertently reinforce this behavior.

These issues will be addressed by the various DBT change strategies. See "Change Strategies" below.

Medical Assessments

Ongoing medical assessment is important when working with adolescents who have disordered eating. It is critical that this be established early in the treatment. The data from blood testing, weight monitoring, and other assessment tools will provide important information to the practitioner about behaviors. Many adolescents are averse to being weighed or to knowing their weight, and this exposes adolescents to emotions that are difficult for them. The practitioner will share with the adolescent all feedback from the medical assessments.

Change Strategies

Change strategies will focus on helping the adolescent use skills to manage her overwhelming emotions in healthier ways. There will also be a focus on helping the parents structure the environment to minimize power struggles around food and to reinforce healthier lifestyle changes.

Cognitive Restructuring

The practitioner challenges the adolescent's beliefs about body shape, weight, and self through a variety of techniques:

- using Socratic questioning, such as "What evidence do you have for the thought that thinness equates with success?" or "What are some other variables that make your friends appealing besides their weight?" (These types of questions are designed to challenge the adolescent to arrive at different conclusions.)

- conducting behavioral experiments in which the adolescent eats and does not compensate for eating (for example, by excessive exercising) to assess the impact of this on weight and mood

- recognizing the role of distorted thinking (catastrophizing, predicting the future, and so on) on mood and behavior

- identifying and challenging underlying core beliefs

- replacing black-and-white thinking with continuum and dialectical thinking

- using the adolescent's growth curve, as provided by the medical provider, to track and provide an objective source of evaluating weight, as a way to address cognitive distortions about weight

Exposure

As with many conditions, exposure asks the adolescent to experience an unpleasant emotion while practicing tolerating the emotion until it passes. This is a very effective way to learn a new response to a trigger, and it will be employed when possible in the treatment of disordered eating. Eating with the practitioner or in session is a way to practice exposure. It is important that the practitioner not allow the adolescent to leave the session to vomit after eating to ensure the exposure's therapeutic effectiveness.

Discussing and monitoring weight with the adolescent is also a form of exposure. Adolescents may have the mistaken belief that purging is an effective weight-management technique. As they begin to eat in a more managed way, the weight checks and discussions demonstrate to them that their weight is more likely to remain stable and provides reinforcement for continuing the plan.

Contingency Management Through Structuring the Environment

Family work with adolescents who have disordered eating is essential, because the home is often the scene of aggression, power struggles, and the disordered eating. A practitioner who tries to adopt the dual role of working with both the adolescent and the parents may find it difficult to accept the nondialectic thinking of both the parents and the adolescent and may be pulled into developing plans that calm the parent and dysregulate the adolescent, or vice versa.

A separate parent coach begins work by validating the parents' concerns and anxieties, providing welcome and necessary support to the parents. Understandably, the parents experience their own painful feelings, which also must be addressed:

- fear about the disordered eating and the long-term impact on the health of their adolescent

- fear about the increasingly dangerous behaviors in their home

- confusion about the changes they see in their adolescent

- disappointment and frustration that their home feels so tense and they constantly have to watch everything they say or do

- anger and disappointment that they cannot trust their adolescent and cannot live in a safe environment in which they do not have to lock up their own things

- embarrassment about not being able to control their child and having to use treatment and, at times, hospitalization

When parents feel that someone understands how they feel, they are able to be less angry, less reactive, and less likely to be drawn into power struggles and dangerous situations. This enables them to be more effective in their parenting strategies.

When working with adolescents who have eating disorders, it may be helpful for a separate parent coach to help parents in various ways:

- increase their reliance on the treatment team to assess their daughter's health, in order to lessen their emotional reactivity and their own anxiety

- help the parents focus on priority targets while minimizing their anxiety over less urgent behaviors.

- encourage parents to manage their interactions about food in effective ways

- aid the development of contingency management plans that reinforce healthy decisions and choices and that are less punitive around unhealthy eating

- help the parents to recognize the ways in which they may trigger the adolescent to become angrier and develop plans for responding to escalating anger and danger

Chain Analysis of Family Behaviors

It is sometimes helpful to the parents and the parent coach to chain an incident in the home. In a nonjudgmental and validating environment, the parents may be able to see the ways in which they inadvertently escalated their adolescent's mood and behavior and then are better able to make effective choices and decisions the next time a similar situation arises. Below is an example of a parent chain:

Vulnerability Factors
We always feel like we are "walking on eggshells,"
and we are afraid to say anything.

She had agreed to eat what the nutritionist recommended,
and she has not been following through. This made us angry.

↓

Prompting Event
We found bags of potato chips in her room. We confronted her
and told her that she could not use the Internet, per our contract with her

↓

She became very angry and continued to use the computer and the Internet.

↓

We began to yell at her and she began to yell back.

↓

We became angrier and did not like that we could not control our own daughter.

↓

Thoughts
We thought this was totally unreasonable and that
she should follow our rules. It is still our house. And we are only
trying to follow the advice of the nutritionist.

↓

Behaviors
When she continued to use the computer, we attempted to take it away from her.

↓

Behaviors
She continued to scream at us, telling us that
we did not understand that she needed to use the computer.

↓

Thoughts

We thought she could no longer behave this way, that she was
disrespectful and that we could not let her do anything she
wanted in our house without following any rules.

↓

Physical Sensations

We were breathing heavily, feeling tension in our necks
and butterflies in our stomachs.

↓

Behaviors

We gave up and let her have the computer. We were worried about what
might happen if she became angrier. We left her alone and went into our own room.

↓

Consequences

The next day we were all exhausted. We took all of the snack food out
of her room and reminded her of the rules that she had to follow.

↓

Consequences

We felt very defeated and felt that we could not control her eating
or any other behavior. We did not engage her any further.

↓

She apologized for breaking the rules and asked us to take her somewhere.
We agreed because we were glad that she apologized.

Parent coach response to the chain. The coach would note a number of things about the interaction and point out areas in which a different response from the parents might have led to a different outcome to this chain:

- The parents followed through on their contract in telling their daughter that she could not access the Internet if she had food in certain areas of the house.

- By validating their daughter's concerns about the Internet, they might have de-escalated her emotional reactivity.

- Using mindfulness or other distress-tolerance techniques can be effective in lessening their emotionality when their daughter is not following their rules.

- Slowing down and being mindful would allow parents to think clearly about effective responses that do not escalate the situation further.

In addition, the parent coach will acknowledge that the parents are doing the best they can:

- Their frustration and anxiety is understandable, even if they can acknowledge that their daughter was doing the best she could at the time.

- Despite their frustration, the parents were able to let go and move on when their daughter apologized, which reinforced her apology. And, by moving on, the parents acted effectively.

Parents will be encouraged to find ways to respond to their daughter with wise mind (Linehan 1993b), reduced emotional reactivity, and the ability to walk away when their daughter is not following the rules or being cooperative. They will be reminded that reasonable discussion cannot occur in the midst of emotion dysregulation, whether theirs or their daughter's. The parents and parent coach can work together to develop a more effective behavioral plan with relevant reinforcers for healthy eating and less reinforcement for unhealthy eating.

Skills Training

Because of the complex interaction of interpersonal issues, mood, and the reinforcing nature of disordered eating, all the skills have relevance to adolescents and their parents. Learning alternative ways to manage stress can lessen reliance on disordered eating. Mindfulness skills are particularly useful as adolescents learn to observe and describe body sensations that are associated with hunger and fullness. Adolescents are taught to act on these sensations or not act as appropriate. For example, an adolescent who binges is taught to recognize the feeling of hunger and to eat in response to this feeling until she experiences a sense of fullness, rather than eating out of boredom or for emotion management. For an adolescent who periodically restricts eating, mindfulness of hunger and effective response by eating without judgment is encouraged and reinforced. Practicing mindful eating can occur within skills group. Skills training groups also offer exposure to urges through snack breaks and provide some opportunities for participants to see others whom they respect eat in a healthy way.

Phone Coaching

Phone coaching is used for managing self-harming urges in the moment (desire to restrict, binge, purge, or overexercise), skills generalization (reminders of ways to distract or self-soothe other than eating or exercise), and repair of problems in the therapeutic relationship (such as anger at the practitioner for "making" the adolescent eat or mandating visits to the doctor).

During coaching calls, the practitioner does not reinforce the behaviors they are extinguishing (restricting, purging, and so on) by talking about them; she talks only about skills for restoring adherence to the structured eating schedule. This might take the form of helping the client use a DBT skill, or it may be nutritional problem solving by helping the adolescent consider a food she will eat in exchange for a food she fears, as long as it meets the same nutritional needs. It is therefore critical that practitioners treating clients with disordered eating are fully informed about nutrition and meal planning. Adolescents with disordered eating are frequently very confident in their knowledge about eating and restricting (though this knowledge is not always accurate), and the practitioner will need to stay alert to effectively dispute inaccurate information and convey her professional command of this subject.

Adjunctive Services

Psychoeducation groups for nutrition are a cost-effective way to impart necessary information about the impact of restricting, how the body responds to purging, the effects of starvation on cognition, and other relevant topics. If not provided in a group setting, this information will need to be provided to the adolescent in the treatment.

Hospitalization is sometimes indicated, given the serious medical risks—such as electrolyte imbalances and abnormal cardiac functioning—that can occur when adolescents have disordered eating. Decisions made about hospitalization rely on feedback from medical practitioners about the medical risk of the client. The practitioner always maintains a focus on keeping the adolescent alive first and in treatment second, so that the disordered eating and emotion dysregulation can be effectively treated.

Summary

In this chapter, we talked about the specific ways in which DBT treatment can be applied to adolescents with disordered eating that is related to emotion dysregulation or for which other treatments have not been effective. The basic tenets and skills of DBT are applied to this population with special consideration given to the advice and feedback from medical personnel about the physical health of the adolescent. The connection between disordered eating and emotion regulation forms the basis of the treatment. Teaching healthy ways to manage emotion is a major goal of this work.

CHAPTER 11

Disruptive Behaviors

Many adolescents who come to treatment have several comorbid behavioral issues and diagnoses, including attention-deficit/hyperactivity disorder and learning disabilities that impact impulsivity, judgment, and behavior. Practitioners may work with adolescents previously diagnosed with oppositional defiant disorder, conduct disorder, or intermittent explosive disorder. An adolescent may be referred or brought into treatment because of aggressive or threatening behaviors, risk taking that leads to dangerous outcomes, stealing, running away, or refusal to attend school. Parents may describe "rages," hitting, blocking the parents' path out of a room, or other "out of control" behaviors. Behaviors may lead to police involvement, and parents may fear that they, or another member of the family, will be physically injured. The practitioner may find an adolescent who does not want to be there, who thinks that he is "just fine the way he is," who resents anyone who will try to change him, who may be "uncooperative" in the session, or who may be verbally threatening to the practitioner.

The DBT framework provides a nonjudgmental understanding of the behaviors of these adolescents, and the DBT practitioner will remain accepting and nonjudgmental while observing limits and safety for himself and his client.

The adolescent's biologically based predisposition to emotion dysregulation might lead to behavioral dyscontrol and a vicious cycle in which the risky behaviors lead to additional dysregulation and the behaviors continue, as can be seen in the diagram below:

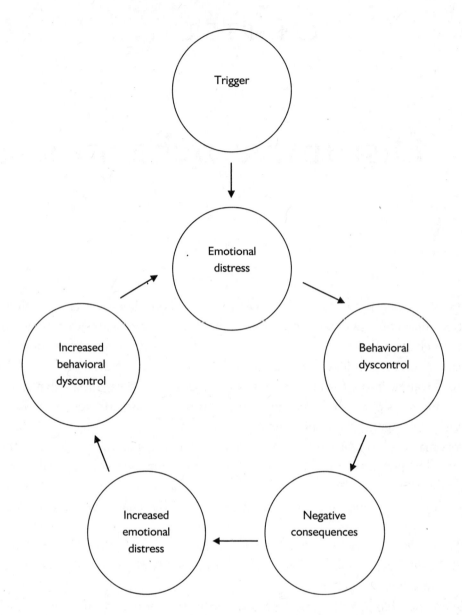

The adolescent will learn in DBT that he can make decisions about using effective and less dangerous behaviors that will help him meet whatever goals he may have (including getting out of therapy or getting his parents or other authority figures to leave him alone). While the adolescent may see no way out of this cycle of problems, he may also not recognize that his life can improve if his behavior does.

Some adolescents might also participate in risk taking or disruptive behaviors as a way to feel more energized and connected to the world. Some adolescents seek a higher level of stimulation in general, and because their behaviors are stimulating, they will want to do them more often. In this case, the stimulation reinforces the risk-taking behavior. The cycle for these adolescents is illustrated in the diagram below:

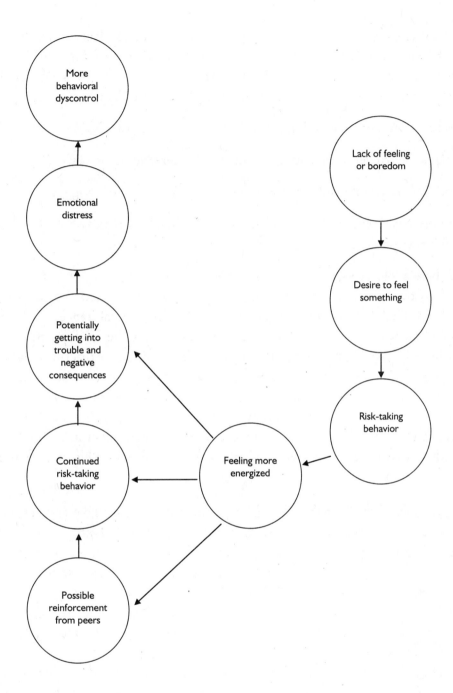

The practitioner maintains awareness that behavioral patterns labeled as oppositional, conduct disordered, or disruptive are the result of a complex combination of biological, environmental, and emotional vulnerabilities, including impulsivity, learning, and processing issues. Adolescents with these behaviors are not "bad"; they are doing the best they can with what they have at the moment *and* will need to learn and apply skills to many areas of their lives in order to change the self-destructive cycle of behavioral dyscontrol.

DBT was developed initially to target impulsive behavior (suicidality) and, not surprisingly, initial research indicates that skills training is effective with incarcerated male and female adolescents (Shelton, Kesten, Zhang, & Trestman, 2011; Trupin, Stewart, Beach, & Boesky, 2002). DBT for these and other adolescents who have disruptive behavior problems serves several purposes:

- helps to lessen the vulnerabilities that lead to emotional distress

- identifies the triggers and reinforcers for the problematic behaviors

- provides skills for safe and less disruptive management of these triggers

- reinforces healthier responses to triggers or emotional distress by both the adolescent and the environment

Many of these adolescents have ended previous therapies without positive results and may be mistrustful of any therapeutic experience (and most adults). They are used to being blamed and not being understood. The DBT validating, nonjudgmental, and dialectical stances will be necessary to gain any commitment to treatment. The focus of treatment for the DBT practitioner seeing an adolescent whose behavioral problems stem from intense emotional reactions and/or from the desire to experience more emotional intensity will be on making sure that the adolescent learns how to access and manage his emotions safely, keeping him engaged in treatment, helping him understand how his choices lead to sometimes unintended consequences, and helping him make behavioral changes that will have a positive impact on his life. We will illustrate how DBT can help adolescents who have disruptive behaviors by discussing Andre, who is introduced in the vignette below:

> Andre is a thirteen-year-old eighth grade student at the public middle school. He had problems in day care with kicking and biting when frustrated; and he was diagnosed with ADHD in first grade and a mild receptive and expressive language disability in third grade. He also has a history of difficulty with teachers and impulsive aggression, and was diagnosed with oppositional defiant disorder in fifth grade.
>
> After numerous unsuccessful therapies, he comes to DBT because he was suspended from school for throwing a chair at a boy who took his seat in a class, and then threatening to kill the teacher who intervened.
>
> Kids at school do not want to be around him, and he has conflicts with family members, authority figures, and peers. His parents are concerned that he is beginning to hang around some older kids from the high school who smoke and skip school, and they worry that he may pick up these behaviors. Andre makes it clear to the practitioner in a somewhat aggressive manner that he does not want or need to be in treatment, and will not cooperate.

Theoretical Dialectics

The DBT practitioner will balance validation of this client's experiences (which does *not* include accepting his behaviors as effective) while encouraging behavioral control during sessions. The practitioner must accept that the client is doing the best he can, while also making it clear that some of his behaviors are not effective in the long run and will need to change if he wants his life to improve. The differentiation, for the practitioner, between accepting the client and his emotional experiences and *not* validating his behaviors must be made over and over again. Remaining nonjudgmental in this dialectic will challenge the practitioner, the client, and the family.

A central paradox is the adolescent's typical experience of discomfort (boredom or emotional distress) and his desire to end that experience as quickly as possible, which does not allow for the development of skills to manage the emotion effectively. The dialectic is that the adolescent develop skills to tolerate the discomfort *and* also use skills strategically, when necessary to manage or end the discomfort effectively and skillfully.

Another dialectic is that adolescents who exhibit disruptive behaviors often feel as though they are seen as either "bad" on the one hand or "stupid" on the other. They frequently report that, seeing no other options, they would rather appear "bad" than "stupid." Their aggressive responses sometimes occur when they do not understand what is being asked of them and they do not want others to find this out. The aggression serves as a distraction for others and allows the adolescent to deny his level of confusion. The synthesis of this dialectic is that the adolescent develop skills to tolerate the discomfort *and* also use skills strategically, when necessary, to manage or end the discomfort effectively and skillfully.

Often parents are concerned with the level of "disrespect" that the adolescent shows toward the parents, or their belief that he "won't listen." This is a dialectic for the practitioner as well as he tries to balance validating and not minimizing the very real concerns and feelings of the parents with the importance of prioritizing and treating behaviors that may be life threatening, or get in the way of effective treatment.

Case Conceptualization and Goal Setting

Behavioral problems can be conceptualized as problems associated with mood dysregulation, limited ability to tolerate distress, and impulsivity (Daughters, Sargeant, Bornovalova, Gratz, & Lejuez, 2008). These problems may be exacerbated by an environment that is chronically invalidating. In Andre's case, the practitioner recognizes that he has a biological predisposition toward impulsivity and difficulty with language skills. It is understandable that these two factors combine to make it likely that Andre will respond with impulsive physical aggression when he is overwhelmed emotionally, unable to fully process what is being asked of him or to effectively relate his experiences, needs, or feelings to others. The impulsive and aggressive responses have likely been reinforced because the focus shifts to his behaviors rather than the initial request; and as a result,

Andre has not learned how to manage these interactions and experiences in a more functional way. The practitioner recognizes that Andre is overwhelmed, possibly frightened, highly reactive, and looking for relief; and he recognizes too that Andre has probably felt and been misunderstood by others, and perhaps does not understand himself.

Positive and Negative Impact of Behaviors

The practitioner will work with Andre on understanding both the positive and negative impact of aggressive behaviors and using more skillful behaviors. The impact of these behaviors can be seen in the chart below:

Behavior	Positive Impact	Negative Impact
Aggressive/threatening behaviors	• feels in control • feels powerful • experiences feelings • gets others to leave him alone and let him do what he wants • is included by some kids who like the behaviors	• faces possible legal problems • experiences loss of trust and freedom • experiences loss of some friends and activities • lives with parents who feel disappointed or angry • feels shame and guilt
Skillful behaviors	• is able to have more friends and activities • enjoys more freedoms • has less difficulties in school and at home	• feels less stimulated and energized • feels less satisfied in the short term

Validation and Acceptance

The practitioner needs to be especially genuine in validating these mistrustful adolescents and must be careful to not validate what might be dangerous or otherwise lead to further problems. The practitioner will be sensitive to, and will validate, these feelings and experiences of the adolescent:

• He is doing the best he can, even though his behaviors get him in trouble.

• He feels as if nobody understands him and may be tired of explaining himself to others.

- He may feel some shame and guilt about his behaviors, even if this may be difficult to admit.

- He does not want to be in therapy, resents that he has been told he has to go, and may see participating in therapy as giving in to authority, which has misunderstood and mistreated him in the past.

- He wants people to leave him alone and let him do what he wants to do.

- He will not want to "earn" trust or privileges that he feels entitled to.

The practitioner will skillfully focus on change, while validating that the adolescent's behavior makes sense given his lack of skills and other factors:

Dialogue: Early Validation

Practitioner: Andre, how did you feel about coming here today?

Andre: (sarcastically) Are you kidding me? I've had it with all these bitches trying to tell me what to do.

Practitioner: You're being pushed around a lot? By whom?

Andre: My teachers, my parents, kids at school...

Practitioner: Wow, no wonder you're feeling so upset.

Andre: Yeah, and I'm sure you're going to tell me the same things I've heard before. I'm sick of it.

Practitioner: I see what you mean; I would feel the same way if I'd been through all you've been through.

Andre: Nobody really gets it.

Practitioner: Since you're here, would you be willing to help me understand what's been going on? I'll let you know what I'm thinking as we talk so you'll know whether I'm like all the others.

Andre: Well, what do you want to know?

In this dialogue, the practitioner validates the suspicion and anger Andre feels about being taken to treatment. He also engages him in a collaborative, rather than an authoritative, approach.

Priority Targets and Goal Setting

The initial phase of treatment with adolescents like Andre focuses on collaboratively understanding the function of their behaviors and establishing a commitment to change. It is essential that the practitioner work on goals that are meaningful to the adolescent at every stage of treatment. A relentless display of respect and deference to the adolescent is consistently effective in engaging "resistant" and angry adolescents in the treatment process.

In every session, the practitioner will continue to adhere to the priority targets of DBT and will focus on life-threatening behavior first, therapy-interfering behavior second, and quality of life–interfering behavior third. If Andre does not bring his daily log, misses a session, or otherwise behaves in a way that interferes with the treatment, the practitioner will use behavior chains and problem-solving techniques—always done collaboratively, respectfully, and nonpunitively—to resolve these issues so the therapy can be effective and productive. In the above vignette, Andre is not exhibiting life-threatening behaviors, and the anger outbursts and school suspension will be addressed after any issues that impact the treatment. The impulsive and emotional threat to kill the teacher would be considered a quality of life–interfering behavior because it does not cause any physical harm to Andre himself. However, if this threatening behavior leads to dangerous results for Andre, the practitioner might reassess the priority of this behavior. These behaviors can be seen in the chart below:

Priority	Specific Behaviors
Life-threatening behaviors	None known at this time
Treatment-interfering behaviors	Not committing to treatment
	Being verbally aggressive with the practitioner
	Not completing treatment expectations
Quality of life–interfering behaviors	Skipping school, school suspension
	Being aggressive toward others
	Threatening others
	Possibly using substances
	Having conflicts with parents
	Behaving impulsively

Client's Goals

The practitioner will spend the time necessary to delineate positive goals of treatment that are relevant to the adolescent and that can be addressed using therapeutic techniques. Goals stated by the adolescent, such as "I want people to stop bugging me" will be accepted by the practitioner, and together he and the client will work on what behavior changes will have to be made so that others will not "bug" him. The practitioner will help the adolescent delineate the positive outcomes of his goal ("I won't get in trouble anymore") and target these behavioral outcomes as goals for the adolescent.

When the practitioner meets with Andre, he will collaboratively establish goals that Andre is willing to work on. These goals might include:

- getting parents, teachers, and other kids to leave him alone

- being able to go out with the friends he chooses and do what he wants

- not going to a school where he feels misunderstood

Practitioner's Goals

The practitioner will help Andre link his goals with the larger goals of behaving in safer and more skillful ways. Doing so will lead to these results for Andre:

- fewer incidents of aggression and threatening others

- managing conflicts with parents and teachers more effectively using interpersonal effectiveness skills

- managing painful emotions through distress tolerance rather than impulsive and aggressive behaviors

- maintaining consistent attendance at school so that Andre can learn to manage school and his behavior there effectively

Practitioners who work with adolescents who have disruptive behaviors need to be mindful of the emotional distress that may drive this behavior and remain nonjudgmental and accepting as goals are established and treatment progresses. The practitioner will work collaboratively to validate and integrate the goals of the adolescent into the treatment. He will also look for opportunities to address treatment-interfering and quality of life—interfering behaviors that the adolescent, at first, might not recognize as ones that negatively impact his life.

Gaining Commitment

The practitioner will spend time addressing and validating concerns and complaints about previous unsuccessful treatment attempts, in the service of gaining a commitment to this treatment. The practitioner will also present opportunities for the adolescent to "choose" to engage in DBT, while also emphasizing some of the negative consequences if he chooses not to participate. He will demonstrate his willingness to approach the work in a collaborative way, and ask the adolescent to give the treatment a chance by focusing on the goals that have been jointly developed for a specified period of time. The practitioner will link the goals of the adolescent to the use of skills in other situations as a way to gain commitment to changing priority targets. He will also return to the importance of commitment throughout the treatment as necessary.

Ongoing Assessment Tools and Strategies

Assessing adolescents whose behaviors are impulsive, disruptive, high risk, or dangerous to others is essential to understanding the function of the behavior and the consequences that may be maintaining those behaviors. These adolescents are often seen by others as "problematic" or simply "difficult," and they rarely accept responsibility for their behaviors. Others might assume that they "should just learn how to behave"; the practitioner will need to overcome preliminary assumptions to gain enough understanding and insight to bring about change in those behaviors.

Daily Log

The daily log will be modified to include behaviors that interfere with the client's functioning. Categories to consider tracking are anger outbursts, fighting, lying, and engaging in high-risk behaviors (speeding, stealing, graffiti, gang activity, and so on). The daily log provides the practitioner and the adolescent with essential information for understanding behaviors. If the adolescent does not complete the daily log, as is usually the case (at least initially), the practitioner patiently, collaboratively, and gently completes it together with the client, and shapes this behavior over time.

Chain Analysis

Adolescents will often say that they "don't know" what caused a certain behavior, may blame others for the behavior ("he made me mad"), or believe that their behaviors just occur, without devoting much insight into what may have caused them. The adolescent's lack of insight and reticence to accept responsibility for the behavior initially makes it very difficult to complete the chain analysis. The adolescent will resist attempts to discuss behaviors that he would rather forget about and that might cause him to feel shame or guilt or that might reactivate his anger. Despite the difficult task this creates for the practitioner, the process of working on the chain and the insights learned from it make it an essential tool in understanding the behaviors of the adolescent and helping him to change those behaviors that cause negative consequences for him.

Andre's initial understanding of his behaviors might look something like this:

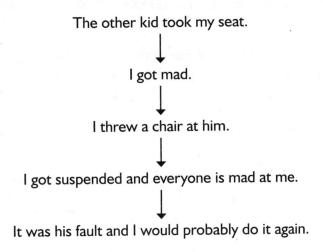

A practitioner will use validation to understand the dilemmas and feelings that Andre is experiencing and accept his explanations, even as he tries to get to the details of what Andre was thinking and feeling (emotionally and in his body), the specifics of his behavior, and the details of the consequences that he experienced.

A more detailed chain might look like this:

I hate school. The kids hate me and make fun of me.

↓

This kid took my seat.

↓

I thought, *He can't disrespect me like that. Who does he think he is?*

↓

I could feel myself getting mad; my face got red,
my heart was pounding, and I made my hands into fists.

↓

I thought, *I can't let someone treat me like that. I'm not weak.*

↓

I thought, *I'll show him that he can't mess with me.*
That will teach all the kids to leave me alone.

↓

I really wanted to hit someone.

↓

I saw an empty chair and just picked it up and threw it.

↓

When the teacher tried to help the other kid,
I got even madder and said I would kill her.

↓

I got suspended, which is great.
I can hang with some of my friends and watch TV.

↓

My parents are mad at me and tell me
that they don't know what to do with me.

↓

I thought, *It doesn't matter. Nothing will get better anyway.*

Some issues become clear from looking at this chain:

- Andre is already vulnerable when he goes to school because he does not feel comfortable or that he fits in with the other kids. This would mean that he would be more susceptible to getting angry or out of control.

- He thinks that not responding is a show of weakness, and he feels as if he needs to show some strength to his peers.

- He did not know how to respond to his desire to hit someone and did not have alternative skills available to him.

- The suspension, meant to be an aversive consequence, is actually reinforcing because it takes him out of the school, which he doesn't like, and allows him to stay home and do what he does like. This consequence would serve to maintain, rather than extinguish, his behavior.

- He feels hopeless about his future and himself.

Practitioners will be aware of the difficulties of engaging adolescents who have disruptive behaviors and may have to be particularly creative and sensitive in responding to the requests and needs expressed by the adolescent. It is important for the practitioner to be aware of the mistrust these adolescents have for authority figures and always work in a way that emphasizes collaboration and mutual respect.

Change Strategies

When disruptive behaviors are the major focus of treatment, the change strategy used continually is contingency management, to strengthen safer and less aggressive behaviors and to help those behaviors generalize to many areas of the adolescent's life. The adolescent will also need to learn new skills to manage his frustration, disappointment, and anger so that he does not create even more problems by his responses to these emotions.

Contingency Management Through Structuring the Environment

Adolescents who have disruptive behavior problems are often effective at getting the environment to meet their needs through their aggression and threats. Parents and teachers may avoid placing demands on an adolescent or may "give in" rather than confront an already angry adolescent whose behavior can become more dangerous. It is thus important for the practitioner or parent coach to teach the individuals in the adolescent's environment to be aware of several things:

- The adolescent *can* learn new ways to manage the complicated interplay of biology, learning, and emotional factors that leads to aggressive or unskilled (rather than "bad" or "oppositional") behaviors.

- It is more effective for promoting change to use reinforcement of adaptive behaviors rather than punishment of disruptive behaviors.

- It is important to notice when responses to behaviors may inadvertently reinforce rather than punish them.

- It is important to notice those instances when the adolescent uses skillful means of getting his needs met and to try to be particularly responsive to healthy requests (rather than ignore them).

- Developing a calming environment minimizes the triggers to the adolescent's emotional system.

- It is important to help the adolescent engage in activities that build his sense of competency and self-esteem.

The practitioner may serve as a consultant to the environment with the adolescent's knowledge or permission, with the goal of eventually teaching the adolescent to do this for himself. The practitioner is aware that the adolescent will need to effectively act as his own advocate, will model this initially, and will then gradually encourage the adolescent to apply the skills he is learning directly to people at school, at home, and in the community.

Practitioners who work with parents of adolescents who have disruptive behavior issues must also be validating of the difficult circumstances parents face. They are often quite confused about these behaviors, feel blamed by others, and may be embarrassed when out-of-control behaviors result in calls to the police. Parents find it hard to develop effective consequences for behaviors and are understandably anxious about the risks their adolescents are taking. They will respond to a practitioner who understands these issues, who will not push them to respond in ways that are uncomfortable, and who can validate their fears and concerns.

Skills Training

Many of the behavioral and temperament traits of adolescents with disruptive behavior are similar to those of adults who meet criteria for borderline personality disorder. Both groups typically have difficulties with interpersonal interactions, mood management, impulsivity, and responding effectively in a crisis. All of the DBT skills are relevant to youth who have disruptive behavior.

Behavioral contingencies can be very effective within the skills training modality to shape behaviors for participation in the program, homework completion, and bringing materials to group.

Given the high rate of language and reading disorders present among youth with these behaviors, the practitioner might consider using understandable and relevant vocabulary, frequent demonstration, and the addition of pictures to the skills training handouts when necessary.

Behavioral Principles

Adolescents often respond well to the "lesson in psychology" that behaviorism skills offer. They are asked to think about the kinds of changes they'd like to see in others and encouraged to try to shape the behaviors of teachers, parents, and friends so that the skills are more meaningful to them. They also begin to understand the ways their own behaviors have been shaped over time, and are taught to reward themselves for working toward the changes that are important to them.

A note on anger management. Punching a pillow or punching bag when upset, as is widely recommended by some for anger, is deliberately not recommended. These behaviors reinforce a response that involves aggression when upset and often contributes to an increase, rather than a decrease, in aggression. Given the impulsive nature of these symptoms, practitioners might recommend nonviolent substitutes (running, doing push-ups or sit-ups to exhaustion, and so on) that allow for the de-escalation of aggression without the link to punching or other aggressive behaviors.

Mindfulness

Mindfulness teaches participants to simply notice what is happening, without judging it and without doing anything about it right away; this leads to opportunities for cognitive restructuring and delayed responding. Mindfulness also serves as a competing response or "positive opposite" to the impulsivity so prevalent in these behaviors. Skills trainers need to focus on teaching mindfulness experientially to be effective with the learning styles of these adolescents.

Interpersonal Effectiveness

Because emotional intensity increases the likelihood of an angry or aggressive response, interpersonal effectiveness skills are necessary for creating more collaborative interactions. The practitioner uses these skills directly with the adolescent, modeling the skills and pointing out when the use of the skills has helped avert a less than productive response. Many adolescents may have had few, if any, collaborative, respectful, nonjudgmental interactions with an authority figure, and it is necessary to teach by example and modeling whenever possible, providing for a new learning experience.

Emotion Regulation

The information that comes from behavior chains and the story of emotions is vital for helping adolescents understand how their emotions develop and where and how they can make changes in the way they manage their anger, frustration, embarrassment, shame, and other distressing emotions. Behavior chains and stories of emotion are taught and reviewed without judgment, and with heavy doses of validation. Practitioners are encouraged to use stories from their own lives to make the material relevant, personal, and interesting.

Acting opposite, specifically being kind and using a half smile (Linehan, 1993b) with those who provoke anger, is particularly effective despite being difficult to teach. Modeling opposite action over and over again within the treatment when the adolescent is hostile and threatening (by validating, setting limits, responding with kindness) is very effective at de-escalating intensity. Practitioners must deliberately model the skills, which legitimizes them and allows the adolescent to learn from personal experience.

Exercise is strongly encouraged for adolescents in DBT treatment and for those with anger-management issues. It helps to lessen vulnerability to negative emotions, and has particular relevance for adolescents who have impulsive and disruptive behaviors. Being part of an organized team or pursuing a fitness goal teaches collaboration, mood management, and focus on goals. With acknowledgment that adolescents with disruptive behavior problems may be suspicious of engaging in certain activities, exposure to yoga in the skills group as a mindfulness activity or participation in a yoga class may be effective in helping adolescents manage their mood more skillfully.

Distress Tolerance

Adolescents have a tendency to escalate and make things worse for themselves when they feel vulnerable, so a high priority with adolescents who "act out" is to teach them skills that keep the problem from getting worse (Linehan, 1993a). Helping the adolescent find distracting or soothing activities allows the intensity of the moment to pass and disengages the adolescent from responding in an increasingly aggressive manner, or helps the adolescent remove himself from a difficult interaction. Urge surfing, or allowing aggressive urges to come and go without acting on them, is another effective technique for building in a delayed response.

The distress tolerance skill of contributing (Linehan, 1993b) has particular relevance. Encouraging an adolescent, especially one who has always been told that he does nothing "right," to participate in an activity that develops competency and results in positive feedback is invaluable for helping him develop positive self-regard. Adolescents with very serious behavior histories have responded tenderly, responsibly, and effectively in volunteer environments with animals, children, the elderly, or peers with special needs, providing a situation in which everyone benefits.

Additional Skills

Three additional skills—the CALM skill, lovingkindness meditation, and progressive muscle relaxation—help adolescents develop tools for dealing with challenging situations. Each can be taught in a skills group setting or in individual therapy.

CALM. This strategy, which focuses on in-group behavior, is part of a modified DBT program for adolescents with oppositional defiant features (Nelson-Gray et al., 2006). It consists of four skills

Connecting: responding to others and interacting warmly, which cultivates connections with others in the group

Attending: using body language and eye contact that indicates interest in others

Listening: not interrupting, listening to the person who is speaking

Manners: acting courteously in group

Lovingkindness meditation. This strategy is a combined mindfulness and opposite action technique that encourages participants to show kindness and understanding to themselves and others (Salzberg, 2002). This skill increases empathy for self and others and may lead to more effective interactions with both peers and authority figures.

Progressive muscle relaxation. This is another opposite action technique. As such, progressive muscle relaxation asks adolescents to systematically relax their bodies to interrupt the fight-or-flight response common in angry reactions (Nickel et al., 2005).

Cognitive Restructuring

Adolescents with aggressive and disruptive responses have almost always had a long history of conflict with others; they also often have particular views of themselves and the world, like the belief that they are victims, a mistrust of authority, and a need to be on the offensive. They typically misperceive threat, seeing attacks where none exist. Or they may respond to a perceived problem in a peer relationship with an aggression that, in driving others away, creates a self-fulfilling prophecy. The practitioner patiently challenges these beliefs and misperceptions through the use of behavior chains and the story of emotions. Many adolescents have been mistreated by people in positions of authority, and it is important to validate that experience while working toward a measured and rational response to interactions with authority. The practitioner continues to teach through example in the therapeutic relationship itself.

Exposure

The goal of this change procedure is to have the adolescent expose himself to the experience he fears or avoids and to find skillful alternatives. This exposure could take a number of forms: tolerating an unfair accusation and coming up with a strategic response rather than exploding in rage; tolerating the feeling of boredom and finding a method for managing it that is not self-destructive; or tolerating the feeling associated with lack of competence and skill, and learning to develop those skills rather than deflecting the focus onto his disruptive behaviors.

The adolescent learns to tolerate and manage unpleasant emotions and urges by experiencing them, first in the therapy session and later in the natural environment, and not resorting to the behaviors that have caused problems in that environment and brought him to treatment. This process must be carefully explained to adolescents in treatment, and all attempts to use exposure should be reinforced and shaped while gently not allowing the adolescent to avoid the exposure or distract the treatment process from it.

As the adolescent learns what triggers his anger or disruptive behaviors, the practitioner helps him find ways to strategically manage some of the triggers through avoidance. For example, an adolescent may be encouraged to advocate for a change in teachers, avoid a certain environment, or otherwise avoid certain triggering situations. However, such avoidance will not always be possible, and skills for managing the anger once triggered will remain a focus of treatment.

Phone Coaching

Phone coaching is traditionally used in DBT with behaviors that are life threatening or to preserve the therapeutic relationship. With disruptive behaviors, phone coaching can be a very effective means for coaching the adolescent through a potentially life-altering interaction. For example, an adolescent calls his practitioner after an argument with his neighbor, who has complained about a party, and has a plan to destroy property to get even with him. The practitioner is able to coach the adolescent through skills that will help him tolerate the anger and desire for revenge until it fades so that he does not make things worse by acting on them. The phone call itself is an attempt by the adolescent to cope effectively, and should be reinforced with support and positive regard by the practitioner. It also serves as a delay tool, and allows the adolescent to think through options and not respond impulsively. When the adolescent phones for coaching, it is a signal that he is connected to the practitioner, buying into the treatment, and making an effort to change, all of which should be encouraged, celebrated, and reinforced.

Summary

Working with adolescents who have disruptive behavioral problems is always a challenge for a practitioner. In this chapter, we presented the ways practitioners can use DBT effectively with these adolescents to reach mutually agreed-upon goals while also maintaining their own limits and expectations. The usefulness of this approach with aggressive and challenging-to-treat youth should not be underestimated. Using DBT to teach, strengthen, and generalize more effective behaviors can help lessen aggression and threatening behaviors with enormous benefit to the adolescent, as well as to families and society as a whole.

PART 4

Practitioners and DBT

CHAPTER 12

Becoming a DBT Practitioner

In this book, we have explained and discussed the principles of DBT practice as they relate to adolescents who have a variety of emotional and behavioral difficulties based on a vulnerability to emotional dysregulation. We have laid out the functions and modalities of comprehensive DBT that have been researched and found to be effective.

All of the modes of DBT (Linehan, 1993a) must be present if the practitioner is "doing comprehensive DBT." The practitioner must, at a minimum, offer these services:

- individual DBT therapy based on priority targets, using daily logs and chain analysis

- a separate skills training component that presents the skills in each of the five modules— mindfulness, distress tolerance, emotion regulation, interpersonal effectiveness, and walking the middle path

- phone coaching so that the adolescent can speak to the practitioner between sessions to share good news, repair issues in the relationship, and, most importantly, receive coaching on how to use skills to avoid unsafe behaviors

- consultation to the environment (including parents) in order to ensure that skills are practiced in the natural environment and that adaptive behaviors are reinforced while less than adaptive behaviors are *not* inadvertently reinforced

The practitioner must also participate in a consultation team that helps her to maintain a dialectical and nonjudgmental stance. The consultation team also helps the practitioner remain mindful of opportunities for structuring the environments (therapeutic and the larger world) to encourage and reinforce adaptive behaviors.

DBT, for those who practice it, is a treatment framework, a way of thinking, and also a set of skills that are as valuable for the practitioner as they are for the client. Skills and principles are often explained to clients and their parents through the practitioner's personal experience with them.

Mindful awareness, thinking dialectically, and maintaining limits and behavioral contingencies are as much a part of the treatment for the practitioner as are the priority targets. DBT practitioners must come to believe in the concepts, apply them to their own lives, and apply them to their clients in a way that is totally natural and genuine.

Being a DBT Practitioner

For a practitioner to implement DBT in her work it requires ongoing learning, practice, and feedback from others. If a practitioner is not prepared to do comprehensive DBT, she can consider beginning to think dialectically, nonjudgmentally, and with validation and acceptance of clients.

Ongoing research is attempting to assess what is or are the most effective aspect(s) of DBT. Skills are being identified as a very important component of DBT and a necessity in bringing about change (C. Swenson & K. Koerner, personal communication, December 2, 2012). We have provided many of the skills throughout this book. To learn more about them, see the Resources section.

Teaching skills can be a part of a practitioner's individual work as well as part of skills training groups. It is also very much a part of individualized parent coaching. Practitioners will have to be well versed and well practiced in DBT skills in order to know when to teach them, how to teach them, how to model them, and how to coach clients to use them. The skills—mindfulness, distress tolerance, emotion regulation, interpersonal effectiveness, and walking the middle path—are invaluable in helping adolescents (and their parents) learn both to regulate their emotions safely without creating more problems and to develop the life they want to have.

If you choose to teach DBT skills or use some of the principles, you may wonder if that makes you a DBT practitioner. A DBT practitioner should be prepared to incorporate the five modalities we listed above into her practice. If you are not able to create a comprehensive DBT model in your practice, then we suggest you describe your work as "DBT informed" or otherwise indicate that you incorporate some DBT practices into your work. Transparency is a very important aspect of DBT, and it is important that you be transparent about what you can and cannot provide to your clients, the limits of your experience and services, and whether or not you are providing comprehensive DBT.

The Importance of Coaching

Coaching is an invaluable modality of DBT and one that causes much concern from practitioners who are just beginning to implement DBT. They worry about the time it takes to provide coaching and the disruption to their nonoffice hours. These concerns are understandable and have to be taken into account when deciding how to develop a practice. Each practitioner has to be able to observe her own limits. When clients in skills groups do not have DBT individual therapists, they miss the opportunity to receive coaching when they are in crisis. Skills group facilitators worry more about those clients who cannot access their individual therapist for coaching when self-harm and/or suicidality are concerns. These issues continue to come up in the authors' consultation teams as we try to provide the safest and most effective services for our clients who do not receive comprehensive DBT. We struggle to provide our clients with the most skills that we can give them while also trying to decide how to provide the most effective and evidence-based services. We have come to recommend having DBT individual therapists best practice for the adolescents who attend DBT skills groups, as the comprehensive package is the most effective set of services we can provide.

Moving Forward

As research continues and more and more practitioners begin to appreciate the structure, philosophy, and effectiveness of DBT, the work will continue to evolve. As is the case of any dialectical framework, "the only constant is change" and change *is* constant. The concepts in this book are presented with awareness and acceptance that while the principles will remain, an ever more effective treatment framework will evolve.

We present the following thoughts about going forward in developing the most effective DBT practice that you can:

- DBT is not just for borderline personality disorder or for individuals with emotion dysregulation. Many adolescents can benefit from the skills training and from work on emotion regulation.

- All parents can benefit from learning the skills through individual instruction, parent coaching, or a parent DBT skills training group. Parents find that the skills enrich their own lives as well as help them parent more effectively. They also benefit greatly from being able to talk honestly and openly to other parents in skills training groups, which helps them feel less isolated or alone.

- Individual adolescent therapists benefit when a separate parent coach is able to work with the parents. This system allows the adolescent's therapist to focus on the relationship with the adolescent while the parent coach is able to focus on the needs of the parents and their parenting strategies. This separation of the roles also enables the parent coach to help the parents observe effective limits without in any way compromising the ongoing relationship between the adolescent and his therapist.

- Research is ongoing about what modalities of DBT may be most effective even when not connected to the other modalities of treatment. This research will be important for practitioners to be aware of as they choose to implement DBT into their practice. It may guide decisions about which modalities will be implemented.

- Mindfulness is an important skill and very important for practitioners to practice themselves. Every consultation team begins with a mindfulness exercise, and practitioners are encouraged to practice on their own. Developing focused and purposeful awareness helps practitioners in their own lives and in their sessions with their clients as well.

- The importance of a consultation team cannot be minimized and is an invaluable modality in DBT. It helps every practitioner become more effective while also receiving the support and validation necessary in doing this very difficult work.

- Practitioners should continually search for the most effective way to work with at-risk and challenging adolescents and their parents. Change for practitioners is sometimes as hard as it is for the clients they treat, and it is also equally necessary. DBT strategies and protocols may seem counterintuitive to what they have previously learned. It requires self-disclosure, awareness of self, and an acceptance that practitioners can also interfere with treatment. Sometimes providing effective treatment means that practitioners may have to make compromises and sacrifices while also continuing to observe their own limits. As is true for clients, the more the skills are practiced, the easier they become. DBT practitioners benefit from the ongoing learning that DBT demands and from how much they continue to grow through this learning.

Clients and their parents may ask if change is really possible and if these skills really work. Those practitioners who utilize DBT concepts, principles, and skills need only look to themselves for the answers to these questions. DBT practitioners find that their lives are greatly enhanced when they use these skills themselves. Mindful awareness, living in the present moment, acceptance of self and others, validation of self and others, using distress tolerance to manage difficult emotions, and taking a nonjudgmental stance provide guidelines for the personal as well as the professional lives of practitioners. The benefits are enormous for clients and their parents—and for the practitioner as well.

Resources

ADOLESCENTS

Books to Use with or Recommend to Adolescents

Adolescent Mental Health Initiative—books by and for adolescents about various disorders. The books can be found at

http://global.oup.com/academic/content/series/a/adolescent-mental-health-initiative-amhi
/?cc=us&lang=en

New Harbinger Self-Help Books for Adolescents (Instant Help Book for Teens Series):

Anxiety Workbook for Teens by Lisa M. Schab

The Bipolar Workbook for Teens by Sheri Van Dijk and Karma Guindon

Don't Let Emotions Run Your Life for Teens by Sheri Van Dijk

Stopping the Pain: A Workbook for Teens Who Cut and Self-Injure by Lawrence Shapiro

Stress Reduction Workbook for Teens by Gina Biegel

PARENTS

Books to Recommend to Parents

Acquainted with the Night by Paul Raeburn

Borderline Personality Disorder in Adolescents: A Complete Guide to Understanding and Coping When Your Adolescent Has BPD by Blaise A. Aguirre

The Buddha and the Borderline by Kiera Van Gelder

Loving Someone with BPD by Shari Manning

Parenting a Child Who Has Intense Emotions by Pat Harvey

Stop Walking on Eggshells by Paul T. Mason and Randi Kreger

An Unquiet Mind by Kay Redfield Jamison

Wasted and *Madness* by Marya Hornbacher

Will's Choice by Gail Griffith

PRACTITIONERS

Books for Enhancing Clinical Skills

Acquiring Competency and Achieving Proficiency with Dialectical Behavior Therapy by Cathy Moonshine

Cognitive-Behavioral Treatment of Borderline Personality Disorder by Marsha Linehan

Dialectical Behavior Therapy: Children and Adolescents by Connie Callahan

Dialectical Behavior Therapy in Clinical Practice by Linda Dimeff and Kelly Koerner

Dialectical Behavior Therapy with Suicidal Adolescents by Alec Miller, Jill Rathus, and Marsha Linehan

Doing Dialectical Behavior Therapy: A Practical Guide by Kelly Koerner

Dialectical Behavior Therapy Skills, 101 Mindfulness Exercises and Other Fun Activities for Children and Adolescents: A Learning Supplement by Kimberly Christensen, Gage N. Riddoch, and Julie Eggers Huber

The Expanded Dialectical Behavior Therapy Skills Training Manual by Lane Pederson

Skills Training Manual for Treating Borderline Personality Disorder by Marsha Linehan

PRACTITIONERS AND FAMILIES

Websites that Provide Resources, Research, and Information

ADAA—Anxiety and Depression Association of America

www.ADAA.org

Resources, information, and updated research about anxiety and depressive disorders

Behavioral Research and Therapy Clinics

blogs.uw.edu/brtc/publications-assessment-instruments/

Has many of the assessment tools needed to assess suicidality in adolescents

Behavioral Tech

www.behavioraltech.com

Resources and information about DBT practitioners and about trainings from the developers of DBT

DBT Self-Help

www.DBTSelfHelp.com

Provides a good description of DBT skills

DBT Therapists' Wiki

practicegroundprojects.wetpaint.com/page/DBT+Therapists%27+Wiki

A collection of resources for practitioners developed for and by individuals who practice and research DBT

DBT Handouts, Protocols & Client Learning Activities

practicegroundprojects.wetpaint.com/page/DBT+Handouts,+Protocols+%26+Client+Learning+Activities

Handouts and charts developed by experts in the field of DBT

International Society for the Improvement and Teaching of Dialectical Behavior Therapy (ISITDBT)

isitdbt.net

Provides information about an annual DBT conference and the process of accreditation

National Alliance on Mental Illness (NAMI) Child and Adolescent Action Center

www.nami.org/template.cfm?section=child_and_teen_support

Information about many emotional disorders, advocacy, and education

National Education Alliance for Borderline Personality Disorder (NEA_BPD)

www.borderlinepersonalitydisorder.com

Many resources, videos, and audios about DBT, validation, and other skills

OTHER RESOURCES

Apps for Use in DBT

To purchase, visit the App Store at www.apple.com.

Buddha Board—practice in accepting the moment

DBT Diary Card and Skills Coach—has diary cards (daily logs) and skills that can be individualized for each adolescent

i-Qi Timer—timer for mindfulness meditation

Lotus Bud—mindfulness bells and timers

PTSD Coach (Veterans Affairs)

Serenity—a mindfulness app

Transform Your Life—awareness practice

Readings for Use in DBT Individual Sessions, Skills Groups, and Consultation Teams

The Book of Awakening by Mark Nepo

Peace Is Every Step by Thich Nhat Hanh

Quiet Mind by David Kundtz

Radical Acceptance by Tara Brach

The Song of the Bird (and other titles) by Anthony de Mello

Wisdom Tales from Around the World by Heather Forest

Zen Shorts by Jon Muth

References

Barlow, D. H., Farchione, T. J., Fairholme, C. P., Ellard, K. K., Boisseau, C. L., Allen, L. B., & Ehrenreich-May, J. (2010). *Unified protocol for transdiagnostic treatment of emotional disorders: Therapist Guide.* New York: Oxford University Press.

Blume, A. W. (2012). Seeking the middle way: G. Alan Marlatt and harm reduction. *Addiction Research & Theory, 20*(3), 218–226.

Bornovalova, M. A., & Daughters, S. B., 2007, How does dialectical behavior therapy facilitate treatment retention among individuals with comorbid borderline personality disorder and substance use disorders? *Clinical Psychology Review, 27,* 923–943.

Bornovalova, M. A., Lejuez, C. W., Daughters, S. B., Rosenthal, M. Z.., & Lynch, T. R. (2005). Impulsivity as a common process across borderline personality and substance use disorders. *Clinical Psychology Review, 25,* 790–812.

Bridge, J., McBee-Strayer, S., Cannon, E., Sheftall, A., Reynolds, B., Campo, J., et al. (2012). Impaired decision making in adolescent suicide attempters. *Journal of the Academy of Child and Adolescent Psychiatry, 51*(4), 394–403.

Buckner, J. D., Keough, M. E., & Schmidt, N. B. (2007). Problematic alcohol and cannabis use among young adults: The roles of depression and discomfort and distress tolerance. *Addictive Behaviors, 32,* 1957–1963.

Burns, D. D. (1999). *Feeling good: The new mood therapy.* New York: HarperCollins.

Carey, B. (2011, June 23). Expert on mental illness reveals her own fight. *New York Times,* A1.

Chapman, A. L., Gratz, K. L., Tull, M., & Keane, T. (2011). *The dialectical behavior therapy skills workbook for anxiety: Breaking free from worry, panic, PTSD & other anxiety symptoms.* Oakland, CA: New Harbinger Publications.

Cougle, J. R., Timpano, K. R., & Goetz, A. R. (2012). Exploring the unique and interactive roles of distress tolerance and negative urgency in obsessions. *Personality and Individual Differences, 52,* 515–520.

Crowell, S. E., Beauchaine, T. P., Hsiao, R. C., Vasilev, C. A., Yaptangco, M., Linehan, M. M., et al. (2011). Differentiating adolescent self-injury from adolescent depression: Possible implications for borderline personality development. *Journal of Abnormal Child Psychology, 40,* 45–57.

Daughters, S. B., Sargeant, M. N., Bornovalova, M. A., Gratz, K. L., & Lejuez, C. W. (2008). The relationship between distress tolerance and antisocial personality disorder among male inner-city treatment seeking substance abusers. *Journal of Personality Disorders, 22(5),* 509–524.

Davenport, J., Bore, M., & Campbell, J. (2010). Changes in personality pre- and post-dialectical behaviour therapy borderline personality disorder groups: A question of self-control. *Australian Psychologist, 45,* 59–66.

Dimeff, L. A., & Koerner, K. (2007). *Dialectical behavior therapy in clinical practice: Applications across disorders and settings.* New York: Guilford Press.

Dimeff, L. A., Koerner, K., & Linehan, M. M. (2008). Dialectical behavior therapy for substance abusers. *Addiction Science and Clinical Practice. 4(2),* 39–47.

Fruzetti, A. E. (2005, October). *Validating and invalidating responses in families.* Paper presented at Borderline Personality Disorder: Historical and Future Perspectives Conference, sponsored by NEA-BPD and McClean Hospital, Burlington, MA.

Howell, A. N., Leyro, T. M., Hogan, J., Buckner, J. D., & Zvolensky, M. J. (2010). Anxiety sensitivity, distress tolerance, and discomfort intolerance in relation to coping and conformity motives for alcohol use and alcohol use problems among young adult drinkers. *Addictive Behaviors, 35,* 1144–1147.

Kabat-Zinn, J. (2012). *Mindfulness for beginners: Reclaiming the present moment—and your life.* Boulder, CO: Sounds True, Inc.

Kim, Y., Moon, S., & Kim, M. (2011). Physical and psycho-social predictors of adolescents' suicide behaviors. *Child and Adolescent Social Work Journal, 28,* 421–438.

Klonsky, E. D., & Muehlenkamp, J. J. (2007). Self-injury: A research review for the practitioner. *Journal of Clinical Psychology, 63,* 1045–1056.

Koerner, K. (2012). *Doing dialectical behavior therapy.* New York: Guilford Press.

Koerner, K., Dimeff, L., & Swenson, C. (2007). Adopt or adapt? Fidelity matters. In L. A. Dimeff & K. Koerner (Eds.), *Dialectical behavior therapy in clinical practice: Applications across disorders and settings* (pp. 19–36). New York: Guilford Press.

Linehan, M. M. (1993a). *Cognitive-behavioral treatment of borderline personality disorder.* New York: Guilford Press.

Linehan, M. M. (1993b). *Skills training manual for treating borderline personality disorder.* New York: Guilford Press.

Manning, S. (2011) *Loving someone with borderline personality disorder.* New York: Guilford Press.

McMain, S., Fayrs, J., Dimeff, L., & Linehan, M. (2007). Dialectical behavior therapy for individuals with borderline personality disorder and substance dependence, In L. A. Dimeff & K. Koerner (Eds.), *Dialectical behavior therapy in clinical practice: Applications across disorders and settings* (pp. 145–173). New York: Guilford Press.

Merikangas, K. R., He, J., Burstein, M., Swanson, S. A., Avenoli, S., Cui, L. et al. (2010). Lifetime prevalence of mental disorders in US adolescents: Results from the National Comorbidity Survey–Adolescent Supplement (NCS-A). *Journal of the American Academy of Child and Adolescent Psychiatry, 49,* 980–989.

Miller, A. L., Rathus, J. H., & Linehan, M. M. (2007). *Dialectical behavior therapy with suicidal adolescents.* New York: Guilford Press.

Nakamura, B. J., Pestle, S. L., & Chorpita, B. F. (2009). Differential sequencing of cognitive-behavioral techniques for reducing child and adolescent anxiety. *Journal of Cognitive Psychotherapy, 23(2),* 114–135.

Nelson-Gray, R., Keane, S., Hurst, R., Mitchell, J. Warburton, J. Chok, J., & Cobb, A. (2006). A modified DBT skills training program for oppositional defiant adolescents: Promising preliminary findings. *Behavior Research and Therapy, 44,* 1811–1820.

Nickel, C., Lahman, C., Tritt, K., Loew, T. H., Rother, W. K., & Nickel, M. K. (2005). Short communication—Stressed aggressive adolescents benefit from progressive muscle relaxation: A random, prospective, controlled trial. *Stress and Health, 21,* 169–175.

Perepletchikova, F., Axelrod, S., Kaufman, J., Rounsaville, B., Douglas-Palumberi, H., & Miller, A. (2011). Adapting dialectical behaviour therapy for children: Towards a new research agenda for paediatric suicidal and non-suicidal self-injurious behaviours. *Child and Adolescent Mental Health, 16(2),* 116–121.

Rizvi, S. L., Dimeff, L. A., Skutch, J., Carroll, D., & Linehan, M. M. (2011). A pilot study of the DBT coach: An interactive mobile phone application for individuals with borderline personality disorder and substance use disorder. *Behavior Therapy, 42,* 589–600.

Salzberg, S. (2002). *Lovingkindness: The revolutionary art of happiness.* Boston: Shambhala Publications.

Sanderson, C. (2001, April 26–27). DBT skills training. Class notes. Orange, CT.

Shelton, D., Kesten, K., Zhang, W., & Trestman, R. (2011). Impact of a dialectic behavior therapy–corrections modified (DBT-CM) upon behaviorally challenged incarcerated male adolescents. *Journal of Child and Adolescent Psychiatric Nursing, 24,* 105–113.

Stahl, B., & Goldstein, E. (2010). *A mindfulness-based stress reduction workbook.* Oakland, CA: New Harbinger Publications.

Swenson, C. (2012, June 28–29). Doing DBT to adherence and with confidence: An advanced course. Class notes. Middletown, CT.

Trupin, E. W., Stewart, D. G., Beach, B., & Boesky, L. (2002). Effectiveness of a dialectical behaviour therapy program for incarcerated female juvenile offenders. *Child and Adolescent Mental Health, 7(3),* 121–127.

Wisniewski, L. (2012, October 4). Integrating CBT to treat eating disorders into a DBT program. Class notes (interactive online class). Cleveland, OH.

Wisniewski, L., & Kelly, E. (2003). The application of dialectical behavior therapy to the treatment of eating disorders. *Cognitive and Behavioral Practice, 10,* 131–138.

Wisniewski. L., Safer, D., & Chen, E. (2007). Dialectical behavior therapy and eating disorders. In L. Dimeff & K. Koerner (Eds.), *Dialectical behavior therapy in clinical practice: Applications across disorders and settings* (pp. 174–221). New York: Guilford Press.

Pat Harvey, ACSW, LCSW-C, has been providing clinical social work services to individuals with emotion dysregulation and their families for over thirty years. Harvey trains mental health professionals in dialectical behavioral therapy (DBT) skills and philosophy by facilitating trainings and workshops at organizations and conferences across the country, and helped to develop one of the first DBT-based group homes for adolescents. The focus of her practice is providing DBT-skill group and individual coaching to parents and other family members of youths who have emotion dysregulation. She is cofounder of the Metro DBT Consortium and coauthor of *Parenting a Child Who Has Intense Emotions*.

Britt H. Rathbone, ACSW, LCSW-C, provides psychotherapy services to adolescents and their families in the greater Washington, DC, area. He is consistently voted one of Washington's best therapists for adolescents, and actively teaches graduate students and trains other professionals on issues of adolescent development and clinical treatment. He has been providing DBT services to adolescents since 2002, and is cofounder of the Metro DBT Consortium.

Index

Register your **new harbinger** titles for additional benefits!

When you register your **new harbinger** title—purchased in any format, from any source—you get access to benefits like the following:

- Downloadable accessories like printable worksheets and extra content

- Instructional videos and audio files

- Information about updates, corrections, and new editions

Not every title has accessories, but we're adding new material all the time.

Access free accessories in 3 easy steps:

1. Sign in at NewHarbinger.com (or **register** to create an account).

2. Click on **register a book**. Search for your title and click the **register** button when it appears.

3. Click on the **book cover or title** to go to its details page. Click on **accessories** to view and access files.

That's all there is to it!

If you need help, visit:

NewHarbinger.com/accessories

new harbinger
CELEBRATING
40 YEARS